Contents

CO-AMT-021

Russia and the Wider World in Historical Perspective

Paul Dukes

Russia and the Wider World in Historical Perspective

Essays for Paul Dukes

Edited by

Cathryn Brennan
Centre for Russian, East and Central European Studies
King's College
Aberdeen

and

Murray Frame
Lecturer in History
University of Dundee

First published in Great Britain 2000 by
MACMILLAN PRESS LTD
Houndmills, Basingstoke, Hampshire RG21 6XS and London
Companies and representatives throughout the world

A catalogue record for this book is available from the British Library.

ISBN 0–333–68300–5

First published in the United States of America 2000 by
ST. MARTIN'S PRESS, INC.,
Scholarly and Reference Division,
175 Fifth Avenue, New York, N.Y. 10010

ISBN 0–312–22926–7

Library of Congress Cataloging-in-Publication Data
Russia and the wider world in historical perspective : essays for Paul
Dukes / edited by Cathryn Brennan and Murray Frame.
    p.   cm.
Includes bibliographical references and index.
ISBN 0–312–22926–7 (cloth)
1. Russia—Relations—Foreign countries.   2. Soviet Union–
–Relations—Foreign countries.   I. Dukes, Paul, 1934–   .
II. Brennan, Cathryn, 1950–   .   III. Frame, Murray.
DK66.R87   1999
303.48'247'009—dc21   99–40355
                                                            CIP

*DK
66
.R87
2000*

This book is printed on paper suitable for recycling and made from fully managed and sustained
forest sources.

10   9   8   7   6   5   4   3   2   1
09   08   07   06   05   04   03   02   01   00

Printed and bound in Great Britain by
Antony Rowe Ltd, Chippenham, Wiltshire

Preface

Few national histories can be comprehended without some reference to the modulating international contexts in which they have evolved. This elementary observation is particularly true in the case of Russia. The history of Russia's relations with the wider world strikes at the very heart of how it emerged as a European and world power. Indeed, it remains central to any understanding of Russia's political and economic position in the world today, not least because several of the key dilemmas it raised are still not fully resolved (most obviously Russia's ambivalent relationship with Europe and the United States). There is an ongoing dialogue between Russia and the wider world, a search for a settled definition of its place in the global order, which, as the essays in the present volume amply demonstrate, has deep roots and remarkably resonant parallels in the past. Moreover, Russia's historical interaction with the wider world functioned, and must be considered, at a variety of levels: it has involved not only diplomacy, wars and treaties, but a complex process of cultural, social and economic relations operating with fluctuating degrees of intensity and influence.

The essays in the present volume are devoted to the general theme of Russia's relations with the wider world since the seventeenth century. Of course, significant formative interaction with the wider world antedated the early modern period. Central to the emergence and consolidation of Kievan Rus' was the lucrative trade and commerce conducted between the Eastern Slavs and the Byzantine Empire, whence Kievan Rus' acquired several distinctive characteristics of Russian culture, not least Orthodox Christianity, the Cyrillic alphabet and many traits of the Russian architectural style. The Kievan period is also the story (though certainly shrouded in myth and legend) of how the first 'Russian state' was established by the Varangians (Norsemen) from Scandinavia when, according to the chronicles, the Eastern Slavs, ravaged by constant feuding between loose-knit principalities, requested that an outside authority impose a unified political order over them. Having gradually consolidated its position as an important power at the eastern extremity of the European continent by its interaction with Byzantium and Scandinavia, Kievan Rus' was weakened by another external force, the Mongols, who swept in from Asia in the thirteenth century, sacking the city of Kiev itself in 1240. Historians continue to debate the impact on Russia of the ensuing two centuries of Mongol domination. Certainly they contributed to the rise of Moscow, which initially collaborated with the Golden Horde but later led the fight against it. Some scholars have even attributed the development of Muscovite autocracy and serfdom to the military, administrative and tax-collecting methods bequeathed by the Mongols, and the power vacuum occasioned by the eventual retreat of the Khan certainly provided Moscow with reason to undertake some early territorial expansion to the east.

The progress made by the Muscovite state in asserting its domination of the Russian lands was not yet sufficient to enable it to withstand the political and social fragmentation of the Time of Troubles (1598–1613). This began as a dynastic dispute, but soon escalated into a wider conflict involving a debilitating war with Poland–Lithuania and Sweden. Foreign invaders were ultimately repelled, and the restoration of relative stability was symbolized in 1613 by the emergence of a new ruling dynasty, the Romanovs. Throughout the seventeenth century, international developments continued to play a major role in determining the course of Russian history. Lingering conflict with Poland, Sweden and the Ottoman Empire ensured that the problem of external security remained high on the agenda, and the various reform measures pursued by the nascent absolutist state (in particular the modernization of the army and the formal enserfment of the peasantry) were intended to address that fact. Meanwhile, Ukraine's struggle against Poland led to union with Moscow in 1654, thereby extending Russian influence to within reach of the Black Sea; and the question of security was no longer confined to European Russia, as rapid absorption of Siberia took Russia to the Pacific Ocean by the end of the 1630s, leading it in 1689 to conclude its first agreement with China (Treaty of Nerchinsk). The whole process of expansion to the east gave rise to the issue of Russia's relationship with Asia. Is Russia a European or Asian country? Or is it Eurasian, combining characteristics of both? Moreover, *where* are Russia's boundaries? Since the formative period of Kievan Rus', its borders have fluctuated with remarkable regularity, contributing to the problematic of identity. If Russia is a colonizing state, where does Russia end and its colonies begin? Such perennial questions entertain no concise answers. The point here is that, in general outline, the early economic, political and cultural history of the Russian lands cannot be extricated from their interactions with, and relationships to, the wider world.

The progressive emergence of Russian absolutism in the seventeenth century was accompanied by growing mutual awareness and contact between Russia and the wider world, particularly Western Europe, a development that provides the starting point for the present collection of essays. In its search for sustainable security the Russian state consumed the military and technical expertise of foreign specialists, notably under Peter the Great, while displaying official enthusiasm for the forms of elite Western culture, such as the shaving of beards. Technical and cultural Westernization coexisted with much popular hostility to foreigners, a theme which forms the subject of the opening essay by Lindsey Hughes. The increasing awareness and knowledge of Russia in Europe at that time is then highlighted by Graeme Herd, who illustrates the role played by General Patrick Gordon as an intermediary between Russia and Western Europe. Gordon helped Peter the Great continue the process of reforming the Russian army, which was soon strong enough to defeat Sweden and secure a foothold on the Baltic, signalling Russia's arrival as a major European power. The Russian Empire had acquired not only an important strategic position, but a centre of Enlightenment culture. As attested by Roger Bartlett in his essay on the Masonic clergyman Georg Ludwig Collins, the Baltic region, in particular Riga, functioned as a kind of intellectual interface between Russia and Europe. Yet the links stretched far into Europe, not simply the 'near abroad'. Dmitry Fedosov explores Russia's links with another country on the European periphery, Scotland, which were long-standing and diverse, and which point to a remarkable affinity between the two countries.

Increasing contact with the wider world served to define what made Russia similar and dissimilar to it. By the mid-nineteenth century this had generated the passionate debate between Westerners and Slavophiles, the former locating Russia firmly within the traditions of Western civilization, the latter emphasizing its unique Slavic characteristics (notably the peasant *mir*) and eschewing the West as a developmental model. Many Slavophiles advocated that Russia act as protector of the Orthodox Christian Slavs outside the Empire too, particularly those of the Balkans. The tsars were certainly prepared to mobilize the imperial army in aid of fellow Slavs, for instance in the 1877–8 Russo-Turkish War; but, as David Saunders demonstrates by comparing Russian attitudes to the Ukrainians within the Empire and to the Slavs of the Balkans outside it, this had more to do with *raison d'état* than religious or ethnic solidarity. After Russian interests in the Near East suffered a humiliating setback at the Congress of Berlin (1878), attention turned for a while to the Far East; but the costly conflict with Japan which ultimately ensued (1904–5) resulted in even greater humiliation for tsarism, providing added momentum to the 1905 Revolution and the increasingly vehement demands for political and social reform. The chief result was the establishment of the first State Duma and the beginning of Russia's 'constitutional experiment'. Many historians have pointed to the weakness of the new constitutional order as evidence that Russia was too 'backward' to evolve a Western-style parliamentary system, even that historical circumstances necessitated an 'Oriental-despotic' form of government. Robert McKean argues instead that the deficiencies of the Duma Monarchy were comparable to those encountered by other constitutional experiments in Europe since the French Revolution, suggesting that the Russian experience was quite in keeping with that of mainstream European history.

The revolution of 1917 and the rise of the Soviet Union fundamentally redefined Russia's relations with the wider world. In the space of a few decades Russia was to be transformed from a European power broadly evolving along Western capitalist lines into a global superpower formally committed to the overthrow of capitalism and the spread of communist revolution. The Bolsheviks initially considered their survival to be dependent upon the outbreak of revolution elsewhere, and for several years they endeavoured to foment communist-led uprisings beyond Russia and the USSR. The early prospects for Soviet-led internationalization of the revolution were enhanced by the presence in Russia immediately after 1917 of many European and Asian peoples who had been uprooted by the calamities of the First World War. John Erickson illustrates how some of these were drafted into Red Army International units designed to spread the revolution while fighting a civil war for its very survival in Russia. Boris Starkov then explores attempts by the Bolsheviks to instigate communist revolution in parts of Europe and Asia in the 1920s. Although such attempts had diminished by the end of the 1920s as the Soviet Union pursued an official policy of 'socialism in one country', general suspicion and hostility towards the USSR remained. This was mitigated only temporarily during the Great Patriotic War when the Soviet Union fought with the Allies against the Axis. Sarah Davies here examines the popular impact of the Soviet government's attempts to portray the (capitalist) Allies in a more favourable light than it had done prior to the war. The triumph of the Red Army in 1945 testified not only to the remarkable character of the Russian and Soviet peoples, but also to the economic advances made in the 1930s. These helped to lay the basis of Soviet superpower status, and as European global hegemony atrophied in the years after 1945, superpower rivalry with the United States became the pre-eminent feature of world politics, making Russia more significant a country than ever, as the two sides competed for influence around the world. The proliferation of colonial vacuums was a crucial consideration in that wider strategic game, the process of decolonization in the Eurasian land mass proving to be of particular concern to the Soviet Union, a theme explored by Jean Houbert in his essay. Finally, some of the key issues regarding Russia and the wider world in historical perspective are considered in concluding remarks by James White, who also discusses the important contribution made to our understanding of that theme by the present volume's honorand.

A Note on Paul Dukes

This book has been produced in honour of one of the most distinguished scholars of Russian history, Professor Paul Dukes, a prolific and stimulating contributor who has persistently strived to locate Russian history in its wider, particularly comparative, contexts. Hence the general theme of this collection. The occasion is his retirement from university teaching, but most emphatically this does not signal the end of a career, rather the beginning of a new stage in it, one that the honorand insists will be even *more* active in terms of research and writing! In the space available here, we can survey only the broad outlines of an immensely rich and productive career thus far.

Paul Dukes was born on 5 April 1934 in Wallington, Surrey, then in the outer suburbs of London. At Wallington County Grammar School he was taught by the late Dr E. N. Williams, fondly remembered by him as 'an inspirational teacher of history, and of much else besides'. One of the subjects that first took his interest was the Boston Tea Party: the mixed implications of ordered ceremony and wild frontier, he says, proved an irresistible blend. As an Exhibitioner in history at Peterhouse, Cambridge, from 1951 to 1954, Paul Dukes enjoyed American history most. With the aid of a Fulbright Travelling Scholarship he worked as a Teaching Fellow at the University of Washington, Seattle, from 1954 to 1956. While there he produced an MA thesis on American colonial history under the supervision of Max Savelle, completing most of the writing during a subsequent spell at the University of Virginia, Charlottesville.

As a national serviceman from 1956 to 1958, Paul Dukes learned Russian at the Joint Services School for Languages in Crail, Fife. From 1958 to 1959, he taught American history for the University of Maryland in France and Germany, continuing this work in England from 1959 to 1964 while studying for his PhD in Russian history at the School of Slavonic and East European Studies, London, under the supervision of Hugh Seton-Watson and John Keep. In 1964, he began lecturing at the University of Aberdeen, where, apart from a few visits to other universities, including Auckland (1974) and Cornell (1988), he has remained ever since.

Paul Dukes' *oeuvre* spans a considerable range of subjects, as attested by his extensive bibliography (see pp. 220–2). His first book, *Catherine the Great and the Russian Nobility*, based on his PhD thesis, was published in 1967. Therein he examined the relationship between crown and nobility under Catherine through the materials of the Legislative Commission of 1767, and the book remains a standard work on that subject. His commitment to advancing our understanding of eighteenth-century Russia was underlined in 1968 when he presented the inaugural paper to the very first meeting of the Study Group on Eighteenth-Century Russia. Since then, he has been a regular contributor to the Study Group and its annual Newsletter.

Meanwhile, his interest in comparative American–Russian history had been aroused by the famous observation on the subject by Alexis de Tocqueville, which prompted him to pursue this topic through to a short book, *The Emergence of the Super-Powers* (1970). As well as bringing out two volumes of documents on aspects of Russia in the age of Catherine the Great, he next turned his attention to the history of Russia as a whole, completing a survey on medieval, modern and contemporary aspects of the subject by 1974, now in its third edition, *A History of Russia c. 882–1996*. In this project his aims were to give Soviet as well as other historians their due, to integrate political developments with economic and cultural in a manner that few historians of Russia had previously attempted, 'to reveal the limitations of an exclusively national approach to Russian history and to contribute to its analysis in a comparative framework' (Preface to the first edition) – aims the study achieved with exemplary clarity and erudition.

In terms of approaches to historical enquiry, Paul Dukes at this time adhered to most of the views advanced by E. H. Carr in *What is History?* (1961) although, he claims, in a rather unfocused manner. His academic motives stemmed more generally from the belief that the Cold War had produced distortions in Russian history as well as in intellectual enquiry in general. This concern led to a series of major publications which had the collective aim of rising above the narrower, exclusionist perspectives of Cold War historiography by placing Russian history more fully within the framework of Western and world history. They were: *October and the World* (1979), a study of the Russian Revolution in diachronic and synchronic global perspectives; *A History of Europe, 1648–1948* (1985), a survey aspiring to an even-handed treatment of the eastern and western parts of the European continent as well as of the wider global context; *The Last Great Game* (1989), a study applying a Braudelian approach to the Cold War; and *World Order in History* (1996), an examination of the ways in which Russian history has been integrated with the history of the West since the eighteenth century.

At the same time, Paul Dukes continued with his work on the history of eighteenth-century Russia, while developing a closer interest in the seventeenth century. This resulted in the publication of *The Making of Russian Absolutism, 1613–1801* (1982; second edition 1990), a compelling study notable in particular for its refreshing emphasis on the importance of Peter the Great's predecessors to the construction of the modern Russian state, and for its location of the apogee of Russian absolutism in the reign of Catherine the Great. The seventeenth and eighteenth centuries also provided the setting for another developing research interest, the emigration of North-East Scots to serve as mercenaries throughout Europe, mostly in Russia. Although he first looked upon this subject as a 'local curiosity', the longer Paul Dukes remained at Aberdeen the more he realized that it was, in fact, a topic of wide significance, and it led to a series of articles which will form part of a major study, provisionally entitled 'Romanovs and Stuarts: Studies in an Old Relationship'. He also developed an appreciation of North-East Scottish culture.

Meanwhile, burgeoning Western interest in contemporary developments in the Soviet Union and Eastern Europe led in 1989 to the foundation of the Centre for Soviet and East European Studies at Aberdeen University under Paul Dukes' direction. Now called the Centre for Russian, East and Central European Studies and still run by Paul Dukes, it remains highly active in convening seminars and conferences, publishing bulletins and collections of original papers, and, in particular, organizing visits to Britain of leading Russian academics, as well as overseeing student trips to Russia. In the midst of all this, Paul Dukes still finds the time and energy to be an active member of several national and international academic bodies, including the International Commission on the History of the October Revolution. He is also an advisory editor of *History Today*.

Still to some extent a disciple of E. H. Carr, Paul Dukes claims that with retirement it is time for himself to 'aspire to the role of teacher before it is too late'. This ostensibly odd comment from someone who has spent his career teaching, not least by example, in fact reflects an underlying philosophy of education which Paul Dukes has consistently adhered to, namely that it should not involve one generation of scholars dictating historical knowledge and an academic agenda to another, but rather should encourage the unfettered exploration of areas and ideas, not least those previously uncharted by scholars. To do this effectively, as Paul Dukes does, requires a special gift as a teacher. But the comment also indicates a belief that, at the same time, experienced scholars have some duty to reflect and pronounce on the nature and future of their discipline. Paul Dukes' message to posterity, which is still evolving, may most succinctly be described in a word as 'pandisciplinarity'. It follows on from a previous and continuing interest in comparative history, and is leading in a direction which, he claims, is not yet totally clear. At the time of writing, Professor Dukes is at work on two projects: a survey of the rise and fall of the superpowers from 1898 to 1998, and a monograph provisionally entitled 'The Uninvited Guest: Soviet Russia and the Washington Conference of 1921'.

It is testimony to the influence and accomplishment of Paul Dukes, and to the genuine esteem in which he is held, that this collection is only one of several that could have been produced. Many other subjects which reflect the honorand's wide interests could have formed the general theme of the book, and many other colleagues with whom Paul Dukes has collaborated over the years could have contributed. Restricted space obviously meant that it was impossible to include them all here. In the end, having settled on the broad theme of Russia and the wider world, the editors felt that the profile of contributors should reflect three constituencies: the honorand's peers, his Russian colleagues, and younger scholars. The individual contributors to this volume in a sense represent these broader constituencies and their members, who are too numerous to mention by name, but who all wished this project particular success because of its honorand. As he is a modest man, we will refrain from embarrassing Paul Dukes with the encomia about him which we encountered in the course of communicating with various people about this book; suffice to say that the honorand should not doubt the extent to which he is widely admired and fondly thought of, not just as a scholar but as a gentleman in the best sense of the term. Finally, we wish to thank the contributors for their co-operation and patience, Paul Dukes for supplying details of his career provided above, and the many people, again too numerous to name individually, who supported and advised on this book at different stages and in various ways.

CATHRYN BRENNAN
MURRAY FRAME

Notes on the Contributors

Roger Bartlett is Professor of Russian History at the School of Slavonic and East European Studies, University of London. His research interests focus on the economic, cultural and social history of the Russian Empire and on Imperial Russia's relations with other European countries. He has recently published, with Erich Donnert, *Johann Georg Eisen (1717–1779): Ausgewählte Schriften. Deutsche Volksaufklärung und Leibeigenschaft im russischen Reich* (1998).

Cathryn Brennan is Honorary Secretary of the Aberdeen Centre for Russian, East and Central European Studies. She is a specialist on the Russian Far East and is currently researching the history of the Far Eastern Republic.

Sarah Davies is Lecturer in History, University of Durham. Her publications include *Popular Opinion in Stalin's Russia* (1997).

John Erickson, FBA, FRSE, FRSA, is Honorary Research Fellow in Defence Studies and Professor Emeritus, University of Edinburgh. His many publications include *The Soviet High Command, 1918–1941* (1962; reprinted 1984); *The Armed Services and Society* (1969); *Stalin's War with Germany*, vol. 1: *The Road to Stalingrad* and vol. 2: *The Road to Berlin*, (reprinted 1993–4); *The Soviet Ground Forces: An Operational Assessment* (1986); and *Soviet Military Doctrine: The Significance of Operational Art and the Emergence of Deep Battle* (1997).

Dmitry Fedosov is Senior Research Fellow at the Institute of General History, Moscow. His publications include *Rozhdennaia v bitvakh: Shotlandiia do kontsa XIV veka* (1996) and *The Caledonian Connection. Scotland–Russia Ties: Middle Ages to Early Twentieth Century* (1996).

Josephine Forsyth (translator) is retired Lecturer in Russian at the University of Aberdeen. Her publications include studies of Leonid Andreev and Anton Chekhov.

Murray Frame is Lecturer in History, University of Dundee. His publications include *The Russian Revolution, 1905–1921: A Bibliographical*

Guide to Works in English (1995) and *The St Petersburg Imperial Theatres: Stage and State in Revolutionary Russia, 1900–1920* (1999).

Graeme P. Herd is Lecturer in the Department of Politics and International Relations, University of Aberdeen. He has published several articles on seventeenth-century Russia. His current research focuses on contemporary Russian security issues, with particular reference to the Baltic region.

Jean Houbert is retired Lecturer in the Department of Politics and International Relations, University of Aberdeen. He has published many articles on global politics and decolonization, most recently 'Decolonisation in Globalisation', in *Globalisation and Europe*, edited by R. Axtmann (1998), and 'Russia in the Geopolitics of Settler Colonisation and Decolonisation', in *The Round Table* (1997).

Lindsey Hughes is Professor of Russian History at the School of Slavonic and East European Studies, University of London. Her publications include *Russia and the West: Prince Vasily Vasilievich Golitsyn (1643–1714)* (1984), *Sophia, Regent of Russia, 1657–1704* (1990), and *Russia in the Age of Peter the Great* (1998). Her current research is on the culture of the royal court in early modern Russia.

Robert B. McKean is Reader in History at the University of Stirling. His main publications include *St Petersburg between the Revolutions: Workers and Revolutionaries, June 1907–February 1917* (1990), and, as editor and contributor, *New Perspectives in Modern Russian History* (1992). He has recently written several articles re-examining the Russian constitutional monarchy of 1906–1917.

David Saunders is Reader in the History of the Russian Empire at the University of Newcastle upon Tyne. His publications include *The Ukrainian Impact on Russian Culture, 1750–1850* (1985) and *Russia in the Age of Reaction and Reform, 1801–1881* (1992). His contribution to the present volume is one of a series of articles on the Ukrainian–Russian relationship in the second half of the nineteenth century. He is at work on a social history of the Russian Empire between 1800 and 1917.

Boris A. Starkov is Professor of Soviet History at the University of Economics and Finance, St Petersburg. His publications include many articles on the Stalin period, and *Dela i liudi stalinskogo vremeni* (1995).

James D. White is Reader in Russian and East European Studies, University of Glasgow. He has published articles on various aspects of Russian history, particularly on the 1917 revolution. He is the author of *The Russian Revolution 1917–1921: A Short History* (1994) and *Karl Marx and the Intellectual Origins of Dialectical Materialism* (1996), and is currently working on a biographical study of Lenin.

1
Attitudes towards Foreigners in Early Modern Russia

Lindsey Hughes

> *May our sovereigns never allow any Orthodox Christians in their realm to entertain any close friendly relations with heretics and dissenters – with the Latins, Lutherans, Calvinists and godless Tatars (whom our Lord abominates and the church of God damns for their God-abhorred guile); but let them be avoided as enemies of God and defamers of the church.*

(Patriarch Joachim, 1690)[1]

> *Wise is the man and the nation which is not ashamed to adopt what is good from strangers and foreigners; foolish and ridiculous is he who will not leave off his bad ways and accept what is good from others.*

(Archbishop Feofan, 1722)[2]

It is a historical commonplace that Peter the Great's attempts to 'Westernize' Russia required the import of foreign specialists, goods, vocabulary and ideas, and the export of his own subjects, by force if necessary, for periods of study abroad. Within a few years the religious scruples so vehemently expressed by Patriarch Joachim in 1690 were suppressed in favour of the pro-foreign statements formulated by reformist churchmen such as Feofan Prokopovich, the foremost propagandist and apologist for Peter's apparent violations of tradition. Foreign-sounding St Petersburg (Sankt-Piter-Burkh, as it was originally rendered) became a sort of experimental laboratory for social and cultural engineering, where the average Russian nobleman became 'like a

1

foreigner in his own country: even when fully grown he had to learn artificially what people usually absorb from direct experience in infancy'.[3] This essay will not pursue the question of whether Peter ultimately succeeded in 'Westernizing' Russia and Russians, but will explore the narrower topic of Russian attitudes towards foreigners in their midst, with special reference to Western Europeans and to the changes that occurred between the Muscovite and Petrine periods. Attitudes towards non-Christians evolved in a rather different context and will not be considered here.

Peter was hardly setting a new trend when he encouraged foreigners to come to Russia. According to the Primary Chronicle, the first such invitation was issued in about AD 860, when warring Slavic tribes called in a band of Varangians or Norsemen to impose 'order'. This incident, best regarded as a founding myth reflecting both general Scandinavian influence and tribal dissensions, is interesting for our purposes because of the strong emotions aroused by the theory that foreigners founded the early 'Russian' state. Famously, Gerhard Friedrich Müller's 1749 lecture on the arrival of the Norsemen was interrupted by the outburst (in Latin) of the Russian academician N. I. Popov: 'You, famous author, dishonour our nation!'[4]

The 'invitation to the Varangians' is just one of many examples of alien intrusion and invasion which punctuate Russian history and which shaped Russians' perceptions of outsiders. In fact, the cities of Kievan Rus' had extensive commercial and political links with foreign countries and princely intermarriage with 'the West' was common. It was the Mongol invasions of 1237–40 and the subsequent two centuries of alien domination which inaugurated a new phase of foreign relations, during which Russia became isolated from its western neighbours. Muscovy's emergence as an independent state in the fifteenth century coincided with the fall of Constantinople to the Ottomans in 1453 and the conversion of neighbouring Lithuania to Catholicism, events which encouraged Moscow to regard itself as the bastion of Orthodoxy and centre of universal Christendom. Moscow was variously New Rome, New Jerusalem, New Constantinople.[5] But at the same time as it isolated itself ideologically, Muscovy was more and more drawn into European politics and trade as it became the recipient of missions from the Holy Roman Empire and trade delegations from England after Richard Chancellor's chance landing on the White Sea in 1553. Balancing pragmatic needs against exclusivist theories was a tricky business.

Western Europeans visiting Muscovy in the sixteenth century record few instances of outright hostility to themselves in person, but were struck by Russian claims to be the only true Christians. This attitude was symbolized by the jugs, bowls and cloth, first described by Sigismund von Herberstein, with which the tsar washed hands 'defiled' by contact with Catholic envoys.[6] The staunch English Protestant Giles Fletcher was one of the first to make an allegation which appeared regularly in travellers' accounts well into the eighteenth century. The tsars, he wrote, prevented their subjects from studying and travelling abroad in order to maintain their 'servile condition', nor did they 'suffer any stranger willingly to come into their realm out of any civil country for the same cause ...'. He mentions attempts in 1589 to banish foreign merchants to border towns 'and to be more wary of admitting other strangers hereafter into the inland parts of the realm for fear of infection with better manners and qualities than they have of their own'.[7] This policy, he believed, was reinforced by the clergy, who discouraged the tsar from innovation and the 'novelty of learning' for fear that their own ignorance would be unmasked.[8] Later in his book Fletcher extended the blame beyond the state and church authorities to the 'self pride' of the Russians in general.[9] He flattered Queen Elizabeth I, the recipient of his account, by his references to Russia as 'a tyrannical state (most unlike your own)'.[10] More than a century later we find the British engineer John Perry making very similar observations: the Russian clergy were

> void of Learning, so they were wary and cautious to keep out all Means that might bring it in, lest their Ignorance should be discovered. To which End they insinuated to former Emperors, that the Introduction of foreign Languages might be a Means of introducing foreign Customs and Innovations, which might in time prove not only dangerous to the Church, but to the State too.

Perry constantly reminded his readers just how fortunate they were to be British.[11] Similarly, the Danish agent Just Juel (in Russia 1709–11) wrote: 'In general in financial affairs and in other respects conditions in Russia are extremely hard and we Danes should thank the Lord God for his special kindness to us.'[12]

In the sixteenth century a number of European countries forged trade and diplomatic links with Russia, while Russian rulers made selective use of foreign personnel and expertise. The first foreigners' quarter in Moscow was established during the reign of Ivan IV (1533–84).[13] The Time of Troubles at the beginning of the seventeenth century was a setback to the aspirations of both sides, when the embers of xenophobia were fanned into flame by foreign invasions. There were strong denunciations of the Poles who came to Moscow in 1605–6 in the retinues of the First False Dmitrii and his Polish Catholic bride Marina Mniczek, and even stronger reactions in 1610–12 to the Polish troops who violated the sacred heart of the tsardom by occupying the Kremlin in support of the claims of King Sigismund of Poland to the vacant Muscovite throne.[14] In the meantime Swedes invaded part of the lands of Novgorod in violation of a defensive alliance made with the Russians, closing Russia's tenuous link to the Baltic for almost a century. For a while the outside world was almost universally perceived as hostile: 'Latin guile' and 'Lutheran heresy' to the north and west, Turkish and Tatar 'infidels' to the south and east.[15]

The Russian terminology of 'foreign-ness' emphasized religious differences. Foreigners who converted to Orthodoxy were no longer *inovertsy* (adherents to other beliefs), hence no longer foreigners. Roman Catholics were *latyny* or *latini*, although the term sometimes referred generally to West Europeans. Although *liuterany* and *kalvinisty* appeared in religious tracts, North European Protestants were more commonly known as *nemtsy* – *nemets* (m.), *nemka* (f.) – the modern Russian term for 'German'. This was not just a colloquialism – it appears, for example, in the Law Code (*Ulozhenie*) of 1649 – but it frequently carried negative connotations.[16]

Popular and religious attitudes ran counter to state needs. While the 'Troubles' sharpened hostility towards foreigners, they also exposed technical and economic deficiencies which could be remedied in the short term only by increasing contacts with outsiders. But in order to attract foreign experts and traders to Russia, notorious for its unenticing climate and alien culture, the government was compelled to grant various privileges and exemptions. From the 1630s onwards 'new model' infantry regiments were formed, staffed by foreign officers. Weapon makers, iron founders, fortification experts and explosives experts were hired. Trade resumed, with lively competition between the Muscovy Company and the Dutch. Protestant communities built churches in Moscow, Dutch Reformed in 1639 and Lutherans in 1643. There were also churches in Nizhnii Novgorod, Astrakhan and Archangel, while in Novgorod, Pskov and other towns, smaller foreign communities conducted services in their homes.[17] Catholics (far fewer in number, although there was no outright ban on employing them) received permission to build a church in stone only in 1695. Before that they worshipped in a modest wooden chapel.[18]

Local opinion lagged behind official tolerance. In 1643 the priests of ten Moscow churches submitted a petition to Tsar Mikhail:

> In our parishes Germans have built churches (*ropaty*)[19] on their properties close to [Orthodox] churches (*tserkvi*), and the Germans keep Russian servants in their homes and Russians suffer all manner of defilation from those Germans, and, without waiting for the sovereign's permission, the Germans are again buying residences in our parishes, as are German widows, and they run all manner of taverns in their homes; and many parishioners who live in our parishes want to sell their homes to the Germans, because the Germans buy the properties and the land at a high price, twice what Russians pay and more, and because of these Germans our parishes are emptying.[20]

Religious and moral fears mingled with economic motives: when parishioners disappeared, priests' incomes declined. The royal response was an order for demolition of existing foreign churches and their removal beyond the city walls.[21]

Anti-foreign feelings intensified at the beginning of the reign of Mikhail's young son Aleksei, who succeeded him in 1645. Aleksei was much influenced by a group of Orthodox churchmen known as the Zealots of Piety (*revniteli blagochestiia*), among them his confessor Stefan Vonifat'ev and Patriarch Joseph (1642–52), whose campaign to cleanse and revive Orthodoxy included a heavy anti-foreign bias and 'Puritanical' elements.[22] Foreigners were barred from hiring Russian servants and the sale of tobacco (a pernicious foreign habit) was banned, as were musical instruments for secular entertainment. 'German' influence on icons was denounced, the patriarch warning that they should not be 'depicted after the manner of the Latin and German deceivers, for it is not fitting that icons should reflect human lusts'.[23] This was all accompanied by a largely unsuccessful campaign to persuade foreigners to convert to Orthodoxy, which reached a height in 1652 when the Scottish colonel Alexander Leslie was tried on charges of taking pot-shots at the crosses on a church, together with his wife who was said to have thrown an icon into a fire and forced her Russian servants to eat dog meat during fasts. Both agreed to convert.[24] (Adam Olearius mentions an assault on a foreign church by a mob who pulled off the roof and threw out the altars and pulpits in response to the alleged desecration of icons.[25]) Another leading member of the Zealots, Nikon, who succeeded Joseph as patriarch in 1652, is said to have been outraged when he inadvertently administered a blessing to some 'Germans' in a crowd, which led to a ban on the wearing of Russian dress by foreigners.[26]

Tsar Aleksei and his advisers were equally influenced by laymen, especially merchants, who resented the exemption of foreign traders from certain taxes and customs dues and other privileges they enjoyed, for example with respect to brewing and the purchase of estates. During the Moscow riots of 1648 anti-foreign statements were heard and merchants' appeals for foreigners to be excluded from Russian commerce were supported by other members of the Assembly of the Land which tried to resolve the situation. There were even calls for the expulsion of foreign mercenaries.[27] This was the background to the removal in 1649 of English merchants from Moscow to Archangel, on the pretext that their fellow countrymen had committed regicide.[28] Chapter 19, article 40 of the Law Code of 1649 repeated both prohibitions on 'Germans' buying land and property in the city and the ban on foreign churches, which were to be located 'beyond Zemlianii gorod [one of Moscow's outer suburbs] distant from the churches of God'.[29] Chapter 20, article 70 stated: 'Unbaptised foreigners in Moscow and the provincial towns shall keep in their houses only foreigners of various different creeds as slaves.' It was claimed that in the past Orthodox servants had suffered 'oppression and profanation' at the hands of foreign masters, dying without confession and prevented from observing fasts. 'And accordingly now Russians shall not be in the houses of unbaptised foreigners for any reason whatsoever.' Article 71 made provisions for foreign slaves in foreign households who wished to convert to Orthodoxy to be redeemed from their owners.[30]

The edict of October 1652 removing 'unbaptised' foreigners to their own self-contained suburb on the eastern outskirts of Moscow, known as the 'New German Quarter' (*Novo-nemetskaia sloboda*), or Foreign Quarter, was fully in keeping with these developments.[31] It may have suited foreigners, too, who according to Olearius asked to be moved following assaults and humiliations; they also escaped the fires that periodically engulfed the centre of Moscow and lived in greater safety. In 1678 Bernard Tanner, a member of a Polish delegation, was told that foreigners moved 'because the Russians outdo them in drunkenness'.[32]

Confining 'Germans' to a virtual ghetto failed to stem the spread of foreign influences. When Archpriest Avvakum, leader of the Old Believer religious sect, exclaimed: 'Poor Russia, what do you want with German ways and customs?' he had in mind a number of developments, of which shaving provides a significant case history. Avvakum refused to bless the son of the boyar V. P. Sheremetev when he appeared before him in such 'depraved fashion' (*bludoliubnyi obraz*).[33] The Orthodox and Catholic priesthoods had long been in dispute over the matter of facial hair – a late seventeenth-century Russian tract warned that 'Latin Jesuits, Dominicans, Bernardines and others not only shave their beards but also their moustaches and look like apes or monkeys'[34] – but the problem was exacerbated in the latter half of the seventeenth century when the fashion for being clean-shaven spread through the urban classes in most Western countries, lasting into the following century and beyond. The beard became a more potent symbol than hitherto of the separateness of Orthodox Russians from foreigners. 'Look often at the icon of the Second Coming of Christ', another tract warned, 'and observe the righteous standing at the right side of Christ, all with beards. At the left stand the Muslims and heretics, Lutherans and Poles and other shavers of their ilk, with just whiskers, such as cats and dogs have. Take heed whom to imitate and which side you will be on.'[35] The message can be found in graphic form in frescoes of the Last Judgment depicting clean-shaven men in Western dress descending into hell.[36]

In the later seventeenth century such warnings became all the more urgent as a few Russians began to adopt Western fashions. Tsar Aleksei decreed: 'Courtiers are forbidden to adopt foreign and German (*inozem-skikh i nemetskikh*) and other customs, to cut the hair on their heads and to wear robes, caftans and hats of foreign design, and they are to forbid their servants to do so.'[37] Aleksei himself as a child had suits of Western clothing made for him, but these were regarded as a sort of fancy dress for wearing in the privacy of the palace, not suitable garb for public occasions. In 1680 his son Tsar Fedor issued sumptuary laws banning certain items of expensive court dress, which at the same time outlawed specifically foreign styles.[38]

It is significant that the warnings against the aping of foreign manners were directed mainly at the court, for this was where influence was strongest. Many of the foreign specialists who lived in the New German Quarter were employees of the royal household, for example the craftsmen and painters who produced the first Russian royal portraits and painted the scenery for the first theatrical perform-ances, staged at Aleksei's court in the period 1672–6 by German youths under the direction of a Lutheran pastor.[39] Aleksei was fascinated by foreign 'innovations', but he and his immediate successors had the patriarch at their shoulder, reminding them of the dangers. Patriarch Joachim (1674–90) was equally alarmed by developments during the seven-year regency of Sophia Alekseevna, when Russia's entry into the Holy League against the Turks in 1686 brought concessions for foreign Catholics and two Jesuit priests were admitted to Moscow. The failure of Russia's campaigns against the Crimean Tatars in 1687 and 1689 hastened the fall (in September 1689) of the regent and her chief minister Prince Vasilii Golitsyn, who was known as a 'friend of foreigners'. In turn, Joachim, in the Testament referred to earlier, associated military defeat with the policy of hiring foreigners: 'No good can come from allowing a heretic – a non-Orthodox man – to hold in bondage, to command, or to judge the Orthodox Christians in the pious tsarist realm. ... It is true that in olden times and within our memory, foreigners have served in Russian regiments. But what good came of it?' In a postscript he appealed to Tsars Ivan and Peter to ban the churches of 'heretic dissenters', not to adopt 'any new Latin and alien customs, nor to introduce the wearing of foreign dress'.[40]

This statement coincided with a virulent anti-foreign campaign, observed among others by the Frenchman Foy de la Neuville, who contrasted the virtues of the fallen Prince Vasilii Golitsyn, who spoke good Latin, enjoyed meeting foreigners and encouraged foreign travel, and of his cousin Mikhail Andreevich Golitsyn, who had 'a strong inclination towards foreigners', with the vices of those 'brutes' the Naryshkins, Peter's maternal relatives, who after Vasilii Golitsyn's demise imposed restrictions upon foreign entry into Russia and discrimination against Catholics.[41] In October 1689 the Jesuit fathers Georgius David and Tobias Tichavsky were expelled. Two priests were allowed to serve the foreign Catholic community, but the authorities were exhorted to ensure that they did not try to convert Russians, visit them in their homes or turn out to be Jesuits in disguise.[42] After the Protestant mystic Quirinus Kuhlman was burned on Red Square in the same month, the governor of Novgorod was warned to take care that

> such criminals should not enter the country and that foreigners who in future arrive from abroad from various countries at the border ... and claim that they have come to enter service or to visit relatives or for some other business in Moscow, should be questioned at the border ... and detained and not allowed to proceed to Moscow until you receive our royal instructions.[43]

The Scottish officer Patrick Gordon records that the atmosphere for a few months after Sophia's overthrow was so oppressive that he contemplated leaving Russia. On the patriarch's orders he and other foreign officers were barred from attending a banquet in the Kremlin, but the next day eighteen-year-old Tsar Peter dined with Gordon, his special friend, showing that Joachim was fighting a losing battle.[44]

A new era in foreign relations was inaugurated by Peter's Grand Embassy to Western Europe in 1697–8. This in turn brought more foreign specialists to Russia, including new categories such as ship-builders, naval officers, navigators and teachers of mathematics, and culminated in Peter's attack on the long beards and Russian dress of his boyars.[45] In 1702 Peter issued a manifesto which decreed that all foreign officers, merchants and craftsmen must be given every assist-ance, be treated with 'benevolence' and allowed 'unrestricted passage', including freedom to terminate their contracts in the manner 'usually adhered to by the other rulers of Europe'. Free exercise of faith must be tolerated, since 'deriving our power from the All-Highest, we do not pretend to compel any human conscience but readily allow each Christian to work for his own salvation at his own risk'.[46] Peter often visited Protestant and Catholic churches, both abroad and in Russia, for example, for the baptisms, weddings and funerals of the families of foreign shipwrights. He particularly admired Lutheran sermons and in 1702 he even laid the foundation stone of the new Lutheran church of SS. Peter Paul in the German Quarter.[47] But he was not without preju-dice, according to anecdotal evidence at least: 'I would rather see the Muhammedan and pagan faiths in my country than Jews. They are rogues and swindlers', he allegedly said. 'I wish to eradicate evil, not inculcate it.'[48] Jesuits constituted another blank spot: several were expelled from Russia in 1719 following differences with the Austrians over the affair of Tsarevich Aleksei, who fled to the Habsburg lands in 1716. Stählin recounted: 'Peter tolerated all Christian faiths without distinction … only about the Jesuits did he refuse to hear a word or to tolerate them in Russia.' In Peter's view, Jesuits were venal and manip-ulative and could not help interfering in affairs of state. He was sur-prised that they were admitted to so many European courts.[49]

It was not only the need for foreign expertise which led to official reductions in religious sanctions. Peter married off his son, two of his nieces and one of his daughters to non-Orthodox foreigners, abandon-ing the previous practice of supplying *tsarevichi* with brides from Russian boyar families (Peter's own first marriage to Evdokiia Lopukhina in 1689 was a case in point) and keeping *tsarevny* unmarried and in seclusion. A landmark in this respect was the marriage in 1711 of Peter's heir, Tsarevich Aleksei, to Princess Charlotte of Brunswick-Wolfenbüttel. Charlotte was allowed to retain her Protestant faith, although children of the marriage were to be raised in Orthodoxy.[50] There is no doubt that this 'German' marriage served further to alienate Aleksei and conservative opinion from Peter. The principle that 'the marriage of a person of the faith to one of another faith is right and lawful', supported by extensive biblical and historical quotations, was embodied in an edict of 1721 permitting Swedish prisoners of war in Siberia to marry local Russian women. It was still specified that the Orthodox spouse must not be pressurized to convert and that children of the marriage must be raised in Orthodoxy. Priests were to make sure that the wives and children of such marriages were attending church regularly.[51]

Copious examples survive from the 1690s onwards of anti-foreign remarks and protests. An anonymous letter discovered in a church in Moscow, for example, warned that the tsar had been 'seduced by Germans and German women into the Latin faith' and was even being poisoned by them. The author railed against the lowering of moral standards and smoking and advised the tsar to attend church more often to avert a Turkish attack.[52] Anxieties were raised by the Grand Embassy and Peter's attack on traditional beards and dress. One tract listed numerous, mainly foreign 'innovations' regarded as harmful to the soul, including smoking, drinking tea and coffee, German dress, Italian singing and painting, shaving and embalming corpses.[53] Peter consorted with foreigners, later married one, looked like one (being beardless and dressed in foreign clothes), perhaps even was one. 'We don't have a sovereign but a substitute German', some landowners complained.[54] Rumours circulated about Peter's origins, for example the story that his mother had given birth to a daughter, who was exchanged for a baby boy from the German Quarter.[55] It was said that the Germans had put the real Peter in prison and sent a fake tsar.[56] 'The tsar loves Germans, shares their faith and dresses his soldiers in German coats', one critic complained. Another was tortured for denouncing a 'Saxon' fur coat and saying that he would like to hang the person who introduced the fashion.[57] Peter was villified for introducing German stockings and boots, which were identified with the 'cow's hooves' of Antichrist.[58]

Denunciation of foreigners was a staple element in all the major rebellions of the late seventeenth to early eighteenth centuries, even before Peter personally became associated with 'Germans'. There was talk of 'foreign guile' during the *strel'tsy* (musketeer) rebellion of 1682, when two foreign doctors were murdered on suspicion of preparing poisonous potions for the royal household.[59] The four regiments of *strel'tsy* who mutinied in June 1698, thereby prematurely ending Peter's stay abroad, in their petitions to the authorities vowed to kill the 'Germans' who were 'destroying Orthodoxy'.[60] In 1705 the Astrakhan rebels also threatened to go to Moscow and kill any German they encountered, to appeal for the old belief to be restored and for permission not to have to wear German dress or to shave.[61] Three years later the Cossack rebel Kondratii Bulavin declared that 'we cannot be silent on account of the evil deeds of wicked men and princes and boyars and profitmakers and Germans and cannot let them off for leading everyone into the Hellenistic pagan faith and diverting them away from the true Christian faith with their signs and cunning tricks'.[62] The alleged 'German' threat to Orthodoxy was a common element in the popular discourse about the perversion of legitimate power by the interposition of a person or a group of persons between the ruler and his subjects, which in the cases quoted above allowed mutiny and revolt to be redefined as loyal service to the crown for the purpose of eliminating 'traitors'.[63]

In reality, of course, all these rebellions originated in a complex mix of social, economic and personal grievances to which foreigners actually contributed little, but even some of Peter's supporters felt uneasy at his seemingly excessive reliance upon foreign aid. Offended patriotic sensibilities were a strong element in the growing retrospective criticism of Peter's reign from the late eighteenth century onwards. 'Peter, having seen Europe, wanted to turn Russia into Holland', wrote Nikolai Karamzin. 'We became citizens of the world but ceased in certain respects to be citizens of Russia. The fault is Peter's.'[64] Such mild reservations culminated in the more vitriolic attacks of the Slavophiles against 'the system introduced by Peter the Great and the foreign influence which is inseparable from it' which 'sowed the seeds of conflict and destruction in Russian life'.[65] Peter's own publicists strove to counter accusations of immoderate 'xenophilia' with praise for the tsar's selfless efforts for the common good. A story attributed to Pavel Iaguzhinskii, Peter's first procurator-general, himself formerly a Lutheran, makes the point:

> It would be wrong to say that Peter the Great had a blind love of foreigners and foreign customs and their way of life; it is evident from all circumstances that he loved foreigners and treated them graciously only for the benefit of his State ... Once he said in the presence of a number of Russian gentlemen: 'I know that the marked preference that I give to foreigners is not pleasing to all my subjects.

But I have different subjects: some are intelligent and reasonable and observe that I treat foreigners well and try to get them to stay here in order that they [my subjects] can learn from them and adopt their sciences and arts, for the good of the state and for the evident benefit of my subjects. I also have foolhardy and wicked subjects who do not appreciate or acknowledge my good intentions and wish to remain in the old mire of their ignorance. In their stupidity they despise anything good which is new to them and would willingly hinder it if only they could. They do not reflect on what it was like in our country before I travelled to foreign lands and invited foreigners to Russia and how little I would have achieved without their aid in all my undertakings against our strong enemies.'[66]

The future historian Vasilii Tatishchev, one of Peter's orderlies in his youth, recorded how in 1724 Peter countered his challenge to an order to hire academicians in Sweden on the grounds that 'it is pointless to look for seeds when the ground in which to sow them is not prepared' with the following story:

A certain nobleman wanted to build a mill in his village but he had no water. Seeing that his neighbours had lakes and swamps containing plenty of water he at once began, with their consent, to dig a channel and lay in the supplies for a mill which even if it could not be completed in his lifetime, would be taken over and finished by his children who would not want to waste the investment made by their father.[67]

In other words, Peter was working for Russia's future and did not always expect to see immediate results.

Most energetic in his attacks on Peter's critics was Archbishop Feofan Prokopovich of Pskov, who reacted, for example, to allegations that fleets were 'ungodly' by pointing out that God had created seas as a means of communication between countries and anyone who denounced Peter's navy was displaying ingratitude to God.[68] When Peter returned from an extended trip abroad in 1717 Prokopovich was there to extol the mind-broadening virtues of foreign travel.[69] His most energetic attacks were reserved for those who spurned education. His early play 'Vladimir' (1705), about the Christianization of Rus' in the tenth century, featured a group of stubborn and ignorant pagan priests, whose resistance to the new 'foreign' religion brought to mind Peter's unenlightened opponents.

Prokopovich could with justification argue that Peter's attitude to foreigners was 'discriminating'. This was later the approach of Soviet historians, who had to maintain a tricky 'bipolar' approach to the Petrine era, weighing 'progressive' achievements in foreign policy and education and the fact that Peter 'used the West to beat the West' against suspicions of 'rootless cosmopolitanism', not to mention Peter's oppression of the peasantry. In fact, despite popular perceptions to the contrary, after the deaths of his friends Patrick Gordon and Franz Lefort in 1699, 'Germans' had fairly little influence in civilian government or among Peter's close circle. The major exceptions were the vice-presidencies of the Collegiate boards, established in 1717–18, which were reserved for foreigners, and special advisers such as Heinrich Fick, consultant on foreign administrations, and Heinrich Huyssens, tutor to Tsarevich Aleksei and collaborator on the official history of Peter's reign. It has been suggested that there were 'no more than twenty' foreigners in the central government. Indeed, a decision may have been made to reduce their numbers still further on the grounds that foreign personnel were less effective than anticipated in mentoring their Russian colleagues as a result of their poor knowledge of Russian.[70] Foreigners were more numerous in the army and dominated the upper echelons of the navy, although here too Peter tried to reduce their numbers.[71] The Naval Statute specified that the skippers of Russian merchant ships should recruit sailors 'of the Russian nation' (*Rossiiskoi natsii*). No more than a quarter of the crew should be foreigners.[72] Even in the matter of shipbuilding, Peter acknowledged Russia's growing expertise. In 1713 he wrote to F. M. Apraksin criticizing some of the new ships bought in France, England and Hamburg which he had just inspected in St Petersburg: 'They are truly deserving of the name of foster children because they are as remote from our ships as a foster father from a real one, for they are much smaller than ours, and even though there are just as many guns, there is not so much space.'[73]

Self-sufficiency was a stated aim. When in 1700 the merchants Osip and Fedor Bazhennii reported that they had built a water-powered saw mill on their estate 'on the German model, by themselves, without the help of foreign masters', they sensed that this would please the tsar.[74] 'This paper was made here in a mill', states an edict of 1723, 'and we can make as much of it as we need in this country and not only commission it in France.'[75] Peter wrote to his wife Catherine: 'I have another marvel to relate: yesterday in Peterhof the fountain was working, the like of which you won't even see in France.'[76] An anecdote, much quoted in Soviet works, makes the point less delicately: 'It's good to borrow sciences and arts from the French, I would like to see all that in my own country; all the same, Paris still stinks.'[77] Peter was sensitive to outside opinion and also very aware of the need to balance flattery through emulation against national pride. The French minister in St Petersburg, Jacques de Campredon, reported a visit to Peterhof palace in summer 1723 in a dispatch to Louis XV:

> The tsar did me the honour of saying that as I had seen so many beautiful things in France he doubted whether I would find anything of much interest at Peterhof, adding that he hoped that Your Majesty had such a beautiful view at Versailles as here at Peterhof from where one has a view of the sea and of Kronstadt on one side and St Petersburg on the other. I told this Prince that I had good reason to admire the fact that during such a long war and in such a harsh climate he had been able to perfect these beautiful things and that I deemed them very worthy of Your Majesty's curiosity.[78]

Foreigners were obliged to train Russians, which they did with varying degrees of success. It was recognized that 'when the years of apprenticeship [of Russian pupils of tapestry weaving] are completed, it will be possible to send the foreigners back home and use His Majesty's subjects for this work, as a result of which this craft will remain in the Russian empire'.[79] Even so, monopolies sometimes had to be granted to foreign craftsmen at high rates 'because local masters who were trained in Russia are insufficiently skilled' (1726).[80] Records paint a grim picture of relations between foreign teachers and their pupils, partly, perhaps, because good relations rarely gave rise to written evidence. Foreigners' inability to speak Russian often led to misunderstandings, while their clothing, life-style and manners had more in common with those of Russian nobles than with the craftsmen who worked under them.[81] No doubt many of the latter shared the distrust of foreigners expressed by the entrepreneur Ivan Pososhkov, who in the 1720s wrote that 'if any such foreigner wastes his time in idleness (as is the long-standing habit of foreigners), neglecting to teach his pupils – since he has come here merely to wheedle money out of us and then to make off home again – let him be sent home with dishonour ...'.[82]

Not all Russians were so sceptical. The nobleman Fedor Saltykov made several visits abroad and spent three years (1712–15) in England. In a memorandum to Peter (1714), he wrote: 'During my stay in England and Holland amidst the affairs which I was commanded to direct by your all-merciful orders, I also looked thoroughly at their advantages and government and noted examples of what might be done in your realms.'[83] Beggars and orphans might be accommodated and taught useful crafts by churches, as in the decree in operation 'throughout all England in all their parishes'. Thames wherries with liveried oarsmen, the penny post, libraries, the special privileges and rights of free trade in the city of London, methods of cheesemaking – all were worthy of emulation.[84] Saltykov recommended sending 'mature persons who know the condition of the Russian realm' to observe practices in England, Holland and France with respect to taxes, duties, currency and customs and also advised stricter supervision of young Russians studying abroad.[85] In particular, he advocated the spread of masonry and paving techniques 'in the way it is done all over England' beyond the towns into the villages, where Russian peasants might learn to make bricks and tiles in the winter months, or use unhewn stone. In alluding to the stark contrast between town and country in Russia, especially between Peter's 'city of stone' and everywhere else, Saltykov had hit upon a contrast which remained, and in some ways remains, resistant to Peter's attempts at reform and added fuel to the argument that Peter had created two nations – a Westernized, 'alien' urban minority and a largely unreformed, alienated provincial majority.

Peter and his reforms were deeply unpopular for a variety of reasons – they imposed enormous burdens of military service, taxation and labour, they dislocated people, they offended religious sensibilities and national pride. Antipathy towards foreigners was inextricably intertwined in all this. Even members of the tsar's inner circle were not immune. Johannes Korb, in Moscow in 1698–9, reported that the reaction of Peter's loyal servitor Prince Fedor Romodanovskii to the information that Ambassador Fedor Golovin had donned foreign dress in Vienna in 1698 was disbelief that Golovin would have been 'such a brainless ass as to despise the garb of his fatherland'.[86] Years later, Johann Gotthilf Vockerodt, secretary to the Prussian legation in St Petersburg, noted the hatred felt by members of the nobility for lifelong military service, for St Petersburg (which was associated with service) and the navy: 'However tiny his estate, even if he has to follow the plough himself, he still prefers it to being a soldier!' This extended to hatred of foreigners.[87]

It is hardly surprising that the population at large did not immediately adopt 'enlightened' attitudes. Korb observed that 'the main delight of the Muscovite populace is to rob and run riot against the Germans'.

He recorded the following outburst: 'Ye German dogs! You have been robbing long enough at your ease, but the day is at hand when you shall suffer and pay the penalty.'[88] Over two decades later Campredon reported an attack on the wife and servants of the Dutch resident:

> Such incidents are commonplace in St Petersburg as a result of the ignorance (*l'impolitesse*) of the Russians. ... In this country the spirit (*génie*) of the population completely accords with the harshness of the climate, so that even those Russians who learn good manners abroad on returning home see themselves obliged to comply with the general manners of their fellow countrymen.[89]

A few years later the Spanish ambassador, the Duke de Liria, who was much given to moaning, wrote that 'the malice against foreigners is universal; the people are quick to attack our homes and we risk not only injury but even death'. He records an incident in May 1729 when soldiers had refused to put out a fire in the Moscow German Quarter on the grounds that 'it's only Germans and Frenchmen burning'.[90]

The problems discussed in this essay did not, of course, disappear after 1729. The rest of the eighteenth century – the period of the so-called 'Bironovshchina' under Empress Anna, the reign of the German Empress Catherine II, Gallomania, reactions to the French Revolution and the Napoleonic Wars and beyond – offers many variations on the theme. It would be tempting to think that the time is now ripe for a dispassionate reassessment of the whole question of foreigners and foreign influences in Russia, now that the vestiges of Stalinist anti-cosmopolitanism and its toned-down '*détente*' version have faded with the demise of the USSR. Throughout the Soviet era there were ideological barriers to a full and frank examination of questions of borrowing and influence. A striking example may be found in N. A. Baklanova's detailed analysis of the account books of the Grand Embassy, in which she listed copious examples of the goods bought by Peter and his companions – clothing, food, porcelain, scientific instruments – then, as if sensing that these simple material facts might provoke invidious comparisons, added that the

> assimilation of elements of alien culture did not devalue their own cultural heritage in the eyes of [members of] the Embassy, which

was linked with national identity. These facts prove that the assimilation of elements of West European life was not blind imitation, but that they were subjected to serious internal evaluation on the basis of people's own culture.[91]

Such arguments put shopping trips abroad in a new light! It was argued that Peter always chose selectively from abroad, 'creatively reworking' borrowed elements. Limited native achievements received a lion's share of attention; foreign efforts were neglected, for example in the area of painting and fine art.[92] Conversely, Western historians have sometimes been guilty of one-upmanship, assuming Western cultural superiority and exaggerating Russia's backwardness, echoing de la Neuville's assertion that 'without the Germans, who are in Moscow in large numbers, they could do nothing right'.[93] Early modern Russian attitudes also need to be viewed in a comparative perspective; dislike of foreigners, of 'the other', was (is) universal. As Linda Colley amply illustrates, xenophobia – hatred of Catholics, the Scots, the French – was very much part of early modern 'Englishness', which displayed 'a vast superstructure of prejudice'.[94]

In the eighteenth century Western thinkers, from Leibniz onwards, were apt to regard Russia as an object lesson in the potential transplantation of 'civilization', a subject which provoked heated debate between Voltaire and Rousseau, among others.[95] Peter himself believed that 'borrowing' was a temporary phenomenon. In a speech recorded by Friedrich Weber, minister of Hanover in Russia, Peter imagined the 'transmigration of sciences' from ancient Greece, via England, France and Germany to Russia, which had the potential to 'put other civilized nations to the blush, and to carry the glory of the Russian name to the highest pitch'.[96] If this is accurately reported, then it was not the first or the last time that Russia regarded itself as a potential leader of world civilization, rather than as a fringe member doomed forever to 'catch up' with advanced nations. The post-Soviet era is clearly not one of those times: loss of empire and the 'scientific' certainties of Marxist–Leninist doctrine, the collapse of domestic industries, NATO enlargement, European integration, and the resurgence of the Orthodox Church bring with them the growth of nationalism, the denunciation of Western brand names, appeals for the protection of the Russian language, calls for restrictions on foreign 'sects', even attacks on foreigners who flaunt their wealth. The state authorities are faced with a dilemma similar to that encountered on numerous occasions by their seventeenth-century predecessors: whether to give in to the demands of indigenous factional interests – the modern-day equivalents of the Muscovite merchants or hierarchs of the Orthodox Church – or whether to adhere to modernizing policies involving free and open contacts with the outside world. Scholars may take a dispassionate view, but the cursed questions of Russian xenophobia and 'xenophilia', of national pride and imitation, are as potent today as ever they were in the early modern period.

Notes

1. Extract from the Testament of Joachim, Patriarch of Moscow (1674–90), 17 March 1690, in *A Source Book for Russian History from Early Times to 1917*, ed. George Vernadsky, vol. 2 (New Haven, 1972), p. 362. Full text in N. Ustrialov, *Istoriia tsarstvovaniia Petra Velikogo*, vol. 2 (St Petersburg, 1858), appendix 9, pp. 467–77.
2. *Pravda voli monarshei* (1722), attributed to Feofan Prokopovich, trans. and ed. Antony Lentin as *Peter the Great: His Law on the Imperial Succession. An Official Commentary* (Oxford, 1996), p. 279.
3. Iu. Lotman, 'The Poetics of Everyday Behaviour in Russian Eighteenth-Century Culture', in *The Semiotics of Russian Culture*, ed. Anne Shukman (Ann Arbor, 1984), pp. 232–4.
4. See Oleg Pritsak, *The Origin of Rus* (Harvard, 1981), pp. 3–4; Simon Franklin and Jonathan Shepard, *The Emergence of Rus 750–1200* (London and New York, 1996), pp. 38–9.
5. See M. Pliukhanova, *Siuzhety i simvoly moskovskogo gosudarstva* (St Petersburg, 1995). Western scholars have tended to concentrate on Moscow's concept of itself as the successor to Constantinople/Rome, but the symbolic transfer to Moscow of locations in the Holy Land was equally prevalent. Peter Chaadaev, who initiated the Westernist–Slavophile debates of the 1830s–1840s, wrote of this period: 'We were isolated in our schism and nothing that was happening in Europe reached us. ... When Christianity was advancing majestically along the road which had been traced for it by its divine founder and was sweeping generations along with it, in spite of the fact that we called ourselves Christians, we did not budge' (from 'First Philosophical Letter' (1829), in *The Major Works of Peter Chaadaev*, ed. Raymond T. McNally (Notre Dame, Ind., 1969), p. 40).
6. Sigismund von Herberstein, *Description of Moscow and Muscovy*, ed. Bertold Picard, trans. J. B. C. Grundy (London, 1969), p. 62. The bowl also appears in accounts from the 1630s–1650s: *The Travels of Olearius in 17th-Century Russia*, trans. and ed. Samuel Baron (Stanford, Cal., 1967), p. 63, and *Relation d'un voyage en Moscovie écrite par Augustin Baron de Mayerberg* (Paris, 1858), vol. 1, p. 99.
7. 'On the Russe Commonwealth' [1591], in *Rude and Barbarous Kingdom: Russia in the Accounts of Sixteenth-Century English Voyagers*, ed. Lloyd E. Berry and Robert O. Crummey (Madison, 1968), p. 172.

8. 'On the Russe Commonwealth', p. 214.

9. *Ibid.*, pp. 244–5.

10. *Ibid.*, p. 109.

11. John Perry, *The State of Russia (1716)* (London, 1967), p. 209. Perry was an ardent admirer of Peter and his efforts to reform the 'Biggottry and Superstition' of his people (p. 221).

12. Just Juel, 'Iz zapisok datskogo poslannika Iusta Iulia', *Russkii arkhiv* (1892), p. 133.

13. See D. Tsvetaev, *Protestantstvo i protestanty v Rossii do epokhi preobrazovaniia* (Moscow, 1890); A. S. Muliukin, *Priezd inostrantsev v Moskovskoe Gosudarstvo* (St Petersburg, 1909).

14. See Maureen Perrie, *Pretenders and Popular Monarchism in Early Modern Russia: The False Tsars of the Time of Troubles* (Cambridge, 1995); S. M. Solov'ev, *History of Russia,* vol. 14: *The Time of Troubles: Boris Godunov and False Dmitry,* trans. and ed. G. Edward Orchard (Gulf Breeze, 1988), pp. 106–8.

15. Discussion in A. B. Kamenskii, *Arkhivnoe delo v Rossii XVIII veka: Istoriko-kul'turnyi aspekt* (Moscow, 1991), pp. 23–4.

16. See examples in *Slovar' russkogo iazyka XI–XVII veka,* 21 vols (continuing) (Moscow, 1975–). *Inozemtsy* – people from other lands – were foreigners in general. On the Law Code see note 29 below.

17. I. Snegirev, 'O nachale i rasprostranenii liuteranskikh i reformatskikh tserkvei v Moskve', *Moskvitianin,* vol. 6 (1844), pp. 270–80; D. Tsvetaev, 'Polozhenie protestantov v Rossii do Petra Velikago', *Zhurnal ministerstva narodnogo prosveshcheniia,* September–October 1883, pp. 84–5.

18. See Muliukin, *Priezd inostrantsev,* p. 138; D. Tsvetaev, *Istoriia sooruzheniia pervogo kostela v Moskve* (Moscow, 1885).

19. Note the use of separate terms for foreign churches. Only an Orthodox church was a *tserkov'*. A Protestant church was *kirka* (*kerka, kirkha*) or (here), *ropata,* which can also refer to a mosque. A Catholic church is *kostël* (from the Polish).

20. Tsvetaev, 'Polozhenie protestantov', p. 79. For a detailed analysis of events leading to the foundation of the Moscow German Quarter, see Samuel Baron, 'The Origins of Seventeenth-Century Moscow's Nemeckaja Sloboda', *California Slavic Studies,* vol. 5 (1970), pp. 1–18.

21. See *Akty istoricheskie, sobrannye i izdannye arkheograficheskoiu kommissieiu,* vol. 3 (St Petersburg, 1841), no. 92, pp. 114–15.

22. See Lindsey Hughes, 'Zealots of Piety', *Modern Encyclopedia of Russian and Soviet History,* vol. 45 (Gulf Breeze, 1987), pp. 213–15.

23. Quoted in Nikolay Andreyev, 'Nikon and Avvakum on Icon-Painting', *Revue des Études Slaves,* vol. 38 (1961), p. 40.

24. Baron, 'The Origins', pp. 12–14, uses the Swede Johannes Rodes' dispatches for this period (B. Kurts, 'Sostoianie Rossii v 1650–1655', *Chteniia v imperatorskom obshchestve istorii i drevnostei rossiiskikh* (1915), no. 2).

25. *The Travels of Olearius,* p. 281.

26. Baron, 'The Origins', p. 15.

27. See K. V. Bazilevich, 'Kollektivnye chelobyt'ia kupechestva i bor'ba za russkii rynok v pervoi polovine XVII veka', *Izvestiia Akademii Nauk SSSR: Otdelenie obshchestvennykh nauk,* 1932, no. 2; L. Loewenson, 'The Moscow

rising of 1648', *Slavonic and East European Review*, vol. 27 (1948), pp. 146–57; Baron, 'The Origins', p. 9.

28. See *Polnoe Sobranie Zakonov Rossiiskoi Imperii*, vol. 1 (St Petersburg, 1830), no. 9 (hereafter, *PSZ*); Tsvetaev, *Protestantstvo v Rossii*, pp. 53–4; Graeme Herd, 'General Patrick Gordon of Auchleuchries – a Scot in Seventeenth-Century Russian Service', unpublished doctoral dissertation, University of Aberdeen (1994), pp. 30–1.

29. *The Muscovite Law Code (Ulozhenie) of 1649, Part I: Text and Translation*, ed. and trans. Richard Hellie (Irvine, 1988), pp. 160–1; Baron, 'The Origins', p. 11, asserts that these measures were 'consistent with the tendency of the Ulozhenie to classify all people into well-defined and mutually exclusive groups'.

30. *The Muscovite Law Code*, p. 182.

31. See Baron, 'The Origins'. In *The Travels of Olearius*, pp. 279–80, Baron offers several interpretations of the alternative name for the Quarter, Kukui, which happens to rhyme with the word *khui* (Russian for 'penis').

32. Bernard Tanner, 'Opisanie puteshestviia pol'skogo posol'stva v Moskvu v 1678 g.', *Chteniia v imperatorskom obshchestve istorii i drevnostei rossiiskikh* (1891), book 3, pp. 125–9.

33. 'Okh, okh, bednaia Rus', chego-to tebe zakhotelos' nemetskikh postupov i obychaev', in *Zhitie protopopa Avvakuma im samim napisannoe i drugie ego sochineniia* (Moscow, 1960), p. 136 and p. 62. For his views on 'German' distortions in religious art, see Andreyev, 'Nikon and Avvakum'. Avvakum blamed such wickedness on the fall of the church leaders from Orthodoxy, although in fact Patriarch Nikon was equally hard on foreign fashions.

34. Patriarch Adrian's tract on matters of faith (1690s), point 15, against the 'heretical' custom of shaving, in G. V. Esipov, *Raskol'nich'i dela*, vol. 2 (St Petersburg, 1861), p. 87.

35. Quoted in F. Buslaev, 'Drevne-russkaia boroda', *Drevne-russkaia literatura i iskusstvo*, vol. 2 (St Petersburg, 1861), p. 235.

36. See, for example, details from a fresco (1686–8) in the Cathedral of the Holy Wisdom, Vologda, in V. G. Briusova, *Russkaia zhivopis' 17 veka* (Moscow, 1984), ill. 158. *The Travels of Olearius*, p. 50, describes a similar scene.

37. *PSZ*, vol. I, no. 607 (6 August 1675).

38. See P. V. Sedov, 'Reforma sluzhilogo plat'ia pri Fedore Alekseeviche', *Trudy Vserossiiskoi nauchnoi konferentsii 'Kogda Rossiia molodaia muzhala s geniem Petra', posviashchennoi 300-letnemu iubileiu otechestvennogo flota* (Pereslavl'-Zalesskii, 1992), pp. 77–83.

39. See Lindsey Hughes, 'The Moscow Armoury and Innovations in 17th-Century Muscovite Art', *Canadian–American Slavic Studies*, vol. 13 (1979), pp. 204–23; Simon Karlinsky, *Russian Drama from its Beginnings to the Age of Pushkin* (Berkeley, Cal., 1985).

40. Testament of Joachim, pp. 362–3.

41. Foy de la Neuville, *A Curious and New Account of Muscovy in the Year 1689*, ed. Lindsey Hughes (London, 1994), pp. 20–1, 25, 54, 57. On the political background, see Paul Bushkovitch, 'Aristocratic Faction and the Opposition to Peter the Great: the 1690s', *Forschungen zur osteuropäischen Geschichte: Beitrage zur '7. Internationalen Konferenz zur Geschichte des Kiever und des Moskauer Reiches'* (Berlin, 1995), pp. 80–120.

42. *PSZ*, vol. III, no. 1351, pp. 39–40; *ibid.*, no. 1388, pp. 86–7 (no date, 1690).
43. *Ibid.*, no. 1358, pp. 46–7 (29 October 1689); J. Billington, *The Icon and the Axe* (New York, 1970), p. 173.
44. See Gordon's diary, 28–9 February 1690, which contains many details of Peter's early relations with foreigners and his visits to the German Quarter. The original, in Moscow, *Rossiiskii Gosudarstvennyi Voenno-Istoricheskii Arkhiv*, f. 846, op. 15, ed. khr. 1–6, awaits publication in full. Thanks to Graeme Herd (see note 28, above) for xeroxes.
45. On recruitment in Britain, see A. G. Cross, *By the Banks of the Neva: Chapters from the Lives and Careers of the British in Eighteenth-Century Russia* (Cambridge, 1996), pp. 160–76.
46. *PSZ*, vol. IV, no. 1910, pp. 192–5 (16 April 1702).
47. Snegirev, 'O nachale', p. 279.
48. L. N. Maikov, *Rasskazy Nartova o Petre Velikom* (St Petersburg, 1891), pp. 30–1. Jacob Stählin, *Podlinnye anekdoty o Petre Velikom* (Leningrad, 1990), pp. 34–5 (first published 1785) has a more double-edged retort, along the lines that although the Jews were swindlers Peter did not think they would make much profit from trade in Russia.
49. Stählin, *op. cit.*, pp. 35–6. For the act expelling them, see *PSZ*, vol. VI, no. 3356, p. 694.
50. *Pis'ma i bumagi Imperatora Petra Velikogo* (hereafter *PiB*), 13 vols (continuing) (St Petersburg, 1887–), vol. 11 (ii) (Moscow, 1964), pp. 123–5 (10 September 1711). In 1712 Peter himself married a foreigner, albeit a convert to Orthodoxy, an even more controversial case for conservatives since Peter's first wife was still alive.
51. *PSZ*, vol. VI, no. 3798, pp. 401–2 (23 June 1721) and no. 3814, pp. 413–19 (18 August 1721). Prokopovich published a tract on intermarriage, *O brakakh pravovernykh lits s inovernymi* (St Petersburg, 1721).
52. N. B. Golikova, *Politicheskie protsessy pri Petre I* (Moscow, 1957), pp. 131–2. Examples from the late 1690s from the Preobrazhenskii *prikaz*.
53. E. Shmurlo, *Petr Velikii v otsenke sovremennikov i potomstva* (St Petersburg, 1912), *primechaniia*, p. 1.
54. Golikova, *Politicheskie protsessy*, pp. 160–1.
55. M. Semevskii, *Slovo i delo, 1700–1725: Ocherki i rasskazy iz russkoi istorii XVIII veka* (St Petersburg, 1884), p. 66. Golikova, *Politicheskie protsessy*, pp. 149–51, 181, lists several cases of monks and priests spreading this story.
56. Golikova, *Politicheskie protsessy*, p. 169.
57. Esipov, *Raskol'nich'i dela*, vol. 2 , pp. 169–70.
58. Golikova, *Politicheskie protsessy*, pp. 145–6, 213.
59. See Lindsey Hughes, *Sophia, Regent of Russia, 1657–1704* (New Haven, 1990), p. 65. Andrei Matveev, the future diplomat, thought they were killed 'solely out of hatred and antipathy for foreigners': 'Zapiski Andreia Artamonovicha grafa Matveeva', in *Zapiski russkikh liudei*, ed. N. Sakharov (St Petersburg, 1841), p. 31.
60. Golikova, *Politicheskie protsessy*, pp. 101–22; Hughes, *Sophia*, pp. 249–55.
61. Esipov, *Raskol'nich'i dela*, vol. 2, p. 103; A. V. Chernov, 'Astrakhanskoe vosstanie 1705–1706 gg.', *Istoricheskie zapiski*, vol. 64 (1959).
62. *PiB*, vol. VII (i), pp. 600–2 (22 March 1708); Paul Avrich, *Russian Rebels, 1600–1800* (New York, 1972), p. 156.

63. See David M. McDonald '"The Wall" in Russian Political Rhetoric', *Dialogues on Discourse*, vol. 5 (1995), pp. 1–3
64. Karamzin's *Memoir on Ancient and Modern Russia* [1810] ed. Richard Pipes (Cambridge, Mass., 1959), p. 124.
65. See K. S. Aksakov, 'On the Internal State of Russia', in *Russian Intellectual History: An Anthology*, ed. Marc Raeff (Madison, 1966), pp. 242–5.
66. Stählin, *Podlinnye anekdoty*, pp. 47–9.
67. P. P. Pekarskii, *Istoriia Imp. Akademii Nauk*, vol. 1 (St Petersburg, 1870), p. xiii.
68. 'Slovo pokhvalnoe o flote rossiiskom' (1720), in *Panegiricheskaia literatura petrovskogo vremeni*, ed. V. P. Grebeniuk (Moscow, 1979), p. 236; Feofan Prokopovich, *Sochineniia*, ed. I. P. Eremin (Moscow and Leningrad, 1961), pp. 103–12.
69. See Prokopovich, *Sochineniia*, pp. 60–7.
70. Claus Peterson, *Peter the Great's Administrative and Judicial Reforms* (Stockholm, 1979), pp. 138–40. The higher cost of employing foreigners was also a consideration. See a list of wages being paid in February 1716 to various specialists employed by the royal household on the books of the Chancellery of Building. The Dutch gardener Jan Roosen received 500 roubles per annum and Denis Brockett 300 roubles, whereas Russian gardeners got 14 roubles and apprentices 10. The interpreters Tom Witt and Johann Wulff received 300 roubles, but their clerk only 36: *Doklady i prigovory sostoiavshiesia v pravitel'stvuiushchem Senate v tsarstvovanie Petra Velikogo*, vol. VI (i) (St Petersburg, 1901), pp. 135–6. The total wages of 59 foreigners employed in the Chancellery of Building in 1722 was 17,355 roubles, for 1,111 Russians – 11,840 roubles. See L. N. Semenova, 'Inostrannye mastera v Peterburge v pervoi treti XVIII v.', in *Nauka i kul'tura Rossii XVIII v. Sbornik statei* (Leningrad, 1984), p. 208.
71. See L. G. Beskrovnii, 'Voennye shkoly v pervoi polovine XVIII v.', *Istoricheskie zapiski*, vol. 42 (1953), p. 290.
72. *PSZ*, vol. VI, no. 3937, p. 539 (5 April 1722).
73. *PiB*, vol. XIII (i), p. 178 (19 June 1713, to F. M. Apraksin).
74. *PSZ*, vol. IV, no. 1749, p. 4 (2 February 1700).
75. *Leningradskoe otdelenie instituta istorii Akademii nauk*, f. 270, d. 104, l. 531 (December 1723).
76. *Ibid.*, d. 106, l. 36 (9 January 1724).
77. Maikov, *Rasskazy*, p. 34.
78. *Sbornik imperatorskogo rossiiskogo istoricheskogo obshchestva* (hereafter *SIRIO*), vol. 40, pp. 273–4 (letter to Louis XV, 3 September, New Style, 1723). Earlier he wrote that the pavilion named Marly 'does not at all resemble that of Your Majesty' (p. 272).
79. Semenova, 'Inostrannye mastera', p. 207.
80. *Ibid.*, p. 203.
81. *Ibid.*, pp. 211–12.
82. Ivan Pososhkov, *The Book of Poverty and Wealth*, ed. and trans. A. Vlasto and L. Lewitter (London, 1987), p. 282.
83. F. Saltykov, 'Iz"iavleniia pribytochnye gosudarstvu' (1714), in N. Pavlov-Sil'vanskii, *Proekty reform v zapiskakh sovremennikov Petra Velikogo* (St Petersburg, 1897), p. 5. See also M. O. Blamberg, 'The Publicists of Peter

the Great', unpublished doctoral dissertation, Indiana University (1974), *passim*.

84. Saltykov, 'Iz"iavleniia', pp. 21–3.
85. *Ibid.*, p. 41.
86. J.-G. Korb, *Diary of an Austrian Secretary of Legation at the Court of Czar Peter the Great*, trans. and ed. Count MacDonnell, vol. 1 (London, 1863/1968), p. 196.
87. J. G. Vockerodt, 'Russland unter Peter dem Grossen', *Chteniia v imperatorskom obshchestve istorii i drevnostei rossiiskikh* (1874), book 2, part 4, p. 107.
88. Korb, *Diary*, vol. 1, pp. 247–8. Feelings were running high as a result of the *strel'tsy* rebellion. See above.
89. *SIRIO*, vol. XLIX, pp. 360–1 (13 June, New Style, 1721).
90. Duc de Liria, 'Pis'ma o Rossii v Ispaniiu', *Osmnadtsatyi vek*, vol. 2 (Moscow, 1869), pp.147 and 162.
91. N. A. Baklanova, 'Velikoe posol'stvo za granitsei v 1697–1698 gg', in *Petr Velikii. Sbornik statei*, ed. A. I. Andreev (Moscow–Leningrad, 1947), pp. 61–2.
92. See, for example, Peterson, *Peter the Great's Administrative and Judicial Reforms*, p. 415: 'Russian reformers attempted to introduce the Swedish system without considering the fact that the social preconditions necessary for such a loan did not exist in Russia… . Peter and his Senate were not as conscious of the important differences between the Swedish and Russian societies as Soviet historians have argued.' On art, see Lindsey Hughes, 'German Specialists in Petrine Russia: Architects, Painters and Thespians', in *The German Lands and Eastern Europe*, ed. Roger Bartlett and Karen Schönwälder (Basingstoke and London, 1998), pp. 72–90.
93. De la Neuville, *A Curious and New Account*, p. 57.
94. Linda Colley, *Britons: Forging the Nation, 1707–1837* (London, 1992), p. 36.
95. See G. Goggi, 'The Philosophes and the Debate over Russian Civilization', in *A Window on Russia: Papers from the V International Conference of the Study Group on Eighteenth-Century Russia, Gargnano, 1994*, ed. Maria di Salvo and Lindsey Hughes (Rome, 1996), pp. 299–305. Catherine II's project for establishing foreign colonies in Russia was regarded as a further step towards civilization.
96. F. C. Weber, *The Present State of Russia*, vol. 1 (London, 1722–3), pp. 15–16.

2
The Mercenary as Diplomat: the Fall of the House of Stuart and the Rise of the Petrine Order

Graeme P. Herd

The idea that seventeenth-century Russia languished in a state of isolation and stagnation that was only reversed by Peter the Great in the early eighteenth century was for many years a standard interpretation of early modern Russian history. Russia had entered European consciousness after its 'discovery' in 1553 as a 'rude and barbarous kingdom' rapidly expanding its territory under Ivan the Terrible. However, after the chaos and anarchy of the *Smutnoe vremia* ('Time of Troubles', 1598–1613) during which the state all but disintegrated, Russia re-emerged only as a fragile entity, weakly governed and inward-looking, once more relegated to the geopolitical periphery of Europe. Historians were thus able to highlight more effectively the critical importance of Peter the Great's contribution to the development of Russian history: Peter was able, through the force of his personality, inherent ability and strategic vision, to modernize the Russian state and to identify and bridge the cultural divides and religious cleavages which had previously split Russia from the West.

This durable interpretation was eventually overturned by historians of the 'Moscow School', particularly Sergei Platonov, Sergei Solov'ev and Vasilii Kliuchevskii, who, writing in the late nineteenth and early twentieth century, argued that sources hitherto ignored suggested a more evolutionary assessment of Russian historical development.[1] While this 'gradualist' interpretation of early modern Russia remains persuasive, it is still generally assumed that political and cultural knowledge about Russia in the West remained extremely limited until the eighteenth century. In particular, M. S. Anderson's view that news and information about Russia circulating within Britain in the seventeenth century was 'slight', indeed 'fragmentary and inaccurate, less satisfactory in every way than it had been a hundred years earlier' still holds sway.[2]

This essay challenges that view by focusing on Romanov relations with the Stuart royal household in Britain. In particular, study of the role of mercenaries in shaping inter-state communication and policies suggests that the degree of knowledge circulating within Britain about Russia during the latter half of the seventeenth century has been seriously underestimated. British mercenaries, particularly through their interaction with the boyar elite and early Romanov tsars, provided a prism through which early modern Europe comprehended social, political, cultural and, above all, military developments within Russia. These issues are explored here through the activities of one of the most influential mercenaries in Russian service, Patrick Gordon of Auchleuchries, whose greatest contributions to the development of Russian international relations in the seventeenth century were achieved in his roles as both diplomat and cultural intermediary between the Stuart and Romanov courts. He was inextricably bound to both royal houses and his service, as we will see, must be viewed in terms of divided loyalties.

Patrick Gordon was born in 1635 in the parish of Ellon, sixteen miles north of Aberdeen. He left Scotland for Poland in 1651 following the death of Charles I. After eighteen months at the Jesuit College of Braunsberg (he was precluded from entering King's College Aberdeen on account of his Catholicism), he spent the remainder of the 1650s in Polish and Swedish mercenary service. At the time of the Restoration of Charles II, Gordon realized that he would be unable to gain preferment in the Stuart military establishment at a time when it was reducing its size. However, other European monarchs were recruiting, none so heavily as the military establishment of Aleksei Mikhailovich (1645–76), second Romanov tsar and father of Peter the Great. The Russian army, with its reputation for low but regular pay, admitted Gordon with the rank of Major. He died in 1699, the highest-ranking foreigner in the Petrine army. Gordon's contribution to Russian politics had been considerable: he provided crucial support for the Petrine accession in 1689; he helped foster Stuart–Romanov relations as a diplomat and then, after 1688, as a Jacobite; he was responsible for having suppressed the *strel'tsy* revolt of 1698; and he secured Russia's first warm-water port at Taganrog in 1696, following the success of the second siege of Azov.[3]

A detailed examination of Gordon's role in Russian service leads one to conclude that Scottish Catholic officers within the nascent Petrine military establishment made a series of initiatives designed to promote the restoration of James VII and II to the throne.[4] These activities ranged from delaying the recognition by the Russian *Posol'skii prikaz* (Foreign Office) of William of Orange as King of Great Britain, to actively exploring the possibility of raising a mercenary army in Russia to fight on the deposed Stuart King's behalf. More generally Gordon assumed responsibility for informing and advising the Stuart monarchs of Russian foreign and security policy in the latter half of the seventeenth century, a period in which Russia was expanding dramatically. In addition, the story of Gordon, a Scottish mercenary in Russian service, further adds to our understanding of the historical links between Scotland and Russia.[5]

Gordon in Romanov diplomatic service, 1666–7 and 1686–7

There is evidence to suggest that a handful of mercenaries were in Muscovy as early as the late sixteenth century. Certainly, during the *Smutnoe vremia* Scottish, Irish and English mercenaries in Swedish, Polish and Russian armies fought and died on disputed Russian soil. It was not until the 'eastern phase' of the Thirty Years War, which culminated in the siege of Smolensk, that mercenaries arrived in significant numbers (between 2,000 and 3,000). The next phase of recruitment is linked to both the end of the Thirty Years War and the establishment of the Cromwellian regime in Britain. Royalists and Catholics fled for Europe following the execution of Charles I in 1649 and the creation of the Commonwealth. The Restoration (1660) initiated the scaling down of the Stuart military establishment, giving a new impetus to mercenary recruitment into continental armies. The Glorious Revolution of 1688 and the Grand Embassy of 1697–8 encouraged the last two waves of seventeenth-century mercenary recruitment into the Russian military establishment.[6] Patrick Gordon arrived in Russian service as a result of foreign recruitment in the 1660s.

During the mid-1660s Gordon, although primarily recruited for his military capability, was also selected for Russian diplomatic service. His first duty in this regard was to serve as a Romanov diplomatic envoy to the court of Charles II. There is strong, though as yet inconclusive, evidence to suggest that as a result of this mission Gordon became a correspondent of the *London Gazette*, a bi-weekly digest of political, diplomatic and military foreign news created by Charles II. The *London*

Gazette was edited by the Secretary of State's office and counted amongst its correspondents soldiers, diplomats and merchants.[7] Prior to Gordon's arrival in London he had engaged in a steady stream of correspondence with key figures in the Stuart establishment, as well as friends and family in Scotland.[8] In London he exhibited the characteristics that would have made him an ideal candidate for a *London Gazette* correspondent. Gordon was the very model of a loyal Royalist. He was an experienced military officer and an observant, cultured and educated individual. Latin, French, Spanish, Portuguese and Dutch were the main diplomatic languages needed by the sixteen accredited Stuart representatives in Europe. Most had achieved fluency in one language, although two diplomats – and they were to receive special notice – had mastered four languages. Gordon was especially fluent in Latin, had learnt Polish through the 1650s, and by 1666 had mastered Russian. More importantly, he had married into a Catholic Dutch family and could speak High or Court Dutch – only one Stuart diplomat, Blathwayt, ambassador to the Hague, was fluent in this language.[9] Thus, even if judged only by his linguistic abilities, his capability profile would have attracted the notice of the Secretary of State. The possibility of a Stuart diplomatic career in Warsaw, Danzig or The Hague could have followed Russian mercenary service. On Gordon's return to Moscow in December 1666 for the first time newsletters appeared in the *London Gazette* under the byline 'Moscow' although, as was the custom, the correspondent's name was not mentioned.[10] It seems probable then that Gordon played an important role in disseminating information about Russia in Britain, not only as a diplomat but as a correspondent.[11]

While on his mission to London, Gordon had enquired about the possibility of recruitment into Stuart service, but when this was not realized he returned to Russia. During the 1670s and 1680s he was engaged with other mercenaries in heavy fighting in Russia's campaigns in the Ukraine which were designed to contain the constant threat from the Ottoman Empire and their Tatar vassals. Russia's attempts to maintain a geo-strategic balance of power mirrored a struggle for survival within the Romanov dynasty. After the death of Aleksei Mikhailovich in 1676, Fedor Alekseevich, weak and infirm, ruled for only six years. In 1682 Peter's half-sister, Sophia Alekseevna, ruled as Regent (1682–9), while Peter and his half-brother, Ivan V, with whom he was to rule as co-tsar, came of age. At this point Gordon was once again recalled from Russian military duties for Romanov diplomatic service, this time as Sophia's envoy to the last Stuart monarch, James VII and II (1685–8).

While Gordon was in London, an attempt was made by King James to recruit him into the Scottish military establishment. However, this attempt foundered on the twin failure of the Scottish Parliament to overturn the exclusionary Test Acts of 1673 (whereby Catholics were excluded from Stuart military service), and Sophia's outright refusal to countenance losing the experience and professionalism of the highest-ranking foreigner within the Russian military establishment. Indeed, so highly was Gordon valued that, when he pressed for release from Russian service, the Russian response was explosive. Gordon vividly described this episode. Vasilii Vasil'evich Golitsyn, Sophia's Foreign Minister

> did fall out in great passion, against me, and because I vindicated my Self the best way I could, and had the great advantage of reason on my syde, he was the more incensed so that in great heat he ordered me to be writt for an Ensigne & sent away the next day, some Noblemen comeing in, and hearing the contest, did fall all to the Boyars syde & favour, though even against reason & their own judgement began to lay a great deale of blame upon me, & urged me to take other measures, the Boyar also with very high words & threats and reasoning without all reason or the least show of uprightness, nor valuing or considering anything I said insisted that I should acknowledge my error & crave pardon and promise to serve in the future.

Gordon, fearing exile 'to the remotest places of their Empire', was forced to 'acknowledge my error and crave pardon' and was further humiliated when this petition was rejected, 'not being pened in humbled enough tearmes'. As Gordon bitterly concluded:

> The Dumny Diack [Chancellor] Yem. Ignat. Ukainsufit [Ukraintsev] gave me a Copy of a petition which I should cause transcribe & sub-cribe, haveing read it I found some things in it not fitt, wherefor blot-ting out these I caused writt it over, and putt my hand to it albeit it was conceived in as submissive tearme & expression as could be done to God Almighty. When it was read above [in the Kremlin] there was great silence neither did the Princess [Sophia] say any thing all knowing it to be forced from me by threats and compulsion.[12]

Although Gordon was precluded on the grounds of his religious persuasion and strenuous Romanov objections from Stuart service within the Scottish military establishment, on his return to Moscow he assumed, it will be argued, the role of unofficial Stuart royal representative to the Romanovs.

Gordon as Jacobite representative at the Romanov court, 1687–99

By the late 1680s Gordon, having twice served as a Romanov envoy to the Stuart court, could easily be considered the most experienced Russianist that the Stuart diplomatic corps might call upon for advice and advanced intelligence of Russian foreign and security policy. That the Stuart court had no permanent diplomatic representative in Moscow during this period reflects a series of factors, including the dominant role of the Muscovy Company in inter-state relations, Russia's relative weakness as a European power and its peripheral geostrategic location.

Gordon utilized both his position – he had now reached the rank of General – and his connections with the Secretary of State, Middleton, to have his devotion to the Stuart cause officially recognized. In October 1687 Gordon wrote to Samuel Meverell, a Muscovy Company merchant, in London to advertise 'in the gazet there'[13] that on 14 October in Moscow 'Our most gracious soveraigne his birthday with the Usuall Joviality haveing all his Sacred Majesty [James] borne subjects & many descended of them at the feast.'[14] This celebration would have been attended by second- and perhaps third-generation descendants of those mercenaries that had entered Romanov service in the 1630s, 1640s and 1650s, as well as those like Gordon who had entered in the 1660s. It is likely that craftsmen, merchants, doctors and other Scots and English in Moscow, as well as the foreign diplomatic elite – for example, the Polish, Venetian and Dutch residents – would have attended. In December 1687, under the byline 'Moscow: October 22', we read in the *London Gazette*: 'Lieut. Gen. Patrick Gordon ... being his Majesty of Great Britain's birthday, the said General solemnized it here, making a great Entertainment for all his Majesties subjects.'[15]

At the outset of 1688, an *annus horribilis* for Stuart monarchical ambitions, Gordon wrote to the Secretary of State that he 'shall not be wanting in any thing that I can to promote his Sacred Majesties [James] interest in this place'.[16] In the build-up to the overthrow of James, Gordon took it upon himself, as the longest-serving and most highly promoted Royalist in Moscow, to account for the actions of 'his most Sacred Majesty' James. He provided explanations and reasoning which sought to justify and legitimize the Royalist cause within the foreign community of Moscow.[17] A pressing challenge for Gordon was to win through the sea of misinformation, misunderstanding and rumour which swept through Moscow in the late summer and autumn of 1688; victory in this argument within the foreign community, within the Russian Court and especially within the *Posol'skii prikaz* was the prize diplomats were to seek.

In his efforts to overcome this triple challenge, Gordon enjoyed an initial advantage. There existed a group of pro-Stuart mercenaries within the Russian military establishment who could be relied upon – they are identified as among those celebrating James's birthday in Moscow. Some Jacobite communities in the diaspora have been characterized as 'numerous, well-organized, obstinate, competent in intrigue, and with a tradition of secret organization dating back to the Stuart exile during the protectorate'.[18] Certainly, those mercenary soldiers in Russian service during the 1680s and 1690s had mainly arrived either during the 1660s recruitment wave or were first-generation descendants from soldiers who had arrived during the 1650s – that is, soldiers, like Gordon, who had fled the Cromwellian regime. Consequently these men had no first-hand experience of the supposed misdeeds of James Stuart. Having been forced to flee under the threat of expulsion from a violently anti-monarchical Commonwealth, they were predisposed to support James. Many of them were Scottish and Catholic and this provided another tie of loyalty to the Catholic monarch and the Royal House of Stuart.

It can also be surmised that due to the extreme difficulty in leaving Russian service once enrolled – witness Gordon's predicament – mercenaries in Russian service had only a partial knowledge of events in Europe. Such information tended to have been filtered through to the Foreign Quarter by official Stuart diplomatic or governmental sources and dispatches or through family contacts. While the latter could not be vouched for it is not unreasonable to suggest that the former sources would have presented the ruling monarch, James, in appropriately deferential and regal terms, in a manner designed to ensure and promote loyalty to the House of Stuart. Thus the preconditions for Jacobite belief within Russia were stronger than within other European states.

On the face of it the Dutch, at least in Moscow if not the Netherlands, had less information. They relied upon their Protestant envoy to provide pro-Williamite news to be translated for the Russian Court. The main sources of non-Russian-based foreign information came from the envoys of the two pro-Jacobite Catholic Polish and

Imperial Habsburg powers. These powers were involved most closely in the formation of Russian foreign policy through their participation in the Holy League and one might suspect their collective influence would have been strong. Lastly we must look to Gordon, who was in direct contact with the Catholic Secretary of State Lord Melfort, the Protestant Secretary of State Lord Middleton, and leading members of the Scottish political establishment, as well as being a *London Gazette* recipient. He was thus well positioned to provide a pro-Stuart interpretation of the fast-unfolding events. The combined efforts of the official Polish, the Imperial Habsburg envoy and Gordon as unofficial Stuart envoy, should have been sufficient to discredit the usurpation of an hereditary line with an interpretation of events which was consistent, continuously updated and thrice underpinned. What to Russian interests was a Russo-Dutch trading partnership when compared to a pan-European military alliance (the Holy League)?

Yet in August 1688 Gordon was confronted, while dining with Prince Vasilii Vasil'evich Golitsyn, Sophia's chief minister, with the uncompromising assertion:

> wee could well enough agree with your Kings [James] father [Charles I] and brother [Charles II], but wee cannot come to right with this, he [James] is proved proud beyond all measure, I makeing as if I understood only his [James] not sending any [mercenaries and military materiel to help in the Russian Crimean campaigns] hither answered that the King [James] because of his great troubles in his owne dominions, had not leasure to think of business lying so farr off [that is, the Russian Crimean campaigns] as I thought he said more over that the English could not subsit without their comodities as leather, hempe, potash, Tallow & masts to the which I gave a compliant answer.[19]

A month later Gordon dined with 'Elias Tabort [the Dutch resident] where was the B[oyar] K[niaz' Prince] V[asilii] V[asil'evich Golitsyn] and most of that party'.[20] The existence of 'that party' and its composition is of great interest. The clear implication is that the 'party' represented the pro-Orangeist faction within the Russian Court and perhaps we can conclude that Golitsyn headed this powerful anti-Stuart, and hence anti-Jacobite, association. His disposition can partly be explained by the lack of Stuart interest and support for the first Crimean campaigns in 1687, upon whose success the Regency had staked its political credibility and legitimacy – indeed, Golitsyn had already notified the Dutch resident that James was guilty of 'favouring the Turks too much'.[21] In analysing the exchange between Golitsyn and Gordon it is difficult to conclude just what aid Sophia had expected from James – whether it be direct participation in the Holy League (Venice, Poland and Russia) against the Turks or, *in lieu* of direct participation, indirect support through monetary loans or the gift of specialist mercenary troops (engineers and artillery experts) or war supplies. Clearly, for Russia, neutrality was perceived to constitute *de facto* support for the Ottomans.

In order to steal Dutch thunder, Gordon had to be first with news of any events so that he could set the agenda and define the parameters within which the debate over the interpretations would be held; in the growing propaganda war – the Dutch resident in Moscow disseminated pro-Williamite *Dutch Gazette* reports within Moscow – it was important to have one spokesman actively peddling a consistent line. Gordon had the authority to unite Royalist elements within the foreign community and, through his experience, contacts and high military rank, also possessed the status to be given a hearing in Russian governmental circles. He possessed the potential ability to neutralize the anti-Jacobite Dutch propaganda.

Thus in October 1688 Gordon began to propagandize for the Stuart cause by publicizing pro-Jacobite news. The ceremonial occasion of James's birthday launched the Jacobite movement in Russia. Gordon used this focal point as a means of appealing to a sense of patriotism and fostering a political loyalty and allegiance to the ruling Stuart monarch within Moscow's Foreign Quarter:

> Wee celebrated the Kings birthday [James] with those of his sacred Majesties subjects who were here [that is, in Moscow] and others of the best quality among whom the Polls Resident, & were all merry. at parting the [Polish] Resident said to me that the King [James] was happy who had subjects to remember him so cordially at such a distance.[22]

Throughout October 1688 William made repeated attempts to land an army in England and an unopposed landing was eventually made at Torbay on 5 November. The news reached Gordon on 22 November and he immediately responded: 'I was in towne and had much discourse with the 2nd favourite [Fedor Shaklovitii] & some of the Councellors concerning the Holanders design on Our King [James], where I told them the truth.'[23]

Gordon was able to collate information and co-ordinate his campaign with the help of the Polish resident. Hard facts and eye-witness accounts were at a premium. Gordon received through Jacobite sympathizers in Riga 'an extract of a letter from London the 6 November, giveing notice of the Pr[ince] of Orange his arrivall & landing at Torbay, Dartmouth, & Exmouth, he landed the 4th ...'.[24] Without delay, Gordon 'caused translate the extract of the letter from London which was being read befor the Tzaars [Peter and Ivan] & councell, gave great satisfaction'.[25] Following hard on the heels of this success, Gordon 'rode to Pokrofska and dyned by the Boyar with the 2d favourite & diverse where much discourse about the affaires of England. where I told the truth and evenly passionately'.[26] It is likely that Gordon would have interpreted the landings in terms of invasion, William's actions as a war of aggression and strategic aim as attempted regicide – concepts which would have found resonance within the Russian elite.

However, Gordon was to receive 'the lamentable newes' in early 1689 'of the King's [James] & his [Jacobite supporters] haveing been forced by the infidelity of his unnatural subjects to flee & that he was safely arrived at Dunkirk'.[27] William's large army had to haul slow-moving waggons and artillery over impassable roads in order to engage the enemy, but had successfully mounted a winter campaign; James provided only indecisive military leadership. By 1688 Gordon had served in Russia for over twenty-five years. It could be argued that the rigours of an English winter, the small size of the army to be commanded and distances to be crossed and the need for decisive leadership were problems and challenges which would not have unduly taxed Gordon. As Gordon wrote to his Clan Chief, the Duke of Gordon, in exile in Paris:

had I been in a place where I could have been servicable to his M:[ajesty] I should have vented my passion another way. I perceived even when I was there, that the King's too great goodness & credulity in intrusting disaffected & il principled persons in high charges could not but prove fatall. Notwithstanding all that hath fallen out I am sorry that his Matie did not, when I was in Scotland, lay his comands upon me to have stayed there albeit without employment, then might I have had occassion at this by me, to have given proofs of my loyalty and what I can do.[28]

On 13 February 1689, the Crown of Great Britain was offered to William and Mary. William stressed James's misdeeds and cast doubts on the legitimacy of the Prince of Wales. He argued that he aimed to create a free and lawful parliament and that he had been invited by the people to invade.

While the Jacobite movement in Europe responded to these events by pressing for the restoration of the Stuart regime, in Russia the emergent movement was emasculated for a crucial seven months. Gordon, its chief proponent, was, with the backbone of its natural supporters, to be neutralized by the military ambitions of Sophia who, in an effort to bolster political support in Moscow, launched two Crimean campaigns in the later 1680s. The first was unsuccessful and the second, launched in 1689, was to prove disastrous, precipitating Sophia's loss of power later that year.[29]

Gordon left Moscow on 12 February 1689 at the head of the foreign mercenary contingent, not to return until 22 July 1689. On his return, he was to face the political crisis and its aftermath which brought Peter the Great to the fore. In the meantime, in April 1689 the Convention in Edinburgh declared William and Mary joint monarchs and the Scottish Crown was accepted by the House of Orange in early May.

The twin unifying articles of political faith among the Jacobite diaspora were a devotion to the Stuart monarch in exile and a desire to restore the House of Stuart to the British throne. James maintained a court-in-exile which Jacobites across the continent could correspond with. In Rome, Lord Melfort, a Catholic, acted as first Secretary of State and Lord Middleton, a Protestant, as second. Feuds over religion promoted factionalism which undermined this shadow court-in-exile. In Russia no such divisions amongst those who professed to be Jacobites appear to have existed. Indeed, as it has already been noted, the preconditions for Jacobite belief were strong.

Jacobites believed in the theory of kingship by divine, hereditary and indefeasible right. The King's authority came directly from God. The hereditary principle avoided disputes over succession, and indefeasible divine right meant that whoever had the divine right to be King could not lose it no matter what he did. In this respect the Glorious Revolution was seen as sacrilege. Jacobites argued that there was no true *de jure* sovereign governing Great Britain after 1688.

The whole of the foreign community in Moscow had seven months to dwell upon the implications of these seemingly abstract and theoretical concepts of divine, hereditary and indefeasible right, before Russia suffered its own 'revolution' – a crisis in which the foreigners were visibly, and potentially fatally, required to express their political allegiance. The resolution of this Russian crisis – the forced resignation of

Sophia as Regent – left Gordon as the undisputed military power within that foreign community and ideally placed to restart the push in earnest for Russian recognition of King James as the rightful ruler of Great Britain.

In the summer of 1689, following the failure of the second Crimean campaign, the ambitious Sophia appeared to be contriving through self-promotion to legitimize her position within the Russian polity as 'Self-Upholder', 'Autocrat' and Regent. This proposed self-promotion represented a legal and constitutional challenge to Peter's hereditary right to rule as tsar without a Regent. Peter, fearing assassination, fled to the Holy Trinity Monastery and sent a letter to the Foreign Quarter ordering all foreign mercenaries to join him. When Gordon took the letter to Golitsyn he was ordered to remain in Moscow. Gordon wrote in his diary:

> I returned and made ready to be gone, and told the Colonells and other Officers whoe came to me for advice, that notwithstanding any order might be here given, I was resolved to go & would be gone in the evening, where upon all the great & small made ready.[30]

In this moment of constitutional crisis Gordon, as the pre-eminent foreigner, unofficial Stuart representative and confirmed Jacobite, provided the leadership to sway others to share his belief in the hereditary succession of the Stuart and Romanov lines. He thus was central in legitimizing the existing monarchical order within Russia. The distinguishing feature of Jacobite ideological conviction was that William owed his position to conquest, not hereditary right – so too was Sophia attempting to overturn the natural order.

Sophia was arrested and imprisoned in a monastery close to the Kremlin. With the resolution of this Russian political crisis, Gordon now attempted to initiate a pro-Jacobite campaign within the newly emerging Petrine political elite. In particular, he attempted to persuade Russia's rulers to adopt a pro-Jacobite foreign policy. In the 1650s the tsarist anti-Cromwellian policy had taken the form of a refusal to countenance diplomatic ties with the new republic. This was the benchmark against which Gordon's efforts were now to be measured.[31]

William III was able to call upon Moscow's resident Dutch diplomatic representatives, with their substantial expertise in Russian affairs, to secure the interests of his new subjects in Russia. In other European countries and cities those diplomats who had openly supported James could be, and were, replaced. For example, the very day that the Stuart resident in Hamburg, Whyche, left for Spain, the new Orangeist diplomatic representative moved into the vacated diplomatic residence. However, Moscow proved an exception. Gordon's position as Royalist representative, never fully formalized and regularized, was underpinned by his primary duty to his masters, that of military general. His military experience and expertise could not be replaced, and his powerful role within the Russian military establishment and the emerging Petrine political order was underestimated by the Dutch ambassador Johan Van Keller, who wrote in a letter dated 1 November 1689: 'At this Court there is not a single English minister. And the number of English traffikers [that is, Muscovy Company merchants] here is not very considerable either; there are no more than six, four of whom live ordinarily here in town, and two others in Archangel.' He then went on to ask if he should 'take care of the affaires of these few Englishmen'.[32] This impression that no English minister was in residence and that Stuart interests had been left unattended was not to last.

Gordon continued to co-ordinate the Jacobite campaign in Russia. He sought to re-establish contact with the leading members of the old English and Scottish political elites who had fled abroad to form a government-in-exile: 'haveing read in the Gazettes [that is, the *London Gazette*] that the Earl of Melfort was to go from Paris to Rome I did writt to him'.[33] Over the last twenty years Gordon had built up a reliable and efficient communications network stretching across Northern Europe, consisting of merchants, Jacobite residents and *London Gazette* correspondents.[34] Thus it was to these contacts that he first turned, and in a letter to one of these well-briefed individuals he elaborated his campaign to spread Jacobitism in Russia. He was to remind them

> how steddable I have been and am and may be at this Court to the publick good of the Nation. Our Country men here will I hope advise the friends what I have done for them this present, and how I may be able to serve them here also, for there is not a day about wherein I cannot see & speake with his Majesty who is now settled in Government, is gracious to me beyond measure ... what hath happened there doth not in the least diminish my care & endeavours for the welfare of the Nation.[35]

How was Gordon to translate this 'care and endeavours for the welfare of the nation' into positive action which would contribute to the restoration of King James?

Gordon had written in a similar vein to the Earl of Aberdeen, but in a letter to the Earl of Melfort he was more explicit as to his intention. He offered to recruit a mercenary force in Russia to fight on behalf of the Stuart cause, promising to 'spend my lyfe and all I have in the defence of his M[ajesties] just right', and requesting only that King James prepare 'some blanke commission whereby I might engage such good oficers [in Moscow] as I may gett moved to a sense of there [*sic*] duty'. Gordon ended this letter with a postscript: 'P.S. I have gott this court to owne still his Sacred Matie [James] & not to hear of any others.'[36]

Russia was certainly a viable recruiting ground for Jacobite mercenaries, trained professional soldiers, who could have offered their services. It is possible that if Gordon had been able to return to the north-east of Scotland in 1686 when he had first requested permission, he would have been able to strengthen the Scottish military establishment and so bolster the resolve of King James to stand and actively engage the enemy in battle in 1688.[37]

While Gordon was unable to raise an army, his secondary objective to halt the recognition of William of Orange was rewarded with success. William III initiated diplomatic overtures to Russia in an attempt to gain diplomatic recognition for his succession. A letter arrived in Moscow in December 1690, the superscription reading: William III to the 'Czar [Peter] and Great Duke Ivan Alexeiowich'. Russian diplomatic protocol demanded that Ivan V, as co-tsar, should have been addressed with the correct title of 'tsar'. William referred to the 'good and friendly intercourse' as the basis 'whereby the Trade and Commerce of both Nations will be advanced to the mutual benefit and advantage of our respective Subjects and Dominions'.[38] This overture neither made reference to the ending of the Regency in Russia nor commented on the overthrow of James and the accession of William to the throne of Great Britain. Gordon noted that the 'Pretended king of Englands' letter, incorrectly addressed, was not even received by the Russian Court:

The copy of the letter from the pretended King of England, calling himself William the 3rd dated the 3rd of June, [was] interpreted and no further notice taken of it, upon pretension that the Hollands resident his name was not in it, It being sent to him and delivered publickly & solemnly, Another [letter from William to the Romanovs] had been sent befor dated in Aprill but not haveing the full Title [it referred to Ivan as 'Grand Duke'] was returned by the Resident & sent,

so that it sems they must have a third [letter], and then a question if it
shall be received for divers reasons. I went to the Potieny Hosse [Play
Club, a semi-official regimental headquarters/social club used by
Peter] and see his Matie [Peter] who was very gracious to me.[39]

An accurate assessment of Petrine attitudes to the new Williamite
regime in Britain constituted a necessary precondition to reversing the
declining fortunes of Muscovy Company trade with Russia. If, according to normal Muscovite diplomatic practice, treaties were considered
to have been concluded by a sovereign on his own behalf and for his
heirs, that is, in the name of the state, what was the legal validity of
existing trade agreements between Russia and a state which had
deposed its king and overturned the principle of hereditary succession?
Were the treaty commitments agreed upon by James to be upheld by
William? This indeterminate situation certainly allowed Gordon scope
for raising legalistic, diplomatic and constitutional objections to
Russian recognition of the 'Pretender King William'.

The Russian ambivalence in recognizing William was partly a
reflection of a Europe-wide hesitation as to whether the House of
Orange would in fact retain control of the three kingdoms of the
British isles. For example, the British resident in Stockholm wrote to
London: 'tis no purpose to speake to our Ministers here, who will
govern themselves only according to the success of either side, and
therefore are very desirous to know how matters go and are likely to
goe'.[40] In early January 1691 Gordon was able to consolidate his position among the Jacobite community in Moscow but was unable to halt
diplomatic recognition. The day after 'the English & other friends at a
feast with musick by me', Gordon wrote in his diary: 'The Diak
[Secretary] prevailed upon to receive the Pretender King William his
letter to the Tz: Majestie [Peter].' By mid-January 1691, 'the Hollands
resident gave up the letter from the Prince of Orange giveing notice of
his being advanced to the crowne of great Brittaine'.[41] Gordon had
been fighting a rearguard action in an attempt to use his influence to
have the Williamite diplomatic correspondence blocked by the various
layers of Russian bureaucratic officialdom. This attempt had failed.
Perhaps Russia recognized William as it became unlikely James could
regain the throne and as commercial interests pushed for a rejuvena-
tion of trade westwards.

Even after this recognition Gordon was still to request 'books or
papers set out in favour of King James or anything impartiall relating
to the tymes' from relatives in Scotland.[42] That Gordon was willing to

act as a Jacobite propagandist serves to underline the fact that there was a very real debate taking place in Moscow, an information war fuelled by pro-Williamite newsletters taken from the *Dutch Gazette*, translated into Russian, and pamphlets procured by the Dutch resident in Moscow. There is also evidence to suggest that tracts were translated from Dutch by the Russian resident in Amsterdam.[43] In turn Gordon's Jacobite tracts would be highly political in nature, concerned with abstract notions and theories of divine right, hereditary principle, the duty of Christian subjects, the rightful subjugation of statute and common law to the Ancient Constitution. It is thus highly likely that Gordon debated and discussed these issues with Peter – to whom he had daily access – and to this extent Gordon can be considered as Peter's tutor not only in military science but also in constitutional law, kingship, current affairs and international relations.

Ultimately Gordon failed in his efforts to stop the recognition of William III in the Russian Court. This was especially apparent with the arrival of the Grand Embassy to Amsterdam and London at the end of the century. There are a number of other conclusions that can be drawn from this whole episode. The emergence of a Jacobite community within Russia in the seventeenth century has remained an obscure and understudied subject amongst both historians of Russian history and British scholars of the Jacobite diaspora in continental Europe. However, it is clear that Gordon had helped to extend the Jacobite network of contacts with other European monarchs into the Russian Court. This network may well have intersected with the web of European agents who contributed to the *London Gazette*. Certainly, before the Glorious Revolution of 1688 there is strong evidence to suggest Gordon was a *London Gazette* correspondent and it has been demonstrated with certainty that one of the newsletters printed in the newspaper was written by Gordon. Indeed, the depth, scope and accuracy of *London Gazette* newsletters concerning Moscow markedly decrease after the end of 1687 when Gordon stopped sending letters to Secretary of State and editor of the *London Gazette*, Middleton, in London.

This essay demonstrates that the Jacobite court-in-exile had for a period of ten years, from 1689 until Gordon's death in 1699, received continuous and accurate information from an extremely well-placed source within the diplomatic and military establishment of Europe's rapidly expanding eastern power. How effective was Gordon in his role as unofficial Royalist representative? That the Jacobite court-in-exile did not capitalize on Gordon's influence and status within Russia for its own benefit and advantage reveals a lack of strategic vision in the heart of the exiled Jacobite political order. While it would have been unlikely that Gordon would have received permission to raise a Jacobite army in Russia in support of the exiled Stuart King (given Russia's need for trained mercenary soldiers) it is remarkable that James did not send a royal letter to Peter and Ivan requesting their support and continued Romanov recognition of the House of Stuart. Such support, at least, might have proved forthcoming. Thus in any assessment of the role of Gordon, it must be noted that he agitated as a peripheral figure in Jacobite consciousness, far from the Jacobite centres in Paris and Rome.

If the embryonic Jacobite community in Russia failed to halt the recognition of the 'Pretender King William', it did at least inhibit the denunciation of James. This allowed for the consolidation of a Jacobite community which was to bear fruit in the shape of positive efforts to effect the second restoration of a Stuart monarch. Many of the future leaders of Jacobitism – such as Admiral Thomas Gordon, Major General Alexander Gordon of Auchintoul, General James Keith – had the example of Gordon to inspire them, and they were to find Petrine Russia a supportive environment within which they could both improve their military skills and refine their Jacobite radicalism.[44]

Western mercenaries in early modern Russia offered service to the Romanov regime outwith our traditional narrow military conception of mercenary activity. Their service during the seventeenth century shaped and modified the cultural and political orientation of an emerging Great Power on the Euro-Asiatic stage. The extended role of the mercenaries, as diplomats and cultural intermediaries, must also prompt contemporary cultural historians to reconsider the limit and extent to which the idea of Muscovy, or Russia, had entered the intellectual and cultural consciousness of Western Europe during the early modern period, particularly in the early Petrine period.

Acknowledgement

I gratefully acknowledge the advice and comments Professor Lindsey Hughes has contributed to this article.

Notes

1. S. Platonov, *Moscow and the West* (Harrisburg, 1972); S. M. Soloviev, *History of Russia*, vol. 25: *Rebellion and Reform: Fedor and Sophia, 1682–1689*, ed., trans. and with an Introduction by L. A. J. Hughes (Gulf Breeze, 1989); V. O. Kluchevsky, *A History of Russia*, vol. 3, translated by C. J. Hogarth (London, 1913). See also P. Dukes (ed.), *Russia and Europe* (London, 1991).
2. M. S. Anderson, 'English Views of Russia in the Age of Peter the Great', *American Slavic East European Review*, vol. xiii (1954), pp. 200–14.
3. The principal source on Gordon is his diary, held in Moscow at the Rossiiskii gosudarstvennyi voennyi istoricheskii arkhiv (RGVIA), f. 846, op. 15, vols 1–6. Although the diary constitutes the largest single continuous source for seventeenth-century Russian history, it remains unpublished in its original form. In the nineteenth century extracts were translated and published in German and English. *Tagebuch des Generals Patrick Gordon, während seiner Kriegsdienste unter den Schweden und Polen vom Jahre 1655 bis 1661, und sienes Aufenthaltes in Russland vom Jahre 1991 bis 1699*, 3 vols, ed. and trans. M. A. Obolensky and M. C. Posselt (Moscow–Leipzig, 1849); *Passages from the Diary of General Patrick Gordon of Auchleuchries, AD 1635–AD 1699*, ed. Joseph Robertson (Aberdeen, 1859).
4. For a more extensive examination of Gordon's career in Russia see Graeme P. Herd, 'General Patrick Gordon of Auchleuchries – a Scot in Seventeenth Century Russian Service', unpublished doctoral dissertation, University of Aberdeen (1994).
5. This field of historical research lay largely undisturbed until the publication of a seminal article: J. W. Barnhill and P. Dukes, 'North-East Scots in Muscovy in the Seventeenth Century', *Northern Scotland*, vol. 1, no. 1 (1972), pp. 49–63. Since then a steady stream of articles has contributed greatly to our expanding understanding of the importance of these historical links. The contributions of Paul Dukes alone include: 'Some Aberdonian Influences on the Early Russian Enlightenment', *Canadian–American Slavic Studies*, vol. 13, no. 4 (1979), pp. 436–51; 'Aberdeen and North-East Scotland: Some Archival and Other Sources', in *The Study of Russian History from British Archival Sources*, edited by J. M. Hartley (London, 1986), pp. 51–66; 'Problems Concerning the Departure of Scottish Soldiers from Seventeenth-Century Muscovy', in *Scotland and Europe, 1200–1850*, edited by T. C. Smout (Edinburgh, 1986), pp. 143–66; 'Paul Menzies 1637–1694, and his Mission from Muscovy to Rome', *The Innes Review*, vol. 35 (1984), pp. 88–95; 'Patrick Gordon and his Family Circle: Some Unpublished Letters', *Scottish Slavonic Review*, no. 10 (1988), pp. 19–49. See also *The Caledonian Phalanx: Scots in Russia*, by Paul Dukes and others (Edinburgh, 1987) and D. Fedosov, *The Caledonian Connection. Scotland–Russia Ties: Middle Ages to Early Twentieth Century: A Concise Biographical List* (Aberdeen, 1996).
6. G. M. Phipps, 'Britons in Seventeenth Century Russia: a Study of the Origins of Modernisation', unpublished doctoral dissertation, University of Pennsylvania (1971). Phipps argues that there were three phases of mercenary recruitment into Russian service during the seventeenth century. For a different interpretation of recruitment patterns see Graeme P. Herd, 'Bravehearts Abroad: Scottish Mercenaries in Muscovite Service, 1570–1640', *War Studies Journal*, vol. 1, no. 3 (December 1996), pp. 119–29.

7. J. Sutherland, *The Restoration Newspaper and its Development* (Cambridge, 1986); P. M. Handover, *A History of the London Gazette, 1665–1965* (London, 1965). The original newsletters can be read in the British Library on microfilm: PRO, SOPR. MIC. P.2, OGE 70 396.

8. Much of Gordon's correspondence on his return to Russia has been published. See S. Konovalov, 'Patrick Gordon's Dispatches from Russia, 1667', *Oxford Slavonic Papers*, vol. 11 (1964), pp. 8–16; S. Konovalov, 'Sixteen Further Letters of General Patrick Gordon', *Oxford Slavonic Papers*, vol. 13 (1967), pp. 80–95.

9. Peter Wyche, who was to become diplomatic representative in Hamburg, commented tellingly: 'though Germany is so neere England, a learned man observed to me that Arabick and Chaldee are better knowne in our University and Countrey than High Dutch. So that without arrogance, I may say, any other person that is not so qualified must be some yeares hard labour to be fitted to doe the same service' (British Library, Add. MS 37982, fol. 206). P. S. Lachs, *The Diplomatic Corps under Charles II and James II and VII* (New Brunswick, NJ, 1965), p. 55.

10. It is remarkable that a book so recent as Sutherland, *The Restoration Newspaper*, p. 124, shows no awareness that foreign correspondents sent dispatches from Moscow, as well as other East European cities, for example Königsberg, Narva, Danzig, Riga and Warsaw.

11. The argument that Gordon was a *London Gazette* correspondent is advanced further in Graeme P. Herd, 'The *London Gazette* as a Source for Seventeenth-Century Russian History', *Study Group on Eighteenth-Century Russia*, no. 22 (1994), pp. 9–12.

12. RGVIA, f. 846, op. 15, vol. 4, pp. 147–8. Gordon's diary, 25 November 1686. (All quotations from the diary are transcribed as originally spelt by Gordon. When not directly quoting Gordon the standard transcription is used.) See also 'Gordon to the Earl of Middleton, 7 January 1687', British Library, Add. MS 41842, fol. 152.

13. 'Gordon to Meverell, 22 October 1687', British Library, Add. MS 41842, fol. 164.

14. RGVIA, f. 846, op. 15, vol. 4, p. 182 ob. Gordon's diary, 14 October 1687.

15. *The London Gazette*, 8–12 December 1687, issue no. 2302.

16. 'Gordon to the Earl of Middleton, 28 February 1688', British Library, Add. MS 41842, fol. 165; RGVIA, f. 846, op. 15, vol. 4, p. 197, Gordon's diary, 28 February 1688.

17. For example, in July 1688 Gordon was 'at a feast by Elias Tabort, where much discourse about our King [James] haveing st[uck] fast [that is, imprisoned] the ArchBP [Archbishop] of Canterbury and 6 other Bps [Bishops] in the Tower [of London], w[hi]ch I maintained to be reasonable and just'. RGVIA, f. 846, op. 15, vol. 4, p. 207 ob. Gordon's diary, 12 July 1688.

18. F. McLynn, *The Jacobites* (London, 1988), p. 172.

19. RGVIA, f. 846, op. 15, vol. 4, p. 210 ob. Gordon's diary, 30 August 1688.

20. *Ibid.*, p. 213 ob. Gordon's diary, 29 September 1688.

21. *Ibid.*, p. 146 ob. Gordon's diary, 17 November 1686. For background information on Anglo-Russian diplomatic relations for this period see L. A. J.

Hughes. 'V. T. Postnikov's 1687 Mission to London: Anglo-Russian Relations in the 1680s in British Sources', *Slavonic and East European Review*, vol. 68, no. 3 (July 1990), pp. 447–60.

22. RGVIA, f. 846, op. 15, vol 4, p. 215 ob. Gordon's diary, 14 October 1688.
23. *Ibid.*, p. 220. Gordon's diary, 2 November 1688.
24. *Ibid.*, p. 222. Gordon's diary, 9 December 1688.
25. *Ibid.*, p. 222 ob. Gordon's diary, 10 December 1688.
26. *Ibid.*, p. 223. Gordon's diary, 18 December 1688.
27. *Ibid.*, p. 227 ob. Gordon's diary, 13 January 1689.
28. *Ibid.*, pp. 58 ob.–59. Gordon's diary (copy of letter 'For his Grace the Duke of Gordon, at Paris, 15 November 1690').
29. See L. A. J. Hughes, *Sophia, Regent of Russia, 1657–1704* (New Haven and London, 1990); L. A. J. Hughes, *Russia and the West: The Life of a Seventeenth-Century Westernizer, Prince Vasily Vasil'evich Golitsyn (1643–1714)* (Newtonville, Mass., 1984).
30. RGVIA, f. 846, op. 15, vol. 4, pp. 253–3 ob. Gordon's diary, 4 September 1689.
31. Events in London constituted one of the first Western foreign policy issues confronting Peter, and it is interesting to speculate how these events might have shaped his perception of Western Europe in the years before the Grand Embassy.
32. Thomas Eekman, 'Muscovy's International Relations in the Late Seventeenth Century: Johan van Keller's Observations', *California Slavic Studies*, vol. 14 (1992), p. 51.
33. RGVIA, f. 846, op. 15, vol. 4, p. 262. Gordon's diary, December 1689.
34. For one example of that network see the 'Memorandum for Captain William Gordon', Tallinn City Archive, f. 230, op. BB37, no. 46–47.
35. RGVIA, f. 846, op. 15, vol. 5, p. 31 ob. Gordon's diary ('Mr. Samuel Meverell, Mosco 27 Febry 1690'). See also N. Ustrialov, *Istoriia tsarstvovaniia Petra Velikogo*, 5 vols (St Petersburg, 1858–64), vol. I, pp. 309–11 ('Letter to the Earle of Erroll, Mosco, Jan 1690'). Here Gordon describes recent Russian army campaigns and conditions and assesses the current political environment in Moscow.
36. RGVIA, f. 846, op. 15, vol. 5, p. 31 ob. Gordon's diary ('Letter to the Earl of Melfort, Mosco, 8 May 1690').
37. Bruce P. Lenman, 'Scottish Nobility and the Revolution', in *The Revolutions of 1688*, ed. R. Beddard (Oxford, 1991), p. 154.
38. 'William III to the "Czar [Peter] and Great Duke Ivan Alexeiowich" 31 January 1690', Public Record Office (PRO), SP 104/120, fols 1–2.
39. RGVIA, f. 846, op. 15, vol. 5, p. 37. Gordon's diary, 24 December 1690. See also Marc Szeftel, 'The Title of the Muscovite Monarch up to the End of the Seventeenth Century', *Canadian–American Slavic Studies*, 13, nos 1–2 (1979), pp. 59–81.
40. 'Mr. Duncombe to Secretary of State, Stockholme April 9th 1690', PRO, SP 95/13, fol. 120. See also PRO, SP 95/13, fols 163 and 174.
41. RGVIA, f. 846, op. 15, vol. 5, p. 65. Gordon's diary, 18 January 1691.
42. *Ibid.*, f. 846, op. 15, vol. 5, p. 131 ob. Gordon's diary. 'Loveing Cousin', signed 'Yor affectinate Kinsman', 16 February 1691.

43. Yu. K. Begunov, '"*Opisanie vrat chestie* ...": a Seventeenth-Century Russian Translation of William of Orange and the Glorious Revolution', *Oxford Slavonic Papers,* n.s. vol. 20 (1987), pp. 60–93.
44. Steve Murdoch, 'Soldiers, Sailors, Jacobite Spy: Russo-Jacobite Relations, 1688–1750', *Slavonica*, vol. 3, no. 1, (1996/97) pp. 7–27.

3

Foreigners, Faith and Freemasonry in the Eastern Baltic: the British Factory and Pastor Georg Ludwig Collins in Riga at the End of the Eighteenth Century

Roger Bartlett

I

The ancient Hanseatic cities of the Baltic had always been cosmopolitan in their population: the vicissitudes of commerce brought numerous merchants of differing nationality, culture and religion to the Baltic coasts. Together with the Dutch, British shippers and merchants were pre-eminent in the Baltic trade, and representatives of British commercial houses established themselves in most of the principal port cities along the Baltic sea highway. In Königsberg the long-settled Anglo-Scottish community was united in a 'Brotherhood of the Great Britannic Nation'; from the early decades of Peter I's new Imperial Russian capital, the British Factory was a significant presence in St Petersburg.[1]

Commercial factors equally shaped international Baltic relations and the Baltic ports' political status. The mercantilist impulse behind Russia's eruption into the Baltic arena during the Great Northern War (1700–21) was as powerful as any broader political motivation. The Russian conquests finally confirmed at Nystadt (1721) significantly altered previous trading patterns, but they did not damage the principal Livonian ports, Riga and Reval (Tallinn). As Riga became a foremost trading centre of the newly proclaimed Russian Empire, second only to St Petersburg, it also maintained its position in the wider Baltic world,[2] and continued to attract foreigners who could become

45

long-term residents and active contributors to the city's public and social life.[3] Georg Ludwig Collins (1763–1814), of Scottish descent, merchant, Reformed Pastor and prominent Freemason in Riga, is a notable case in point.

The British presence in eighteenth-century Riga[4] was commercially very significant. In 1765 the British Factory there reported to the British Consul-General in Russia, Samuel Swallow: 'It will appear that near one half of all the Exports of Riga to all Parts, are shipt by the British residing here.'[5] Twenty years later William Coxe observed that Riga's trade 'is chiefly carried on by foreign merchants, who are resident in the town. The merchants of an English factory established there enjoy the greatest share of the commerce, and live in a very hospitable and splendid manner.'[6] As elsewhere, the core community consisted of English and Scottish families long resident in the city, although questions of burgher rights in Riga complicated both contemporary status and subsequent historical analysis.[7] In the nineteenth century the British established a separate Anglican congregation. The first chaplain, the Reverend John Ellis, was appointed in 1829, and records of the British Church of St Saviour are preserved from 1830 until the 1930s. Construction of the 'English Church' itself, built of bricks and Bath stone imported as ballast, was begun only in 1852; interrupted by the Crimean War, it was not completed until 1859.[8] The Church still stands and has recently been returned to religious use. Before the creation of the Chaplaincy, most Anglican British joined their Presbyterian and Puritan compatriots in the city's older and cosmopolitan Reformed (Calvinist) congregation, rather than the locally established Lutheran Church; and throughout the period 1830 to 1859 Anglican services were held in the Reformed Church building.

One of the most picturesque sources on the eighteenth-century British Factory is the 'pocket-book' of Thomas Wale (1701–96), containing a life-time's jottings and memoranda.[9] Wale was in business in Riga from 1724 until the 1790s, though he retired physically to Cambridgeshire in 1764. His elder son Gregory (1760–94), German-educated at Mitau (Jelgava) in ducal Courland, was also engaged in the Riga trade. In Riga Thomas married the daughter of a German cleric, 'clergyman and preacher to the Duke of Brandenburgh'. On leaving Riga permanently in 1764, Wale made valedictory donations which clearly indicate his attachment to the Reformed community: to 'the Weisend [*Waisen*] or Orphan House', 'Reformed Poor', 'Pastor Thorwarthy' (*sic*). He also listed 'my godson Collins' and 'my goddaughter Strauch'.[10] During his Riga career Wale had various business partners, including James Fraser, two Auchterlonies, Joseph Fanthropp, and James Pierson (Pearson).[11] In 1782 Wale, Pierson and Co. was the largest exporter among all Riga houses.[12] In 1795 Wale acted for Pierson in the purchase of an estate in England.

Notable among Riga's Scottish merchant clans was the Cumming family. In the middle of the eighteenth century James Cumming ran Cumming, Fenton and Co., with his partner Philip Ibbetson Fenton. On James's death his estate passed to his nephew John, who in 1777 brought out from Britain his younger brother Patrick Cumming (1764–1830). In 1782 the firm ranked sixth among Riga exporters.[13] When Philip Fenton returned to England in 1792, Patrick became John's partner and, subsequently, head of the firm, in which another brother William (d. 1817) was also employed. After spending the Napoleonic years in England (1800–17), Patrick returned to Riga, where he was a prominent citizen, President of the Exchange, much engaged in the affairs of the Factory and of the Reformed Church. Married to a Baltic German noblewoman, he left two daughters and three sons, who continued the business, in association with further Fentons. The firm finally ceased trading in 1876.[14]

Another Scottish member of the Riga Factory in this period was John Hay (1747–1818). Hay had been an assistant to Necker, the subsequent French Finance Minister, before moving (or, possibly, returning home) to St Petersburg, where the Hays were apparently an established family: the lives and deaths of George Hay (d. 1763), and of Robert Hay (1733?–1802) and his family can be traced through the St Petersburg Church registers.[15] John Hay established himself in commerce in the Russian capital and married a Miss Cramp (probably daughter of the rope-maker Robert Cramp);[16] he came from St Petersburg to Riga as partner in the firm of Zuckerbecker and Co. Hay, like Cumming, won great respect in the city, being known, according to an obituary, for his excellent judgement, his choice library, and his diligence as elder (*Kirchenvorsteher*) of the Reformed Church.[17] Together with Philip Fenton he was a member of the five-man committee which in 1786–7 set up a new gentlemen's club in Riga, Die Musse ('Leisure'), designed as 'a permanent club on the same footing as the great so-called English Club in St Petersburg' and based upon the latter's constitution.[18] Either this John Hay, or a relative of the same name (1780–1858), was also one of the first managers of the British Poor Fund. Established by the Factory in 1806 to succour indigent Britons, this Fund became in time the carrying organization for the new Anglican church.[19] The Fund's founding signatories included names which recur repeatedly in the available data on the British community: George Renny and Co.; J. Morison; Balfour and Co.; Ramsay and Garry; Hay and Co.; Hay Pierson and Co.; Mitchell and Co.; Cumming, Fenton and Co.; Hill Jacobi and Co.[20]

Whereas John Hay moved westwards from St Petersburg to Riga, his older contemporary Robert Nettleton travelled in the other direction. An exporter of pitch from Riga, in St Petersburg Nettleton engaged in sugar-refining and became a central figure of the British community; he was also governor of the Russia Company from 1753 to his death in 1774.[21] As these cases suggest, connections and movement between Riga, the Russian hinterland, and the rest of the Baltic littoral and Germany were fluid and easy, and intermarriage was frequent, at least among Protestants.

Another exemplar of the way in which merchant dynasties could establish Baltic networks stretching into the Russian Empire was the Collins family, also of Scottish descent. The family was related to the noted divine John Antony Collins.[22] In the mid-eighteenth century two brothers, Edward and William Collins, migrated to the Baltic, Edward to Königsberg and William to Riga. Both established themselves in commerce: in 1782 William Collins was Riga's second-largest exporter.[23] Edward had 24 children, including 11 sons, one of whom was our hero, Georg Ludwig Collins.[24] Initially Georg wished to follow his elder brother Johann David into the Church. Johann David (1761–1833) subsequently became Pastor of the German Reformed congregation in St Petersburg; there he married the granddaughter of the great mathematician and member of the Russian Academy of Sciences Leonhard Euler. His family stayed in Russia and became assimilated: his son Eduard Davydovich (1791–1840) tutored the future Tsar Alexander II in mathematics.[25] Georg Ludwig was initially less fortunate than his brother: his father failed suddenly in business, and the sixteen-year-old had to enter commerce to make his living. In 1779 he accordingly moved to Riga, where his sister Margaret had married their cousin William Collins junior (1755–1824).[26] The latter found Georg a place in the merchant house of Emmanuel Friedrich Groot, Reformed Church elder and specialist in the silk trade. Here Georg worked, reluctantly, for four years, until his fortunes changed again: on the retirement of his principal from business and with family support, he was able to take up theology. This period in trade, it was said, prompted a love of foreign examples in his sermons, and inspired in him as a disappointed outsider an exaggerated, sometimes excessive sense of the dignity of the churchman's office.[27]

Georg Ludwig Collins studied first (1784) at Königsberg, where he attended Kant's lectures, then (1785) in Leipzig, coming under the spell and enjoying the protection of the noted theologian and preacher G. J. Zollikofer, whom Karl Aner includes among the leading 'neologians' of the period.[28] Here he met Johann August Albanus and Karl Gottlob Sonntag, later his Lutheran colleagues in Riga, outstanding churchmen for whose subsequent move to the north he was partly responsible.[29] In 1787 he returned to Riga as private tutor to the English family Renny, but the following year was offered the post of pastor of the Reformed Church in the city. Duly ordained in Königsberg, in 1788 he entered upon his office, which he held until his death in 1814.

II

The dominant form of Protestantism in the south Baltic provinces was the Lutheran Church, confirmed by Peter I as the official regional Church of Livonia in the 'capitulations' of 1710. The Tsar was a man of firm personal religious faith. He was however largely indifferent to church ceremonial, but acutely aware of religion's political and social importance. While abolishing the Russian Orthodox Patriarchate and despoiling the Orthodox Church of much of its wealth (a process completed by Catherine II in 1764), he legislated to compel his Russian subjects to attend church and his parish priests to report confessions of a criminal or seditious nature. Inviting much-needed foreign specialists and military men to serve in Russia, he extended his predecessors' policy of freedom of religion and of worship (but not of proselytism) for non-Orthodox foreigners.[30] In Livonia this enlightened utilitarian toleration of other faiths reinforced the Russian practice of conciliating local non-Russian elites by leaving their existing rights intact.

The main beneficiaries of this approach were the Lutherans. However, Reformed congregations had also grown up in major Baltic centres and despite difficulties with the Lutheran authorities established their right to worship and to have their own churches. Nicholas Hope has mapped the European distribution of the Reformed religion, strongest in the German west and south-west, but present in the largely Lutheran Prussian lands of the Reformed and tolerant Hohenzollerns, and in northern enclaves supported by Dutch Reformed, Puritan and Huguenot influence. Such enclaves included the Reformed congregations of both Riga and St Petersburg. Despite competition and friction, Hope also emphasizes influences between the confessions, both in the academic sphere where doctrine and elite culture were transmitted, and in the commercial world outside:

> The growing influence of seventeenth-century Dutch Reformed theology, Anglican pastoral theology, and Dutch and English natural-law theory on north-German Lutheran university theology and law, and in Scandinavian sister universities ... is one of the salient features of the half-century 1700–50.
>
> Communication was an important leavening force too. Commerce, using the big river systems of the Rhine and Main, spread Calvinist and Zwinglian churchmanship and spirituality, particularly Dutch Precisionism and British Puritanism, into many Lutheran *Landeskirchen* by 1700. The seaports on the North Sea and along the Baltic coast became points of entry for Dutch and English devotional literature, Dutch and English natural law, and the new moral philosophy of the British and French Enlightenments. Ships and cargoes also continued the Hansa tradition of uniting the entire Baltic region economically and culturally.[31]

Like the Reformed congregation in seventeenth-century Swedish Narva, from which it inherited several members and a silver chalice,[32] the Reformed community in Riga had a significant British contingent. It had the same origins, too, in the religious affiliation of immigrant merchants, and as we have seen, both before and after 1830 it provided a haven for English Anglicans as well as Scottish and other Dissenters. Its recorded beginnings lie in the sixteenth century, and in its early stages it had strong connections to the better-organized and better-protected Reformed congregation in Mitau. In the late seventeenth century attempts were made to obtain authorization for the Riga community's activity from both Amsterdam and Stockholm, seats of competent religious and administrative authority respectively; but the congregation was properly constituted only after the Russian takeover during the Great Northern War.[33] While the 1710 'capitulation' between Russia and the city of Riga guaranteed existing rights of religious freedom, this was at first interpreted by the Riga city authorities as relating to the Lutherans only. With the end of the war in 1721, however, the Reformed congregation sought to consolidate its position: relying on Peter I's known tolerance of European religious diversity, it petitioned the Tsar himself. A copy of this petition opened the Church's Minute Book, begun then by the English merchant and Elder Joseph Fawthrop.[34] According to local reminiscence, Peter gave verbal assent. This was thwarted by the Riga City authorities, but a second petition in 1722 brought a written instruction from the Governor-General, Prince Repnin. Transmitted to the City fathers on 2 August 1722, this became the effective legal foundation document of the Riga Reformed congregation.[35]

In the following years the congregation had to rely heavily upon foreign support. The first Minister, Johann Heinrich Thorvarth, was found in Germany through the good offices of a former Mitau incumbent. Expenditure for the pastor, and for a sexton, cantor and new church buildings, weighed heavily. In 1724 Thorvarth, who had studied in England and Holland, and a Dutch Elder, Cornelio Maten, appealed for help to Amsterdam, whose Reformed Church responded generously. North German cities were less liberal – only Danzig opened its purse wide – and Elder Fawthrop's fund-raising in London was equally disappointing; but in Riga 'the gentlemen of the English Factory' voted an annual donation of 100 Rix-dollars (Reichsthaler Albertus).[36] Finally a systematic fund-raising campaign by a special emissary, Samuel Lauvergne, produced better results, especially in Holland. On 14 August 1727 the foundation stone of the new Riga Reformed church was laid; after further strenuous financial efforts the church was completed in 1733.

The British continued to play a significant part in the life of the Reformed congregation. In about 1740 Joseph Fawthrop, who had returned permanently to London, was instrumental in obtaining a legacy of 2,000 Rix-dollars for the Church, which paid for a house for the pastor, and further help followed. Later Fawthrop himself bequeathed 1,000 Rix-dollars, on condition that the Church erect a memorial tablet to him and give each year an anniversary sermon on human mortality: a custom still observed in 1900.[37] Finally in 1748 a new financial settlement was achieved. More than 50 Amsterdam commercial houses resolved to pay an annual tax to the Church of 4 per cent of their Riga turnover. Meanwhile it had become customary in the British trade for ships arriving in Riga to pay two Rix-dollars each into Church funds and the British Factory, with its regular contribution, 'had become [in the words of one document] the foundation of the Church'. These benefactors now made permanent written commitments. The 'ship tax' agreement was subsequently renewed in 1770, and in the later decades of the century the growth in Riga's trade assured the congregation a regular income.[38]

The new arrangements were codified at a meeting in May 1748 of 'the leading members of the congregation and the English merchants'.

The provisions for the Church's management evidently essentially confirmed the status quo. The Minister was to receive 500 Rix-dollars per annum. The Presbytery was to consist of six Elders and two Deacons; the congregation's financial obligations – specified house and church collections – remained unchanged. Although towards the 1780s the collections declined and the Pastor's salary shrank (400 Rix-dollars in 1788), these arrangements, and the Church's painfully achieved financial security, continued broadly through the rest of the century.[39]

Thorvarth died in harness in 1771 and was succeeded by his assistant (since 1769) Laurenz Schmidt, from the Rhein Palatinate. Like Thorvarth, Schmidt knew Dutch and preached in it to Dutch sailors; it is not recorded whether similar sermons were given in English. In 1788 Schmidt decided to return with his family to his native Pfalz;[40] his successor was Georg Ludwig Collins. The Church's official history ends its sketchy account of Schmidt with the observation: 'It becomes immediately apparent that the first epoch of the history of the Reformed congregation has run its course. With Schmidt's successor the new period of the Enlightenment intervenes mightily in the by now somewhat torpid flow of the congregation's life.'[41]

Collins was chosen by the congregation with speed and unanimity.[42] On his engagement in the autumn of 1788 to Gertrud Dorothea Bulmerincq, daughter of a city alderman, the salary of his post was increased to 600 Rix-dollars, a compliment which doubtless facilitated his marriage in the following January. He and his wife had sixteen children, of whom eleven survived him. Collins became a popular preacher and city worthy, composer of occasional verse and author of numerous published pieces, notably three volumes of sermons and six of 'official speeches on various occasions', and his *Maurerische Monatschrift* (Masonic Monthly).[43] He was active in philanthropy, a member too of the 'Literarisch-praktische Bürger-Verbindung' set up (after a Hamburg model) by Albanus, Sonntag and another prominent Pastor, Liborius von Bergmann, in 1802.[44] He enjoyed extremely cordial relations with his Lutheran colleagues in the city;[45] and the revision of the official Riga hymn-book,[46] in which Collins along with the Lutherans took an active part, evidently reflects the rationalist-modernizing impulse for liturgical reform which made itself widely felt in Northern Europe at the end of the century. (A prominent advocate of such action in Prussia was the Reformed court chaplain Wilhelm Crichton, another Germanized Scot, members of whose family Collins could well have known in Königsberg.)[47]

Collins in fact formed part of an outstanding group of 'enlightened' and rationalistic Riga churchmen, whose merits were admired both by contemporaries and by the succeeding less rationalistic generation.[48] Collins's popular standing with his Riga congregation, within the city, and among his fellow churchmen of other denominations, was amply demonstrated in 1813 on the twenty-fifth anniversary of his taking office. His congregation gave him a commemorative silver vessel and 4,000 roubles; the University of Dorpat conferred a doctorate; K. G. Sonntag, by now General Superintendent of the Lutheran Church in Livonia, dedicated two sermons to him, while the (Lutheran) pastors of the three principal Riga city churches as well as Superintendent Mayer in Reval composed verses for the occasion.[49] According to Collins's obituary a year later in the *Rigasche Stadtblätter*,

> As a distinguished writer in his own field he did honour to Riga even abroad. As preacher he early won influence among a numerous circle of listeners beyond his own congregation, through the religiously solemn and uplifting nature of his sermons and their multifarious and beneficial moral impact, both in the manner of his presentation and in the earnestness with which he observed external forms of piety.[50]

The regard of the British Factory found expression in the decision of the trustees of the British Poor Fund to grant Collins's widow an annuity of 300 silver roubles, which continued for at least ten years.[51]

III

The obituary quoted above commented also on G. L. Collins's role in the life of Riga's Freemasons: 'Certainly also very powerful in spiritual and moral terms was the influence which he exerted in earlier years, from a local Masonic lodge, on one part of the public here.'[52] The first Masonic lodge in Riga, one of the first in the Russian Empire, 'Nordstern' (North Star), was set up in 1750 by the merchants Johann Dietrich von der Heyde and Johann Zuckerbecker, who had become Masons under Danish patronage;[53] some early Riga Masons had also brought the craft back with them from study in Germany. In 1765 Nordstern went over to the strict observance system and was renamed 'Zum Schwert' (The Sword). Other lodges appeared – 'Apollo' (1773); 'Castor' (with a corresponding 'Pollux' in Dorpat, 1778); 'Astraea' (1787, under the British Grand Lodge);[54] 'Zur kleinen Welt im Orient'

(The Little World in the Orient, 1789).[55] They became subject to the Russian Grand Master I. P. Elagin when he was invested with authority by the British Grand Lodge in London. Members included leading names of the province: Johann Gottfried Herder, who spent his early years 1764–9 in Riga; the printer and bookseller Johann Friedrich Hartknoch;[56] the painter Woldemar Freiherr von Budberg; Pastor Liborius von Bergmann.[57] K. G. Sonntag was a member of Apollo from 1789 to the end of 1793, attaining the degree of Master and from 1791 serving as Orator in the lodge.[58] One prominent representative of the numerous Baltic German noble brethren was the wealthy and well-connected Otto Hermann von Vietinghof-Scheel. As the outstanding Maecenas in Riga of his time, Vietinghof founded the Riga City Theatre (1782), which operated in the same building as Die Musse.[59]

If Danish influence can be observed at the foundation of Nordstern, it is conversely the case that the first Copenhagen lodge was established in 1743 from Livonia, by Ernst von Münnich (a relative by marriage of Vietinghof-Scheel). Hubertus Neuschäffer has emphasized the multiplicity of connections between Russian and Livonian lodges and those elsewhere in the Baltic.[60] For Riga itself some lodge membership lists survive which allow closer analysis, and identification of Britons: in 1781 Zum Schwert's 53 members included the English merchants R. King (from Hull) and G. Veston (Weston?), and the Scots J. Cumming and R. Jobson, all listed as Anglicans.[61] Benjamin Whisker, Thomas Gardyne, Gregory Wale – 'Merchant in London' – and another Collins, George Friedrich, all merchants, appear among the 51 members of Castor recorded in 1784, while a William Collins (presumably senior) is noted as 'departed Deputy Master'; in 1797 when the lodge reopened with 49 members, the four British names had been joined by another, William Petrie, later a manager of the British Poor Fund.[62] A list for Zur kleinen Welt of 1793 includes the Lutheran Matthew Benjamin Iork (York?) and, in a later entry, the Reformed Charles Clark, both merchants; Emmanuel Friedrich Groot, lawyer and accountant of the Riga Six-Deputy City Council, also appears, as Honorary Member. 'Master of the Chair and Scottish Grandmaster' is Georg Ludwig Collins.[63]

Georg Ludwig apparently began his Masonic career in Zum Schwert; at any rate by 1792 he occupied the office of Orator in that lodge. But he made his mark in Zur kleinen Welt, to whose mastership he was elected in the same year. Collins himself left a short account in his *Maurerische Monatschrift* (1797) of the early years of his new lodge.[64] Its creator, Christian von Moller, was possibly identical with the founder of the St Petersburg lodge 'Immortality' (1787).[65] His intention in 1789 in Riga was to bring together 'worthy men of the middling estate' and to give them an opportunity to develop their natural abilities as well as to 'express their still undistorted feelings'. The subsequent membership list shows that the lodge's brethren were indeed much more plebeian than their fellows in Zum Schwert and Castor. The lodge opened formally in 1791. There were, however, serious difficulties both with some of its members and its procedures, and also with its accreditation in St Petersburg. First Moller, then his successor Collins, felt obliged to resign. Collins on his election as Master in 1792 had

> considered it both necessary and his duty to stop certain disorders and abuses which had crept in, and especially the now usual rapid progression to higher degrees. Whether this gained him universal applause is a question none will ask who know the common tendency of men to form their judgments in accordance with their passions. ... Disappointed in his expectations, he laid down his office already at the Feast of St John [Midsummer, 13/24 June] of that year. ... That he had in this short time made his lodge well-known throughout Germany, and established connections with the [other Riga] lodges, must be recorded here, while it is more suitable to bury in the archive of oblivion all the unpleasant events of that and the following period.[66]

His successor, one of the few Russian members, Martin Mikhailov, 'Imperial Russian Provincial Secretary',[67] likewise had much to put up with; but when the following year (St John 1793) Collins was re-elected to the Master's hammer, Mikhailov, who stayed on as Deputy, was able to hand over to him, Collins recorded, 'an ore purified of dross and ennobled, whose working gave more pleasure than it called for effort'.[68]

However, this promising development was cut short by political changes and the fall-out from the Novikov affair. Catherine II's initial attitude to Freemasonry had evolved from amused tolerance to scorn for it as mumbo-jumbo and charlatanry. When Russian Masons developed links with Sweden, however, she suspected sedition, and still more so when she discovered that the Moscow Rosicrucians, directed from Berlin, were seeking to entice Grand Duke Paul. In 1792 she meted out fierce punishment to the leading Moscow Mason and publisher N. I. Novikov, formally found guilty only of printing unauthorized and unsavoury books. At the same time, as French and Polish affairs gathered pace, Catherine saw herself confronting an apparent tide of Jacobinism; she tightened security and censorship regulations and in 1794 she banned Freemasonry.[69] Masons throughout the Empire fell silent. A number of public associations set up in Riga in the following years have been seen as public social replacements for the prohibited lodges: this was explicitly the case of the 'Euphonie', a body founded by Collins and others with official permission in 1795.[70] Things seemed to change again with the death of Catherine II and the accession of Paul as Tsar in November 1796. Paul at once released Novikov from prison, and gave government office to several Masons. 'Sweet hope!' concluded Collins in the *Monatschrift* early in 1797, 'now you smile upon us [once more]'. He followed his account of the troubled foundation years of Zur kleinen Welt with an enthusiastic welcome to the reopening of the lodges and of his in particular, a 'drinking song' entitled 'Our Prospects in the Year 1797'.[71] The third, March, issue of the *Monatschrift* carried a song, to the tune of 'God save great George the King etc.', entitled 'Joy over our good Emperor', in which Collins (with unfortunate lack of clairvoyance) celebrated the alleged virtues of the new Tsar.[72]

IV

Collins's *Maurerische Monatschrift* was published in nine issues, January–September 1797.[73] The introduction explains its rationale: Collins wished, and had been asked, to collect and circulate his speeches and writings on Masonic themes. These were not intended as scholarly pieces, to be subjected to rigorous scrutiny:

> I lay this collection to the heart of the better members of humanity, not before the sharp eye of scholarship. All these essays can withstand the examination of sound reason, but I wish to conceal them from art, from science, from any systematic illumination. That is why I publish them only in manuscript for the brethren. Brethren demand less than strangers. ... And I make no secret: ... bitter, mocking and dismissive public censure would cost me my life. That is the reason why despite many advantageous offers I have hitherto published no collections of my sermons – vestigia me terrent – and why I ask the purchasers of this journal to take the greatest care in exercising their rights of ownership.[74]

However, Collins apparently overcame his authorial fears: both the *Monatschrift* and his collected sermons appeared in print, although the former, printed 'as a manuscript', was presumably intended for a restricted Masonic readership. Not all the contents of the *Monatschrift* were written by Collins himself, 'the best belong to my friends, whom I name in some cases':[75] authorship of those whose permission he had not asked was to be indicated only by their initial (in practice also by other symbols). Nevertheless Collins composed the lion's share, 36 out of 57 items, signing his contributions 'G. C ... s'. The introduction, exceptionally, was signed in full, 'George [*sic*] Collins, Minister of the Evangelical-Reformed Church',[76] making explicit his extra-Masonic religious status.

The contents of the nine issues fall broadly into three, overlapping, categories: instructional addresses for the Masonic brethren; songs and poems of an entertaining nature, especially drinking and eating songs; and occasional pieces, particularly associated with deaths and anniversaries. The latter include two programmes, as it were secular liturgies, composed by Collins for lodge ceremonies.[77] The ideology that runs through the publication is not undifferentiated, varying somewhat according to author. Overall however it is – unsurprisingly – Deistic, and emphasizes moral virtues and brotherly rather than divine love. It is nonetheless not incompatible with the character of the journal's composer/editor and with the position of his lodge as, in effect, a public social institution in Riga. An address (not by Collins) at the induction of an apprentice exhorted the newcomer:

> You now belong to a union, which from motives of natural religion – the heavenly revelation of the wise – leads to virtue. Take this impression of your mother lodge with you on your [Masonic] journey, observe and compare; delight in meeting brothers on this road along which you are led, and pass firmly and coldly by wherever alchemy and spirit visions are – imagined. Believe me, Masonry has nothing to do with political relationships. ... As a worthy Mason, make yourself richer in knowledge of Nature, practise brotherly love, become ever more master of your passions. ... [78]

Thus, unlike the Moscow Rosicrucians, this version of Masonry abjured any political dimension and equally avoided the occult. Collins himself wrote in similar terms. In an almost programmatic poem, 'The Genius of Masonry. A Dream',[79] read at the Lodge's anniversary (*Stiftungsfeyer*), he made God his starting point. The dreamer is led by nature's vernal awakening from winter 'into the nearby pine grove/In order to be alone with God.' His prayer to the deity is interrupted, however, by a youth in dazzling white who points the way to the Masonic temple, 'the sanctuary of all wise men, ... the final goal of all paths, ... the holy asylum/For true human feeling.' Looking inward into his own innermost past experience, the dreamer recognizes the presence of the youth throughout his life. In the 'spiritual union' to which the youth dedicates him he finds 'Love, Friendship, Truth' and 'higher-worldly blessings' (*überirdischer Gewinn*[80]): there are consolations too for what are evidently autobiographical distresses, and for the life of the expatriate 'far from the fatherland'. At the end the dream turns out to be reality.

If Masonry here seems almost to have supplanted religious faith, a more personal relation to God speaks through a posthumously published memorial address by the well-known actor and writer K. F. D. Grohmann (1758–94),[81] to whom Collins in his turn devoted a deeply felt and religiously cast memorial poem.[82] Seeking to prove the reality of immortality, Grohmann began with a religious verse on God's power and justice, then justified his use of this 'old church song' to introduce his theme in 'these enlightened new times'. His God is 'omnipotence, goodness and love itself' and therefore cannot possibly allow Man to end simply in physical death. With a passing swipe at the French Revolution, 'the atrocities now [1793] in France', Grohmann concludes: 'No! my brothers, fear nothing! We are made for Eternity! We are [*sic*], through God's power! His goodness and grace will preserve us!'[83]

A later anonymous speaker, speculating on the origin and purpose of the Order, stood nearer to the mystical side of Masonry. Acknowledging its ancient and hermetic origin, but skirting more specific questions as unanswerable, he concluded that 'our sublime goal is essentially higher understanding of Nature and more worthy knowledge (which springs from that) of the highest Architect': a knowledge however neither accessible nor beneficial to the common masses.[84] Collins himself, in a long piece designed for the instruction of First Degree brethren, gave a more prosaic formulation: that the secret to which all Masons should strive is simply 'the ennoblement of our moral nature, in a manner compatible with physical or visible Nature'.[85] After a detailed exegesis of the symbolism of the First Degree initiation, he ended with a verse declaring Masons' devotion to the 'Builder of the World' and their striving for goodness in His honour.[86]

Among the jollier pieces in the periodical is a chorus composed by Collins 'In Praise of Our Sisters' (*Lob der Schwestern*): the only reference to women, a predictably patriarchal paean to the virtue of the good woman, 'the pride of the wise man,/His dearest property', and to the joys of marriage.[87] In his verse Collins showed an ability to turn an apt phrase and rhyme, and to produce fluent and agreeable, if unremarkable, lines.

Collins' *Monatschrift* is an unexceptionable sample of right-thinking Masonic discourse; in the Enlightened late eighteenth century such sentiments sat easily with professed religious beliefs and with Collins's public and professional position in Riga. They fitted also in the mainstream of the non-mystical European (and Russian) Masonic tradition: as Rudolf Vierhaus remarked of German Masonry, 'most Freemasons in the eighteenth century wanted no more than to be model burghers: the lodge for them was an element of sociability and moral self-confirmation'.[88] As elsewhere, the flourishing of Masonic lodges in Riga was part and parcel of the development of sociability, civil institutions and public life; Gvido Straube has even suggested that they served a function prefiguring that of modern political parties.[89] The appearance of Collins's periodical in print, on whatever terms, suggests moreover that the tension between the public discourse sought by Enlightened and civil society, and the secrecy of the Masons, was not a serious problem in this case; and his publication provides a relatively rare insight into the activities of his lodge.[90] At the same time, with the development over the same period of religious awakening[91] (associated in Livonia especially with the name of Julie von Krüdener, née Vietinghof), clergy like Collins might either find a refuge for their rationalism in Masonry or (like Sonntag[92]) move away from the latter to a warmer and more deeply felt faith.

The *Monatschrift* was a response to the renewal of the lodges in 1797. Paul I as Grand Duke had been well-disposed to Masonry, and initially he seemed inclined to legalize the movement again: many lodges, like Zur kleinen Welt, reopened. However Paul decided otherwise and a new ban was imposed later in 1797, only rescinded in 1803 by Alexander I. (Thereafter lodges continued in official existence in the Russian Empire until 1822.) The abrupt end of the *Monatschrift* presumably reflects these developments; and there is little further information on Collins's Masonic activities after 1797. Paul's official prohibition, however, like that of 1794, did not fully prevent further covert and some overt Masonic activity.[93] In September 1796 Collins had published four Masonic songs celebrating the seventh anniversary of Zur kleinen Welt; now in 1799 he printed a Masonic 'cantata'.[94] A source of 1805–6, however, while mentioning Zur kleinen Welt and Collins as its master, notes that the lodge is no longer functioning.[95] And there is another hint, in the commemorative pamphlet composed by his colleagues and admirers on his death in 1814, that Collins's Masonic hey-day was in fact the years before Catherine's ban. Collins's good friend General Superintendent Sonntag, whose position in 1814 had changed from that of the early 1790s, wrote:

> However little the present writer agreed with the deceased about the value of the Free Masonic Order in *our* time, historical justice and truth require him to state that, just as Riga had much to thank Freemasonry for in earlier decades, so Collins also and in particular did much for spiritual and moral education and philanthropy as Master of the Riga lodge called 'Little World', until March 1794, when all Masonic lodges here found themselves under the necessity of ending their work.[96]

In the life and work of Georg Ludwig Collins the histories of religion and of Freemasonry in the Baltic region of the Russian Empire, and of the British and other expatriate communities in its ports, intersect. Collins's life exemplifies the social integration of the foreign merchant communities in their host cities, the normality of marital alliance and assimilation between specific national and cultural strata,[97] and the ease with which educated merchant families could participate in cultural as well as commercial life. Much here still remains unclear which further research may illuminate. In a larger perspective Collins personifies the wide-ranging economic and cultural interchange between the Russian Empire and its Western neighbours along the northern Baltic sea highway. In another formulation his career demonstrates the vitality of the eighteenth-century 'North-European communications network'[98] which united centres of culture and community from Moscow and St Petersburg across national boundaries to Stockholm, Danzig, Copenhagen and Hamburg, further southwards to Leipzig or Berlin, and westwards to Amsterdam, London or Aberdeen.

Notes

1. Karl-Heinz Ruffmann, 'Engländer und Schotten in den Seestädten Ost- und Westpreußens', *Zeitschrift für Ostforschung* (hereafter *ZfO*), vol. 7 (1958), pp. 17–38; Anthony Cross, *By the Banks of the Neva: Chapters from the Lives and Careers of the British in Eighteenth-Century Russia* (Cambridge, 1997).
2. E. Harder-Gersdorff, 'Riga im Rahmen der Handelsmetropolen und Zahlungsströme des Ost-Westverkehrs am Ende des 18. Jahrhunderts', *ZfO*, vol. 44 (1995), pp. 523–4.

3. On eighteenth-century Riga see Henryk Rietz, *Z dziejów życia umysłowego Rygi w okresie Oświecenia* (Toruń, 1977); C. Mettig, *Geschichte der Stadt Riga* (Riga, 1897).

4. On the seventeenth century see R. W. K. Hinton, *The Eastland Trade and the Commonweal in the Seventeenth Century* (Cambridge, 1959); V. V. Doroshenko, *Torgovlia i kupechestvo Rigi v XVII veke* (Riga, 1985).

5. Quoted in Herbert H. Kaplan, *Russian Overseas Commerce with Great Britain during the Reign of Catherine II* (Philadelphia, 1995), p. 45. Britain became the principal market for Riga exports at this time (see Harder-Gersdorff, 'Riga', p. 531, see also p. 543).

6. William Coxe, *Travels into Poland, Russia, Sweden and Denmark [...]*, 3 vols (London, 1784–90), vol. III, p. 268.

7. This problem cannot be discussed here. See, in general, T. Zeids (ed.), *Feodālā Rīga* [Feudal Riga] (Riga, 1978), pp. 276–7 and *passim*; I. Grasmane, 'Rīgas eksporttirgotāji XVIII gs. beigās un XIX gs. pirmajā puse' [Riga's Export Merchants at the end of the 18th–first half of the 19th centuries], *Latvijas PSR Zinātņu Akadēmijas Vēstis*, no. 4 (345) (1976), pp. 69–82. I owe these references to the kindness of Dr Aija Priedite (Riga). See also Harder-Gersdorff, 'Riga', n. 97; Revd Henry John Wale, *My Grandfather's Pocket-Book, AD 1701 to 1796* (London, 1883), pp. 85–6.

8. 'Records of St Saviour's Church, Riga', Guildhall Library, London: Diocese of London, British Church of St Saviour, Riga, Ms 11,228, ff. 1–9; Baptisms, Marriages, Burials 1830–1937: Mss 10,953–10,953B. Cf. Janet M. Hartley, *Guide to Documents and Manuscripts in the United Kingdom Relating to Russia and the Soviet Union* (London and New York, 1987), no. 162.16; also 152.1, 173.22.

9. Wale, *Pocket-Book*. Thomas Wale's papers are held in the Cambridgeshire Record Office: Hartley, *Guide*, no. 39.2

10. Wale, *Pocket-Book*, pp. 121–2, 383 and *passim*. The monies were distributed by his firm's accountant J. H. Thorwarth, namesake and presumably relative of the Pastor.

11. Wale, *Pocket-Book*, pp. 77–80, 244, 331.

12. Harder-Gersdorff, 'Riga', p. 546.

13. *Ibid.*, p. 546.

14. *Rigasche Biographien, nebst einigen Familien-Nachrichten, Jubiläums-Feiern, etc. Aus den 'Rigaschen Stadt-Blättern' v. J. 1810 bis 1879 incl., mit Ergänzungen und Zusätzen ...*, J. G. F[robeen], 3 vols (Riga, 1881–4), vol. II, pp. 1–3.

15. Guildhall Library, Ms 11,192B, *passim*: data kindly communicated by Professor A. G. Cross.

16. Cross, *By the Banks*, p. 68.

17. Frobeen, *Rigasche Biographien*, vol. I, pp. 56–7.

18. R. Büngner, *Die Gesellschaft der Musse in Riga, 1787–1887* (Riga, 1887), pp. 7–8; in general see Rietz, *Z dziejów*, pp. 48–66. On the St Petersburg English Club (founded in 1770) see Cross, *By the Banks*, pp. 27–8.

19. Guildhall Library, MS 11, 227, 'British Poor Fund, 1806': foundation and GM minutes 1806–22, accounts 1808–50s. The later account in MS 11, 228, ff. 1–2 wrongly asserts that two initial British Poor Fund goals were the

establishment of an Anglican minister and church. The original documents are concerned solely with poor relief.

20. MS 11, 227, f. 6. On these firms and families in the nineteenth century see Grasmane, 'Rīgas eksporttirgotāji', especially pp. 80–1.

21. Cross, *By the Banks*, pp. 50–1.

22. *Chronik der deutsch-reformierten Gemeinde in Riga, herausgegeben vom Presbyterium* (Göttingen, 1933) (hereafter *Chronik*), p. 31.

23. Harder-Gersdorff, 'Riga', p. 546.

24. *Dem Andenken des evangelisch-reformierten Predigers zu Riga Herrn Dr. Georg Collins, von Einigen seiner Freunde im Januar 1814* (Riga, [1814]) (hereafter *Andenken*). In general see *Allgemeines Schriftsteller- und Gelehrten-Lexikon der Provinzen Livland, Esthland und Kurland*, bearbeitet von Joh. Friedrich v. Recke und Karl Eduard Napiersky, 5 vols (Mitau, 1827–61) (hereafter R/N), vol. I, pp. 356–61; Rietz, *Z dziejów*, p. 91.

25. E. Amburger, *Deutsche in Staat, Wirtschaft und Gesellschaft Rußlands: Die Familie Amburger in St. Petersburg, 1770–1920* (Wiesbaden, 1986), pp. 37–8; idem, *Fremde und Einheimische im Wirtschafts- und Kulturleben des neuzeitlichen Rußlands. Ausgewählte Aufsätze*, ed. K. Zernack (Wiesbaden, 1982), p. 299. Both J. D. and E. D. Collins were Freemasons: T. Bakounine, *Répertoire biographique des francmaçons russes (XVIIIᵉ et XIXᵉ siècles)* (Paris, 1967), p. 98.

26. On William see Frobeen, *Rigasche Biographien*, vol. I, pp. 119–21.

27. *Chronik*, p. 31

28. Karl Aner, *Die Theologie der Lessingzeit* (Halle, 1929), chapter II, p. 142.

29. *Andenken*, p. 6; *Chronik*, pp. 31–2; Konrad Hoffmann, *Volkstum und ständische Ordnung in Livland: Die Tätigkeit des General-Superintendenten Sonntag zur Zeit der ersten Bauernreform* (Königsberg–Berlin, 1939), p. 26.

30. J. Cracraft, *The Church Reform of Peter the Great* (London and Basingstoke, 1971); L. Lewitter, 'Peter the Great's Attitude towards Religion: from Traditional Piety to Rational Theology', in *Russia and the World of the Eighteenth Century*, ed. R. Bartlett *et al.* (Columbus, Ohio, 1988), pp. 62–77.

31. Nicholas Hope, *German and Scandinavian Protestantism, 1700 to 1918* (Oxford, 1995), pp. 14–17. I am grateful to Dr Hope for assistance with sources and other information.

32. Dirk Erpenbeck, 'Die Engländer in Narva zu schwedischer Zeit', *ZfO*, vol. 38 (1989), pp. 481–97 (490). Erpenbeck has also investigated the British community in Reval: '"Die englischen in Lieflandt negotierenden Kaufleute." Reval und der englische Handel im späten 17. Jahrhundert', in *Reval. Handel und Wandel vom 13. bis zum 20. Jahrhundert,* eds Norbert Angermann and Wilhelm Lenz (Lüneburg, 1997), pp. 209–60.

33. Erpenbeck, 'Die Engländer'; *Chronik*, pp. 8–15.

34. *Sic* in *Chronik*, p. 15 and *passim*: Fanthropp?

35. *Chronik*, pp. 15–16.

36. *Ibid.*, pp. 18–19. On currencies see Harder-Gersdorff, 'Riga', pp. 540–5 and sources.

37. *Chronik*, pp. 23–4.

38. *Ibid.*, pp. 20–3, 28 (quotation p. 23).

39. *Ibid.*, pp. 22–4, 28.

40. *Ibid.*, p. 29

41. *Ibid.*, pp. 29–30.

42. *Ibid.*, p. 30. The selection meeting, at the house of Collegiate Assessor Thomas Zuckerbecker, comprised only 13 members.

43. R/N, vols I, pp. 356–61 and V, p. 134 include 43 entries, many multiple. Additions: *Svodnyi katalog knig na inostrannykh iazykakh, izdannykh v Rossii v XVIII veke*, eds A. I. Kopanev *et al.*, 3 vols (Leningrad, 1984–6) (hereafter *SK*), vol. I, s.v. 'Collins Georg Ludwig', nos 640–55.

44. Guildhall Library, MS 11, 227, f. 9; [A. Bulmerincq], *Geschichte der Allerhöchst bestätigten literarisch-practischen Bürger-Verbindung zu Riga* (Riga, 1852), pp. 1, 25, 33.

45. Cf. contemporary Berlin: Hope, *Protestantism*, p. 235. See also P. H. Poelchau, *Rigas evangelische Kirche im 19. Jahrhundert* (Riga, 1910).

46. *Sammlung alter und neuer christlicher Lieder, in Gemäßheit der 'Allerhöchst bestätigten Allgemeinen liturgischen Verordnung für die evangelisch-lutherischen Gemeinden im Russischen Reich von 1805'* (Riga, 1810): *Andenken*, pp. 13–16.

47. Hope, *Protestantism*, chapter 13; on Crichton, see *ibid.*, p. 287; potential acquaintance with Collins, personal comment of Dr Hope.

48. C. A. Berkholz, quoted in *Riga im 19. Jahrhundert: Ein Rückblick von Bernhard Hollander* (Riga, 1926), p. 10.

49. *Andenken*, p. 8.

50. Frobeen, *Rigasche Biographien*, vol. I, pp. 28–30; cf. *Andenken*, *passim*.

51. Guildhall Library, MS 11, 227, ff. 12 (1814), 15, 18.

52. On Freemasonry in the Russian Empire (including Riga) see A. E. Pypin, *Russkoe masonstvo XVIII v. i pervaia chetvert' XIX v.*, ed. G. Vernadsky (St Petersburg, 1916); G. Vernadsky, *Russkoe masonstvo v tsarstvovanie Ekateriny II* (Petrograd, 1917); T. Bakounine, *Répertoire*; I. de Madariaga, 'Freemasonry in Eighteenth-Century Russian Society', Chapter 7 of her *Politics and Culture in Eighteenth-Century Russia* (London, 1998); D. Smith, 'Freemasonry and the Public in Eighteenth-Century Russia', *Eighteenth-Century Studies*, vol. 29, no. 1 (October 1995), pp. 25–44. In Riga: Rietz, *Z dziejów*, pp. 57–60; G. Straube, 'Brīvmūrniecība Latvijā apgaismība gadsimtā' ['Freemasonry in Latvia in the Century of the Enlightenment'; German summary], *Latvijas Vēstures Institūta Žurnals*, 1992, no. 2, pp. 56–73. In Courland: Erich Donnert, *Kurland im Ideenbereich der Französischen Revolution. Politische Bewegungen und gesellschaftliche Erneuerungsversuche 1789–1795* (Frankfurt a/M, 1993), pp. 43–55. Generally: Ludwig Hammermayer, 'Zur Geschichte der europäischen Freimaurerei und der Geheimgesellschaften im 18. Jh.: Genese-Historiographie-Forschungsprobleme', in *Beförderer der Aufklärung in Mittel- und Osteuropa. Freimaurer, Gesellschaften, Clubs*, ed. H. Ischreyt (Berlin, 1979), pp. 9–69; Hubertus Neuschäffer, 'Anmerkungen zur Frage der Freimaurerei im Ostseeraum im 18. und 19. Jh.', *Journal of Baltic Studies*, vol. XIII (1982), pp. 134–43.

53. Pypin, *Masonstvo*, p. 499. Officers of the lodge Zur kleinen Welt in 1793 included T. Zuckerbecker, listed as Consul of the Dutch Estates General, b. 1768, Reformed religion: Latvian State Historical Archive, Riga (hereafter LVVA), 4038 fonda, 2 apraksts, 1394 lietas, 12 lapuse.

54. A. G. Cross, 'British Freemasons in Russia during the Reign of Catherine the Great', *Oxford Slavonic Papers*, N.S. vol. 4 (1971), p. 45: also valuable on the

Russian context. The United Grand Lodge Library, London holds correspondence from Apollo, Castor and Astraea (Hartley, *Guide*, no. 233.2–3).
55. Pypin, *Masonstvo*, pp. 499–521. Pypin wrongly dates Zur kleinen Welt to 1790; he mentions reports (1760s) of other otherwise unattested lodges in Riga.
56. On the Hartknochs see Henryk Rietz, 'Johann Friedrich Hartknoch 1740–1789', in *Wegbereiter der deutsch-slawischen Wechselseitigkeit*, eds Eduard Winter *et al.* (Berlin, 1983), pp. 89–100, and the same author's article in *Acta Universitatis Nicolai Copernici*, Historia XX, Nauki humanistyczno-spoleczne, no. 158 (1985); also E. A. Savel'eva and A. A. Zaitseva in *Latvijas PSR Zinātņu Akadēmijas Vēstis*, no. 4 (1990), pp. 40–4, 45–52.
57. Bergmann had been member and Orator of a Leipzig lodge in the 1770s: August Wolfstieg, *Bibliographie der Freimaurerischen Literatur*, 3 vols (Burg, 1911–13; Ergänzungsband 1926), nos 3294, 11169, 13936–7. Zum Schwert early established a children's refuge in Riga.
58. Straube, 'Brīvmūrniecība Latvijā', pp. 62–3.
59. Heinrich Bosse, 'The Establishment of the German Theater in Eighteenth-Century Riga', *Journal of Baltic Studies*, vol. 20 (1989), pp. 207–22. On Vietinghof-Scheel, son-in-law of Fieldmarshal Münnich and father of Julie von Krüdener, see *Deutsch–Baltisches Biographisches Lexikon, 1710–1960*, ed. Wilhelm Lenz (Köln-Wien, 1970), p. 836; Rietz, *Z dziejów*, p. 61; Andrew Swinton, *Travels into Norway, Denmark and Russia in the Years 1788, 1789, 1790 and 1791* (London, 1792), p. 114.
60. Neuschäffer, 'Anmerkungen', pp. 139–40.
61. Straube, 'Brīvmūrniecība Latvijā', p. 61.
62. LVVA, 4038 f., 2 apr., 1394 l., 18–19 o.p. lpp. No religious affiliation given. G. L. Collins published a memorial to his 'unforgettable friend Mr. Benjamin Whisker, d. 10 February 1806' (R/N, vol. V, p.134).
63. LVVA, 4038 f., 2 apr., 1394 l., 12–13 1pp. The printed 1793 list gives 56 members, 14 honorary members, 5 serving brothers. Undated handwritten additions make totals respectively 75, 15, 5. Other lists: Wolfstieg, *Bibliographie*, Ergänzungsbd, nos 1233, 1236.
64. G. C ... s, 'Beitrag zur Geschichte der Loge zur kleinen Welt in Riga, vom Jahr 1789 bis 1794', *Maurerische Monatschrift*, Erstes Heft, Jan. 1797 (Gera, 1797) (hereafter *MM*) pp. 8–16. *MM's* pagination is continuous. Wolfstieg, *Bibliographie*, nos 517, 6531; Straube, 'Brīvmūrniecība Latvijā', p. 63.
65. Pypin, *Masonstvo*, p. 521.
66. *MM*, pp.14–15.
67. LVVA, 4038 f., 2 apr., 1394 l., 12 lp. According to Vernadsky (*Russkoe masonstvo*, p. 12) Zur kleinen Welt (very unusually) 'added Russian-language sessions' to its activities after 1790. This is discordant with the very small number of Russian names in the 1793 list. Adequate information is lacking; perhaps this was one of the problems Collins faced at his election.
68. *MM*, pp. 15–16.
69. On Catherine, Masonry, Novikov and the changing climate of the 1790s see Pypin, *Masonstvo, passim*; Isabel de Madariaga, *Russia in the Age of Catherine the Great* (London, 1981), pp. 521–48; Madariaga, 'Freemasonry in Eighteenth-Century Russian Society'.
70. Rietz, *Z dziejów*, pp. 63–4; Mettig, *Geschichte*, pp. 410–12, 415. I have not seen F. Kolberg, *Geschichte der Gesellschaft der Euphonie* (Riga, 1897). By 1800

Riga had a relatively well-developed set of public and social institutions – clubs and coffee-houses, bookshops, newspapers and journals, libraries and reading societies, musical events as well as the rather short-lived theatre – which supported a brisk social life open to the upper strata of burghers and non-nobles, as well as the nobility. See further Part I of Indrek Jürjo, 'Lesegesellschaften in den baltischen Provinzen im Zeitalter der Aufklärung. Mit besonderer Berücksichtigung der Lesegesellschaft von Hupel in Oberpahlen', *ZfO*, vol. 39 (1990), pp. 540–71; vol. 40 (1991), pp. 28–56; idem, 'Die Klubs in Reval im Zeitalter der Aufklärung', in *Reval* (as note 32), pp. 339–62; H. Rietz, 'Das Verlagswesen in Riga in den Jahren, 1750–1810', *Nordost-Archiv*, Jg. 17 (1985), pp. 187–214, 241–64.

71. *MM*, pp. 17–18.
72. *MM*, pp. 76–7.
73. 9 Hefte (Gera, 1797), 288 pp. The copy in the Academic Library of the Latvian Academy of Sciences, Riga, is dedicated by Collins to Liborius von Bergmann, as previous Master of the (a?) Lodge. Wolfstieg lists *Monatschrift*'s contents individually: see Register, s.v. 'Collins' and 'Riga'.
74. *MM*, pp. 5–6.
75. *MM*, p. 6.
76. *MM*, p. 8.
77. *MM*, pp. 244–56, 269–75.
78. *MM*, pp. 34–5.
79. *MM*, pp. 18–27.
80. *MM*, p. 22.
81. *MM*, pp. 40–5.
82. *MM*, pp. 47–51. Other tributes: *MM*, pp. 236–8; *SK*, no. 640.
83. *MM*, p. 45.
84. *MM*, p. 104, further developed pp. 147–8. This speaker noted that the oldest statutes allowed only Christians and freemen to enter the Order (p. 100). The 1793 Lodge membership list included one Jew, merchant Abraham Joseph David, a very rare occurrence at this time.
85. *MM*, p. 169.
86. *MM*, pp. 181–8.
87. *MM*, pp. 107–10.
88. Rudolf Vierhaus, 'Aufklärung und Freimaurerei in Deutschland', in *Das Vergangene und die Geschichte. Festschrift für Reinhard Wittram zum 70. Geburtstag*, eds R. von Thadden *et al.* (Göttingen, 1973), pp. 23–41, reprinted: Rudolf Vierhaus, *Deutschland im 18. Jahrhundert. Politische Verfassung, soziales Gefüge, geistige Bewegungen* (Göttingen, 1987), pp. 110–25 (quotation p. 117); Bakounine, *Répertoire*, Introduction.
89. Straube, 'Brīvmūrniecība Latvijā', pp. 71–3; generally, Hollander, *Riga im 19. Jh.*, p. 11.
90. Cf. Vierhaus, 'Aufklärung' (1987), p. 119; Neuschäffer, 'Anmerkungen', pp. 135–7.
91. Hope, *Protestantism*, chapter 15.
92. Hoffmann, *Volkstum und ständische Ordnung*, pp. 30–1, 41–2; Hope, *Protestantism*, p. 403.
93. Bakounine, *Répertoire*, p. xv and note 15; Pypin, *Masonstvo*, pp. 522–3.
94. *SK*, no. 650; R/N, vol. V, 134.

95. Pypin, *Masonstvo*, p. 521.
96. *Andenken*, p. 7.
97. The civic gap between Germans and 'un-Germans' (Latvians and Estonians) was rarely bridged before the mid-nineteenth century. But see the unusual case in Wale, *Pocket-Book*, p. 186.
98. Cf. Heinz Ischreyt, 'Buchhandel und Buchhändler im nordeuropäischen Kommunikationssystem (1762–1796)', in *Buch und Buchhandel im 18. Jahrhundert* (Hamburg, 1981), Wolfenbütteler Schriften zur Geschichte des Buchwesens, Bd 4, pp. 249–69.

4

Scotland and Russia: a Boundless Bond

Dmitry Fedosov

The notion is often expressed, and I have heard it more than once, that the subject of Russo-Scottish links is rather narrow and restricted. 'Thay haif said, quhat say thay, let thame say.'[1] A negative or dismissive approach can always be adopted, and there is little doubt that any topic has its limitations, as does anyone who attempts to study it. Historians readily sacrifice their entire lives to scrutinize a solitary event, or the career of a single person, or even some facet of it. However, after exploring a theme for years, and seeing no end to it, one is challenged to counter such accusations in a positive way.

Since the history of Russo-Scottish connections is concerned with individuals, families and relatively small groups of people, the subject is indeed a kind of 'chamber history' compared to 'symphonic' developments and global phenomena. But what if we are dealing with the natives of arguably the greatest of the world's smaller countries in terms of cultural achievement, at least according to Englishmen such as Winston Churchill or Horace Walpole?[2] And what if their destination was one of the most powerful empires history has known, and their field of action was its whole expanse from Poland to Alaska, from the Arctic to the Chinese frontiers? What if the unbroken relationship between the two countries spans over five centuries from the Middle Ages to the present? And, because rapid travel across the continent was impossible until recently, there were often several stages along the way via other countries resulting in an international network of Scottish settlements or colonies? Surely, there must be some room for manoeuvre in this field.

I

The sources on both sides are as abundant as they are varied, especially from the seventeenth century onwards. The researcher must literally 'climb paper mountains', as one witty writer put it.[3] Every sizeable collection of documents in Britain or Russia would yield some evidence on the matter. In St Petersburg alone the Historical Archive contains dozens of files on Russian noble families of Scottish origin with their petitions, career records, pedigrees, coats of arms and so on; the Naval Archive is a wealth of information on seafaring Scots who joined the Imperial Russian Navy, besides the priceless correspondence of the Greig family; and the Artillery Museum boasts the official and private letters of Count James Daniel Bruce (1669–1735), Master of the Ordnance under Peter the Great. In addition to random or isolated references of the early period, we possess, for instance, the muster rolls of the tsar's 'regiments of foreign order' recruited in Western Europe by Colonel Alexander Leslie in 1631–2.[4] The rolls are replete with his namesakes and compatriots: Leslies, Robertsons, Gordons, Carmichaels and Crawfords. In many sources, as in life itself, the clannish principle is immediately apparent: wherever you meet a Scotsman, look out for more. A handsome library can be amassed with volumes written by Scots about their Russian experience. Although sometimes underrated, long out of print, or only partially published, their diaries, reminiscences and autobiographies make fascinating reading and have a lot to say on almost any feature of Russian life and history. My own catalogue of such titles (non-fiction only) is nearing a hundred, from David Gilbert's brief description of the Time of Troubles to the twentieth-century impressions of Robert Bruce Lockhart, William Gallacher and Thomas Johnston.

Historians in both Britain and Russia have produced a considerable corpus of works which bear, directly or indirectly, on Russo-Scottish links.[5] In particular, Paul Dukes, A. G. Cross and Harvey Pitcher have enriched and widened our perception of the subject. On the Russian side relevant studies are less systematic and more biographical. N. V. Charykov's monumental book on Paul Menzies stands out, while the towering figures of General Patrick Gordon, Admiral Samuel Greig, Prince Mikhail Barclay de Tolly, Charles Cameron the architect and Mikhail Lermontov the poet (along with his Fife forebears) have all received the attention they deserve.[6] General accounts are also helpful. The index to the latest edition of Sergei Solov'ev's classic *History of Russia from the Ancient Times* mentions scores of Scottish names.[7] Yet, for all that, A. F. Steuart's *Scottish Influences in Russian History* (1913) remains the only endeavour to treat the theme as a whole. His book is still useful, if somewhat superficial; it rarely resorts to Russian sources and ends with the early nineteenth century, probably the richest in this respect. A fresh survey, and a much fuller one, is badly needed, although it will be a formidable undertaking given the scope of the matter in time and space.

My own efforts towards a reappraisal led to the publication of several articles and a concise list of people involved in Russo-Scottish contacts from the Middle Ages to the revolution of 1917.[8] The approach taken there as a starting point for further studies was to identify the individuals and 'clans' who directly contributed to our relations over the ages through their actual presence on, or service for, the other side. I have consciously left out those who, like Sir Walter Scott or Dostoevsky, exerted only a spiritual influence, however strong, on respective cultures, as consideration of such cases would expand the subject beyond reach.

The Scots who appear in Russia can be divided into four categories. First, those who accepted Russian citizenship and settled in the country for good during one or more generations. Second, Scots on temporary service in Russia for periods between several weeks and several decades. Third, British subjects from Scotland who were active in Russia in some specific role: merchants, travellers, diplomats, preachers, engineers and so on. Fourth, persons of Scots birth or descent employed by third countries on missions to Russia, such as the Danish envoy to Muscovy Peter Davidson, '*de Scotia Aberdonensis*', or Spain's first ambassador to St Petersburg, who was a Stuart and a Jacobite. Of course, it was not a one-way relationship, and we must not forget Russian visitors to Scotland, mostly students, tourists and seamen. More of them have pursued the road to the isles than could be expected, including members of the Romanov dynasty and some leading characters of the Empire,[9] but the flow in the opposite direction was by far the mightier.

II

Preliminary biographical study has revealed nearly five hundred Scottish surnames in Russia. The majority of them conceal more than one person, often several families or branches of many generations. The total figure of a few thousand people spread over four centuries is perhaps modest when set against the great migrations of history or, say, the number of German settlers in the Russian Empire (though, of course, Germans did not form a single nation until the later nineteenth century). Nevertheless, given the difficulties of getting into Russia, and the size of Scotland (a population of just over a million at the time of the Union of 1707), the strength of the Scottish contingent in the tsar's dominions is impressive. Russia has not been the only, the first nor the main destination for vagrant Scots, but for sheer vastness and potential it was unsurpassed as the land of opportunity. She sheltered and fostered many a braw lad, and not a few of them became the most famous men of the diaspora. The names most frequently met with in Scotland, especially in the eastern counties, i.e. Hamilton, Gordon, Leslie, Scott, Stewart, Ramsay, Kerr (or Carr), were also among the most common in the adopted country. Every Scottish neuk sent its natives to Russia, and Highlanders were well represented from early on,[10] but not surprisingly the bulk of the migrants came from the east, which has always been oriented towards the busy Baltic route.

The journey did not necessarily follow a straight line, and in many cases the range of activity is incredible. Gabriel Elphinstone, 'a valiant captaine', after a spell in Denmark and Sweden went on an expedition in search of the north-eastern passage to China, was captured by Tatars in Siberia and escaped to Moscow around 1581–5.[11] One soldier of fortune ended up at the tsar's court in 1679 after spending twenty-two years in Sweden, Spain, Poland, Bavaria and Austria.[12] Others arrived via Portugal, Venice, the Ottoman Empire, or, later, the Far East. A significant number of Scots settlers, firmly established in the Baltic region, swore allegiance to the Russian crown as Livonia, Finland and parts of Poland were gradually annexed to the Empire, and played a prominent role in the new administration, armed forces and trade.

As regards their distribution on arrival, prior to the eighteenth century the natural focus was Moscow, where Westerners usually stayed in the so-called 'Foreign Quarter'. From the reign of Ivan the Terrible Scots mercenaries were employed on campaigns all over the Tsardom, and Olearius encountered many of them in Nizhnii Novgorod in the 1630s. With the foundation of St Petersburg in 1703, and its rapid rise, the fame of Moscow was eclipsed. Direct passage by ship to the new capital took only a couple of weeks, and right down to the fall of autocracy the British community of St Petersburg was the most numerous. In 1783, among the 422 parishioners of the city's British chapel (English, Irish, other Europeans, coloured servants, etc.) over a hundred were certainly or probably Scots.[13] The following year the arrival of 140 builders with families, hired in Edinburgh by Charles

Cameron, raised their presence to almost 50 per cent, and in time this proportion steadily increased. In 1865 Peter MacLaren, manager of Macpherson's Baltic Iron and Shipbuilding Works on Vasilevskii Island, was delighted to discover 'seventy Scots families living within a five minutes' walk' of his house.[14] Moreover a substantial Scottish element abided in Moscow (the local British church was consecrated to St Andrew), Kronstadt, Archangel and Riga as well as in small Protestant missions in the Caucasus,[15] Crimea, Astrakhan, Orenburg and Selenginsk near Lake Baikal. In the end very few districts of the Empire remained unfamiliar to the Scots.

Most Scots had similar motives for leaving home. Patrick Gordon frankly explains them in his diary:

> being unwilling, because of my dissenting in Religion, to go to the University in Scotland, I resolved, partly to dissolve the bonds of a youthfull affection, wherein I was entangled, by banishing my self from the object; partly to obtaine my liberty, which I fondly conceited to be restrained, by the carefull inspection of my loveing parents; but, most of all, my patrimony being but small, as being the yonger son of a yonger brother of a yonger house; I resolved, I say, to go to some forreigne countrey.[16]

Personal, religious and financial reasons are given here, to which political ones must be added, certainly in Gordon's case, as he set out from Scotland shortly before it was swallowed by Cromwell's Commonwealth, and to his last breath clung to the Stuart cause.

Ancient Anglo-Scottish feuds inevitably told on the pace of Scottish emigration and sometimes flared up abroad, as when Alexander Leslie shot a fellow officer of the tsar's service, the Englishman Sanderson, at the siege of Smolensk in 1633, 'upon which Murder, the English in a rage drew into a Body to be revenged upon Leslie; the Scots likewise drew into a Body, but the General prevailed with both Parties to mind their Duty'.[17] In the 1650s Scottish loyalists at the Court of Muscovy flourished under the leadership of Generals Thomas Dalyell of the Binns and William Drummond, Lord Madderty, as well as Lord *Sharl Ergart* (presumably Charles Seton, Earl of Dunfermline and Lord Urquhart), who was appointed 'generalissimo' by Tsar Aleksei. Patriotic traditions were later upheld by a band of highly influential Russian Jacobites originally headed by Patrick Gordon, whose son James was wounded at Killiecrankie, and surviving into the 1740s with General James Keith and his brother George, the Earl Marischal, both of whom sought Russian citizenship – in vain because of Hanoverian intrigues.

While old hatred subsided, rivalry remained. In 1763 the uncle of a young mate deplored 'the rage against Scotsmen' in the British Royal Navy.[18] It was evidently not lack of talent or resolution that hindered his advancement; within months Samuel Greig swore an oath of loyalty to Russia as captain of the first rank, to become in due course the commander of her Baltic Fleet, and full admiral. In the later eighteenth century Russo-Scottish contacts reached new heights, so that, according to the observation made in 1805 by an envious English engineer, 'to come from the North side of the Tweed is the best recommendation a man can bring to this city [St Petersburg], the Caledonian Phalanx being the strongest and most numerous, and moving always in the closest union'.[19]

By that time, however, those who formed the Phalanx were roundly known as '*anglichane*', or 'Englishmen'. From the eighteenth century the 'Greater England' syndrome led to the virtual disappearance of the 'Celtic fringe' in the eyes of many, and this attitude still survives today not only in popular imagination, but in scholarly thought as well; even modern Russian editions persevere in styling Adam Smith an English economist and Sir Walter Scott an English writer. What of self-consciousness, then? Could it be that Russian or, indeed, other Scots simply neglected their own background and ancestry, or despaired of ever getting it across to ignorant foreigners? Some might have done so, but there is enough evidence to the contrary.

In 1688 the Lermontov brothers, although wholly russified and converted to Orthodoxy, drew up a genealogy of the Learmonths of Dairsie in Fife, going back to the reign of King Malcolm III (1058–93) and submitted it to the Muscovite authorities.[20] The Moscow-born James Daniel Bruce stocked his library with lives of Wallace and Mary Queen of Scots, interceded with the tsar for captive Swedish officers named Bruce and Hamilton, and attracted his cousins from as far afield as Westphalia and Clackmannan to Russia.[21] During his audiences with Catherine the Great in 1779 the London-born architect Charles Cameron enchanted the Empress with stories of Scotland, and imprinted the device of his chief Lochiel on his book covers. Thomas Mackenzie (*c.* 1745–86), Rear Admiral of the Black Sea Fleet, sported a full Highland attire complete with broadsword and dirk at the time when it was banned in Britain.[22] In 1829 the St Petersburg doctor Thomas Walker, native of Polmont, Stirlingshire, matriculated his coat of arms at the Court of Lord Lyon in Edinburgh; it displayed a saltire on the shield and a 'Scottish fir eradicate proper' (heraldic terms for 'uprooted and naturally coloured') as the crest.[23] In the 1890s Russian Leslies dedicated an Orthodox church on their country estate near Smolensk to St Bartholomew because it was the name of the legendary progenitor of their clan. A Russian officer in World War I, whose mother was an Elliot, entertained a Scottish comrade in arms at the Eastern Front; the former spoke poor English, but the latter instantly recognized the 'braid' accent inherited from his grandfather.[24] In these and other ways roots were treasured, despite the distance in miles or years.

Scoto-Russian contacts, I believe, can be distinguished from Anglo-Russian, not only because the Scots themselves *are* different from the English, as anyone having the slightest acquaintance with Britain in a historical or personal sense would realize, but for other reasons as well. To give one important difference, at least until the mid-eighteenth century 'Russian Scots' were overwhelmingly soldiers while Englishmen mostly engaged in trade of some sort. Secondly, it can be demonstrated that Scots more readily became Russian citizens and served *for*, rather than *in*, their adopted country. Whether their motives arose from habit, attachment, ambition, or something else, is another question, but the results are quite remarkable. There were about a dozen titled aristocratic families of Scottish descent in the Russian Empire (Princes Barclay de Tolly, Counts Bruce, Douglas, Fermor and Balmain, Barons Stuart, Rutherford and Sutherland and so on) against one English (Baron Dimsdale, who never took root in Russia). At a lower social level, among the untitled nobility of British extraction, Scots also prevailed.[25]

Besides, the very essence of the relationship is distinctive. There were several chances for, or attempts at, establishing official links. In 1556 Osip Nepeya, first Muscovite envoy to Britain, after a shipwreck off Fraserburgh, spent over three months in Scotland and had talks with the Queen Regent; in 1601 the Russian and Scottish diplomatic representatives met in London;[26] later in the century Patrick Gordon, as *de facto* Stuart ambassador in Moscow, prevented Peter the Great from acknowledging the outcome of 'The Glorious Revolution' for a long while. In 1718 at the Russo-Swedish peace congress on Aland Islands the parties discussed the possibility of a mutual alliance, one of the aims of which could be the restoration of the Stuarts on their throne;[27] curiously, the Russian delegation was headed by James Bruce, whose kinsmen in Clackmannan were ardent Jacobites. In the end the combination failed, and Scotland departed from the European stage at the very time when Russia made her triumphant appearance.

Yet precisely because Russo-Scottish ties never quite attained an official level, they seem to have remained undamaged by chronic political hostility between London and St Petersburg, except perhaps for the period of the Crimean War. Even then many Scottish names distinguished themselves on the losing side, while others languished in St Petersburg or elsewhere and could hardly wait for a formal peace to resume and expand their enterprises, as did Murdoch Macpherson when he launched his giant Baltic Works at the mouth of the Neva in 1856. The dialogue went on between people and cultures, not states or governments, and can thus be called truly international, in the proper meaning of the word.

III

In the development of Russo-Scottish ties several phases can be identified. The 'Dark Ages' lasted as late as the sixteenth century, and vestiges of that period are barely perceptible. But the legends are haunting. The Declaration of Arbroath opens with the assertion that the Scots originated from 'Greater Scythia', that is, the steppes of Southern Russia, or Ukraine.[28] The very words 'Scythia' and 'Scotia' are strikingly close, which probably gave rise to the myth. The veneration of St Andrew the Apostle traditionally passed from one to the other and was inherited by both the Kingdom of Scots and the Tsardom of Russia. There are grounds to believe that the family of St Margaret of Scotland spent some time of their exile at the court of Prince Iaroslav the Wise, the most powerful ruler of ancient Rus'. It has even been claimed that the future queen was born in Kiev, where her parents had married.[29] Margaret and her mother Agatha were given Greek names, very uncommon for eleventh-century Western Europe. In the same period a Celtic monastic community existed in Kiev and, strangely enough, the earliest British reference to the Tatar devastation of the East is found in the chronicle of Melrose Abbey under the year 1238.[30] Was the dreadful news carried to the brethren by some monk fleeing from Russian lands just before the infidel hordes laid them waste?

After a long hiatus, which coincided with the Mongol yoke over Russian principalities, came the Late Medieval (or Early Modern) revival. From the sixteenth to early eighteenth century the unified Tsardom of Muscovy emerged as a major Eurasian power. A hearty appetite for expansion and endless conflicts with neighbours brought military matters to the fore. Each successive tsar increasingly relied on professional mercenary forces that in many respects proved superior to irregular local levies and *strel'tsy* part-timers. It was also the dominant feature in Scoto-Russian contacts at this stage. Already famed throughout Europe as 'bonnie fechters', Scots infantrymen had a promising start under Ivan the Terrible (1533–84). Nearly a hundred of them, headed by Captains Lingett and Elphinstone, showed how to handle firearms against the Crimean Tatars: 'The Crim, not knowinge then the use of peece and pistolls, stroken dead of their horses with shott they sawe not, cried – 'Awaye with those new divells that com with their thunderinge puffs!'[31]

From then on the Scottish presence in Russia, especially in the army, was a constant and growing factor. Boris Godunov and the False Dmitriis hired Scottish soldiers for their bodyguard, and Captain David Gilbert survived the chaos of the interregnum to tell his story. Innovation in armament, structure and tactics became the order of the day, and it is significant that Russia's first serious military reform was entrusted to the supervision of a Scot. Alexander Leslie's unparalleled recruitment drive of the early 1630s aimed at importing thousands of men, muskets and swords from the West. Even if he fell short of the intended goal, his efforts did bear fruit in the near future. Again, we find a heavy Scottish element among the recruits, notably the officers. In the spring of 1633 Captain James Forbes procured a letter from King Charles I permitting him to enlist in Scotland on Leslie's behalf 200 men for the tsar's employ.[32] In recognition of his role, Leslie received lavish gifts, real estate, the governorship of Smolensk and the rank of first-ever Russian general. His offspring served his 'second homeland' with honour for twelve generations, and reside there to this day.

Recent historical works rightly stress that Peter the Great's transformation of Russia was largely prepared by his predecessors.[33] This is certainly true in the military field. Naturally it was not just the soldiers who flocked to the opulent Romanov court. Christopher Galloway (or Halloway) designed the first clock and water supply system in the Moscow Kremlin, and Scottish merchants, smiths, doctors and so on practised their trade in seventeenth-century Muscovy. But soldiers still prevailed until at least the end of the Great Northern War in 1721. Their numbers were considerable, but their calibre was really astonishing. In the half-century between the 1650s and 1700s alone I have counted fifteen Russian generals of Scottish provenance, and two of them, George Ogilvie and James Bruce, reached the supreme rank of field marshal. No other contemporary foreign party can match this record.

From his childhood to his deathbed Peter the Great was accompanied by a constellation of Scots who helped to shape his outlook and policies. Paul Menzies became his earliest foreign tutor; Patrick Gordon advised him on all urgent matters, especially in time of war; John Chambers commanded his elite Semenovskii Guards; George Ogilvie consolidated his army at a critical point of the war with Sweden; Robert Bruce, the High Commandant of St Petersburg, was responsible for the construction and defence of Peter's beloved 'paradise' city, and as to Robert's brother James, equally skilled as a scholar, statesman, general and diplomat, 'there was nothing he had not a finger in';[34] Robert Erskine was the tsar's personal physician and confidant; and, not least, Henry Farquharson ran Russia's first special educational institution, the Moscow School of Mathematics and Navigation, later the Naval Academy. Given the weight of this party, it is not surprising that the principal Russian order of knighthood, and the saltire chosen by Peter as the banner for his nascent fleet, bear an obvious resemblance to Scottish prototypes. The debt is plainly acknowledged in the original statutes of the Russian Order of St Andrew dating back to 1698.[35]

Peter the Great ushered in a new age in Russian history and opened new horizons in Scoto-Russian ties. Although the signing of army officers went on until the time of Catherine II, the exchange between the two countries became ever more lively and diverse. It now encompassed the naval sphere and trade, industrial development and the realm of culture.

From its very birth the Russian Navy was joined by a throng of Scots: common sailors, officers, shipwrights, engineers, doctors and teachers. They arrived in waves in the 1710s, 1730s, 1764 and later until the end of the century.[36] The string of Russo-Scottish army generals is rivalled by an equally brilliant line of marine leaders. Mention must be made of at least a handful. Thomas Gordon, first British admiral of the Russian Empire and long-standing commander of Kronstadt, led the seaborne campaign that culminated in the capture of Danzig in 1734; Thomas Mackenzie headed the Black Sea squadron after Russia conquered the Crimea in 1783 and laid the foundations of Sevastopol, where local hills still bear his name; John Paul Jones from Kirkcudbright, having 'fathered' the American Navy, became a Russian vice-admiral and proved his worth against the Turks;[37] Henry Baillie liberated Naples from the French in a daring raid in 1799, which won him the admiration of European monarchs and the Russian Star of St Anne, first class. But the first place in this cohort undisputedly belongs to Samuel Greig of Inverkeithing (1735–88), full admiral, reformer of Russia's Baltic Fleet, victor at Chesme and Hogland. Some celebrated naval dynasties were established by these men; all four of Greig's sons followed in his footsteps, and his grandson, after a spell in the Marine Ministry, ended up Minister of Finance under Emperor Alexander II. All told, nearly thirty Russian Scots achieved flag ranks before the destruction of the Imperial Navy in 1917.

The success of Russia's military exertions largely depended on her economic progress. During the eighteenth and early nineteenth century the small workshops and old-fashioned factories were gradually enlarged and upgraded with the aid of Western expertise. Here too Scottish entrepreneurs and engineers, with their proud technological traditions, had a chance to shine. Carron, one of the largest and most advanced iron foundries in the world, dealt with the Russian government from about 1770. In 1786 the Company's director, Charles Gascoigne, accepted the invitation to move to St Petersburg. In his twenty Russian years he did as much as could be done to modernize production by building, reconstructing and directing the biggest works in the Empire.[38] Under his guidance the annual output of cast iron at the Olonets foundries more than doubled, and in the south he established an enterprise at Lugansk making use of the newly discovered ore and coal. Gascoigne's colleagues and followers took over his legacy. Charles Baird created his own industrial kingdom in St Petersburg, including a wharf where in 1815 he devised and launched Russia's primary steamship, the *Elizaveta*. The business further thrived under his heirs Francis and George who naturalized in Russia.

Scholarly and artistic contacts also prospered from the early eighteenth century onwards. James Bruce and Robert Erskine, the most learned men in Petrine Russia, bequeathed their unique libraries and collections to the St Petersburg Academy of Sciences. The architects Charles Cameron, Adam Menelaws and William Hastie stand on a par with any European master of their time. Scots doctors made an extraordinary contribution, directing Russian medical bodies, publishing novel essays and practising modern methods of treatment.[39] Probably the most eminent of them was James Wylie (1768–1854), who rose from regimental surgeon to personal doctor of three Emperors, Chief Medical Inspector of the Army, President of the Medico-Chirurgical Academy and Russia's sole baronet. Their pursuits were very broad indeed: Dr James Mounsey exported rhubarb seeds from Russia to Britain for the first time, while Dr Matthew Guthrie translated and printed the earliest piece of Russian fiction to appear in English, a tale by Empress Catherine the Great.[40] From the mid-eighteenth century traffic between the two countries became bilateral, with a growing number of Russians attracted to one of the hotbeds of European Enlightenment.

The next chapter in the Scotland–Russia story can be dated from the mid-nineteenth century to 1917, but, for all the richness of material, it is the least appreciated. It was no longer customary to engage foreigners for the army or navy, and the majority of peregrine Scots at this stage were involved in various industries which boomed after the abolition of serfdom. Some enterprises continued from the previous age, others were just being established in both capitals or provincial cities. Siberia, the Far East and the outskirts of the Empire emerged as new economic regions with the development of the railway system, machinery, oil processing and so on. Many businesses across the country were owned, managed, consulted and staffed by Scots. In St Petersburg some employees of Macpherson's Baltic and Baird Works lingered on even when they changed hands. In 1890 the textile tycoon Coats struck a deal with his rivals setting up the joint Nevskii Thread Mills with a capital of 12 million roubles;[41] as a consequence, his Paisley workers invaded Russia. In Moscow 'the leading British families were Bells, Gibsons, Hoppers, McGills and Smiths ... all were Scottish not only by birth but by conviction'; the originally Glaswegian Smiths ran their boiler works until 1916, while the biggest department store in contemporary Russia belonged to the firm of 'Muir & Mirrielees'.[42] There was furthermore

> the giant concern of William Miller & Co. whose activities ranged over the whole country. Begun as a partnership for the import of coal and herring, it launched out later into local industry on a large scale. ... It had in Moscow alone a great brewery, a factory for sweet mineral waters including a highly popular cranberry cordial, and the largest stearine works in the country.[43]

The extent of Sir William Miller's Russian fortune is apparent in the grand mansion of Manderston in Berwickshire.

This period presents a colourful mosaic. William Carrick and John MacGregor pioneered photography among the lower townsfolk and peasantry of Russia; a Scot named Denbigh engaged in fur trade, fishing and processing 'sea cabbage' on the island of Sakhalin;[44] Alexander Bisset introduced and supervised tea-planting and manufacture in Georgia; a Clyde shipyard built a luxurious yacht for the Russian Emperor, while 'Shanks & Co.' of Barrhead supplied bathroom facilities to the imperial palaces; in the 1890s football got started in St Petersburg largely by the Scottish labour force who formed the bulk of the first champion side,[45] but when rugby was taught by the Hopper family to their Moscow workers the police banned the game as too violent.

Artistic life blossomed at the turn of the century, and both Russia and Scotland gave birth to some of the most exquisite creations in Europe. It is little known that Sergei Diaghilev's first exhibition (St Petersburg, 1897) was mainly devoted to paintings by the 'Glasgow Boys'.[46] In 1901–2 two great masters of *Art Nouveau*, Fedor Shekhtel and Charles Rennie Mackintosh, held an exchange of their work in Glasgow and Moscow; Shekhtel's fairytale 'Russian village' in Kelvingrove Park, built by 200 Russian carpenters, drew millions of visitors and won him the diploma of the show's best architect.[47] The first British production of a Chekhov play was also staged in Glasgow (*The Seagull*, 1909).

The amicable convention of 1907, negotiated and signed by the British ambassador in St Petersburg Arthur Nicolson, himself a Scotsman, ensured that Britain and Russia fought side by side in World War I. Liaison missions and direct co-operation between the allies were maintained until the collapse of the Eastern Front in 1917, after which Scottish units took part in the unhappy allied intervention in Soviet Russia. For most Russian Scots the revolution and the ensuing civil war meant disaster: some fled leaving all their possessions behind, others lost their lives. The survivors frequently had to change their alien-sounding names and hide their past to avoid trouble. Almost the only remaining channel of communication was the one between the Bolsheviks and Red Clydesiders who were keen to express proletarian solidarity. John Maclean acted as Soviet consul in Britain, William Gallacher went to Moscow to meet Lenin, and Arthur MacManus's wish that his ashes be placed in the Kremlin wall was fulfilled. Today, after a long hibernation, the Scotland–Russia ties are as vigorous as ever, but here we enter a different age.

Finally, it might be argued – not without controversy – that one of the reasons Russia attracted so many Scots, in addition to the opportunities identified above, is that a certain affinity exists between us in terms of national character. I would have dreaded suspicions of prejudice on so elusive and delicate an issue were it not for the fact that my view is shared by a multitude of others on both sides. I would even suggest that no other nation in Western Europe is so like my compatriots. Both peoples dwell in a northern environment with a difficult climate; both are Christian sharing a common Patron Saint; both are polyethnic and culturally diverse; both had to wage fierce and protracted struggles for self-determination; both exerted an enormous influence over large areas of the globe; and both societies have a strong sense of kinship. What one writer describes as 'the fiery imagination, incisive intellect, tough stoicism and gentle affection that are aspects of the Scottish character'[48] can be applied to the Russian nature too. Then there is that famous fighting spirit; experts would doubtless agree that few nations make better warriors than Scots and Russians. On the gastronomic plane, both prefer simple country fare, good (and neat) grain spirits and plenty of sweets. Of course, these are not necessarily positive traits, for 'the fiery imagination' can manifest itself as hopeless idealism, and tenacity as obstinacy, and there are a lot of differences as well. Scottish disposition is of a more active and restless kind, while a Russian normally shakes off his innate indolence when cornered – to perform miracles of valour and ingenuity.

Still, the similarity is there. When I asked Eugenie Fraser,[49] a scion of a Russo-Scottish family, about it, she exclaimed, 'Right you are! Scots *heuch* when they dance, just like us' (she considers herself Russian in the end) – a more profound statement than it sounds, for it instantly evokes the air of unbridled revelry so typical of both cultures.

This closeness, which certainly requires a fuller examination, may account for the tremendous popularity of Ossian, Burns, Scott and Stevenson in Russia. It is also part of the answer why the Scots were drawn there in great numbers and, by and large, felt very much at home, despite all the obstacles, misconceptions and fits of xenophobia. Their own comments in this respect are numerous and eloquent, ranging from details on custom and costume ('The dress of the Russian women is exactly the same as that of the Highland women in Scotland: both have the short jacket, the striped petticoat, and the tartan plaid; and both too, in general, have a napkin rolled about their head')[50] to wider, often very keen and moving, reflections. Robert Bruce Lockhart, who was nearly shot by the Bolsheviks, probably spoke not just his own feelings when he confessed:

> Russia has been the dominant influence in my life. Try as I will, I cannot escape from it. … Even today she haunts me like an unfaithful mistress whom I cannot discard. The experience has affected my subsequent career, my character, and my attitude to life. It has given me confidence and fears, disgust and tolerance, an unrealised desire to forget, and a constantly recurring and at times almost uncontrol-

lable longing to return. Even today my strongest feeling is affection for that country … and for its people, unrivalled in attractiveness as individuals and, in the mass, cruel beyond Western imagination. … I do not lack entirely the canniness of the Scot, but I am still affected by the Russian passion for extremes to the point of sometimes accepting as a reproach my own adherence to the less exacting middle way.[51]

Russian visitors, in turn, are unanimous in their praise of Scottish warmth and hospitality, and the beauties of the country, that in places, as some thought, is not unlike the Russian landscape.[52] For Princess Dashkova, who lived in Edinburgh with her children in the 1770s and ventured out to the Highlands, in her own words, 'it was the most tranquil and happy period that befell my lot in this world'.[53] The Scottish impact abroad was also noticed. Alexander Turgenev wrote in 1836 that 'Walter Scott's native country benefits the homeland of Karamzin and Derzhavin. Tatarization [*tatarshchina*] cannot long endure against this Scottish coal smoke; it will eat into her eyes, and they will clear'.[54] Ironically, Turgenev, a refined man of letters with a perfect knowledge of the European cultural scene, sprang from ancient Tatar stock.

The present article does not pretend to show that Scots formed the main foreign ingredient in Russian history, but be it said that their amazing achievement can stand comparison with any other. The cast of characters is more or less clear, as well as the principal sections and trends of the plot. However, proper study of the subject has really just begun, and many riddles still await solution. In particular: When and how does a Scot turn into a Russian? Why did the migration continue even at the peak of Britain's prosperity? What part did the image of Scotland play in Russia's awareness of the West, and vice versa? These and many other questions must be answered if we want to fully appreciate the past, enjoy the present and foresee the future of Russian–Scottish links.

Notes

1. Words uttered by George Keith, Earl Marischal of Scotland, to those who opposed the foundation of his college in Aberdeen in 1593.
2. '[Scots are] the most accomplished nation in Europe; the nation to which, if any country is endowed with a superior partition of sense, I should be inclined to give the preference' (H. Walpole, *Correspondence*, XV (London and New Haven, 1952), p. 41); 'No other small nation, perhaps excepting the Greeks, has influenced the world as the Scots did' (Scottish Branch, Great Britain–USSR Association, *Shotlandiia* (Edinburgh, 1983), p. 33).
3. Prince Antiokh Kantemir (1708–44).
4. *Rossiiskii gosudartsvennyi arkhiv drevnikh aktov* (RGADA), Moscow, f. 210, op. 1, no. 78.
5. See *The Caledonian Phalanx: Scots in Russia*, by Paul Dukes and others (Edinburgh, 1987), and the bibliography there.
6. N. V. Charykov, *Posol'stvo v Rim i sluzhba v Moskve Pavla Meneziia* (St Petersburg, 1906). His protagonist apart, Charykov gives many details on other Scots in seventeenth-century Muscovy and shows that Tsar Peter's Life Guard regiments were largely a Scottish invention. On Gordon, see A. Brückner, *Patrick Gordon i ego dnevnik* (St Petersburg, 1878); on Greig, see Iu. S. Kriuchkov, *S. K. Greig* (Moscow, 1988); on de Tolly, see D. Bantysh-Kamenskii, *Biografii rossiiskikh generalissimusov i general-feldmarshalov*, vol. III (St Petersburg, 1840), pp. 159–235 (repr. Moscow, 1990); on Cameron, see G. K. Kozmian, *Charles Cameron* (Lenizdat, 1987); on the Russian Learmonths-Lermontovs, see V. N. Storozhev, *Rodonachal'nik russkoi vetvi Lermontovykh* (Moscow, 1894).
7. S. M. Solov'ev, *Sochineniia*, vol. XV (Moscow, 1995), pp. 298–556.
8. D. Fedosov, *The Caledonian Connection. Scotland–Russia Ties: Middle Ages to Early Twentieth Century: A Concise Biographical List* (Aberdeen, 1996).
9. Emperors Nicholas I and Nicholas II with their suites, Grand Duke Constantine, Princess Ekaterina Dashkova, the writers Alexander and Ivan Turgenev, Admiral Fedor Lütke, anarchist revolutionary Prince Peter Kropotkin, Secretary of State Alexander Polovtsov, philosopher and poet Vladimir Solov'ev and architect Fedor Shekhtel, to name a few.
10. So far I have traced 45 'Mac' surnames in Russia (not including the Irish), some of which occur in the seventeenth century.
11. Sir Jerome Horsey, *Russia at the Close of the Sixteenth Century: A Relacion or Memoriall Abstracted owt of Sir Jerom Horsey His Travells*, ed. E. A. Bond (London, 1856), p. 225.
12. 'Count' David William Graham, alias Baron of Morphie. Charykov, *Posol'stvo v Rim*, pp. 578–84.
13. *Rossiiskii gosudarstvennyi istoricheskii arkhiv* (RGIA), St Petersburg, f. 1689, op. 1, no. 1, ff. 60–0v. – *Register of the British Factory Chapel*.
14. F. L. MacLaren, 'From Clyde to Neva', *The Scots Magazine*, n.s. vol. XLIII, no. 4 (1945), pp. 249–54.
15. In the first half of the nineteenth century, the village of Karass in the Caucasus became known as *Shotlandka*, or Little Scotland.
16. *Rossiiskii gosudarstvennyi voennyi istoricheskii arkhiv* (RGVIA), Moscow, f. 846, op. 15, no. 1, f. 3v. – *Diary of General Patrick Gordon of Auchleuchries*.

17. P. Dukes, 'The Leslie Family in the Swedish Period of the Thirty Years' War', *European Studies Review*, vol. XII (1982), pp. 409–24.
18. *Rossiiskii gosudarstvennyi arkhiv Voenno-Morskogo Flota* (RGAVMF), St Petersburg, f. 8, op. 1, no. 54, f. 23v.
19. *The Caledonian Phalanx*, p. 74. I hope I can be forgiven for quoting this passage too often for it is a striking one.
20. *Lermontovskaia Entsiklopediia* (Moscow, 1981), pp. 467–8.
21. Archive of the Artillery Museum, St Petersburg, f. 2, op. 1, no. 38, ff. 583, 586 and no. 39, ff. 173–173v.; Scottish Record Office, Edinburgh, Airth Writs, GD 37/328–9; see also my article 'The First Russian Bruces' in *The Scottish Soldier Abroad*, ed. G. G. Simpson (Edinburgh and Maryland, 1992), pp. 55–66.
22. RGAVMF, f. 243, op. 1, no. 19, ff. 13v.- 15v. Mackenzie wore it in Sevastopol at the last ceilidh of his life.
23. *Lyon Register*, Court of the Lord Lyon, New Register House, Edinburgh, III, f. 69.
24. I. T. Beliaev, *Zapiski russkogo izgnannika*. I am grateful for this reference to his descendant, Mrs Irina V. Kuznetsova.
25. This conclusion is based on my extensive research at RGIA. A huge amount of documents of the Imperial Russian Senate anent hereditary noble status is preserved there (f. 1343).
26. N. E. Evans, 'The Meeting of the Russian and Scottish Ambassadors in London in 1601', *Slavonic and East European Review*, vol. LV (1977), pp. 516–28.
27. *British Diplomatic Instructions* (London, 1922), I, pp. 82–9; S. A. Feigina, *Alandsky Kongress* (Moscow, 1959), p. 155.
28. *The Acts of the Parliaments of Scotland*, vol. I (Edinburgh, 1844), p. 474.
29. G. Ronay, 'The Other St. Margaret', *History Today*, vol. 43 (1993). Cf. Geffrei Gaimar, *Lestorie des Engles*, Rolls Series, no. 91, vol. I (London, 1888), p. 194.
30. *The Chronicle of Melrose*, ed. A. O. and M. O. Anderson (London, 1936).
31. See Horsey, *Russia at the Close of the Sixteenth Century*, pp. 182–4, 225.
32. *Register of the Privy Council of Scotland*, 2nd series, vol. V, pp. 79, 548.
33. See, for example, Paul Dukes, *The Making of Russian Absolutism, 1613–1801*, 2nd edn (London and New York, 1990), chapters 1 and 2.
34. A. F. Steuart, *Scottish Influences in Russian History* (Glasgow, 1913), p. 75.
35. RGIA, f. 496, op. 3, no. 1, f. 6v. I have edited the original of the Statutes for publication.
36. *Obshchii Morskoi Spisok*, vols I–V (St Petersburg, 1885–90).
37. *Istoricheskii Vestnik*, vol. LXXXVII, no. 3 (1902), pp. 1062–85.
38. R. P. Bartlett, 'Charles Gascoigne in Russia', in *Russia and the West in the Eighteenth Century* (Newtonville, Mass., 1983).
39. J. H. Appleby, 'Through the Looking-Glass: Scottish Doctors in Russia', in *The Caledonian Phalanx*, pp. 47–64.
40. *Ivan Czarewitz, or The Rose without Prickles that Stings Not* (London, 1793).
41. A. A. Polovtsov, *Dnevnik*, vol. II (Moscow, 1966), pp. 266–7, 283, 323, 327.
42. H. Pitcher, *The Smiths of Moscow* (Cromer, 1984), p. 21; *idem*, *Muir & Mirrielees* (Cromer, 1994).
43. R. Bruce Lockhart, *My Europe* (London, 1952), p. 13.

44. P. Barlow, 'Chekhov's Far Eastern Scotsman', *Scottish Slavonic Review,* no. 8 (1987), pp. 7–15.
45. This was *'Nevka'* in 1901.
46. *Sergei Diagilev i Russkoe Iskusstvo,* vol. I (Moscow, 1982), pp. 61–3.
47. C. Cooke, 'Shekhtel in Kelvingrove and Mackintosh on the Petrovka', *Scottish Slavonic Review,* no. 10 (1988), pp. 177–205.
48. J. Derrick McClure, *Why Scots Matters* (The Saltire Society, 1988), p. 63.
49. Author of *The House by the Dvina: A Russian Childhood* (Edinburgh, 1984).
50. Andrew Swinton, *Travels in Norway, Denmark and Russia in the Years 1788, 1789, 1790 and 1791* (London, 1792), p. 227.
51. Bruce Lockhart, *My Europe,* pp. 3–4.
52. Unpublished diary of Nikolai Fan-der-Flit (Van der Vliet), who toured Scotland in 1862 (Russian National Library, St Petersburg, MSS department, f. 806, no. 8, ff. 12v., 16–16v.).
53. E. Dashkova, *Zapiski, 1743–1810* (1985), p. 99.
54. *Literaturnyi arkhiv,* I (1938), p. 85.

5
Russia, the Balkans, and Ukraine in the 1870s

David Saunders

In the 1870s Alexander II had to respond to Slavonic awakenings in both the Balkans and Ukraine. In the Balkan case he began by discouraging local freedom-fighters but subsequently intervened on their side; in the Ukrainian case he began by permitting expressions of particularism but subsequently stamped them out. The immediate purpose of the present essay is to explain why the tsar responded in these different ways; the more deep-seated objective is to shed light on the differences between the political opinions of educated Russians and ethnically conscious Ukrainians in the middle of the nineteenth century.

The Balkan crisis of the mid-1870s arose when a Slavonic revolt against Ottoman rule in Hercegovina in June 1875 spread to the adjacent Ottoman province of Bosnia and inclined the nearby autonomous principalities of Montenegro and Serbia to contemplate a war with the Ottomans on behalf of their cousins. A revolt among Bulgarians at the end of April 1876 and the subsequent 'Bulgarian horrors' increased Serbian and Montenegrin enthusiasm for the fray. By the time the two principalities declared war on the Porte on 20 June 1876, many of the tsar's subjects believed he should help them.

Their reasons were various. Some felt a sense of kinship with fellow Orthodox Christians. Some saw an opportunity to reverse Russia's defeat in her last conflict with the Ottomans (the Crimean War). Some stressed the need for the Russian Emperor to look to his laurels at a time when the King of Prussia had become Emperor of Germany and the Queen of England was becoming Empress of India. Mikhail Cherniaev, a retired Russian general who made his way to Belgrade in

April 1876 to take charge of the Serbs' armed forces, was partly motivated by personal ambition.[1] Nikolai Ignat'ev, the tsar's ambassador at
Istanbul, feared Vienna, arguing that

> If Austria–Hungary managed at some point to get the Serbs and
> Bulgarians into her hands in a political, economic, and military
> sense, to strengthen the Poles (who depend on her natural allies, the
> Hungarians), and to bring them closer to the Czechs, Vienna would
> head a Slavo-Catholic federation that would be hostile to us; in that
> event the significance of Russia would be at an end in Europe, and
> serious dangers would arise on our western frontier.[2]

At first the tsar was cautious. In a statement of October 1875 he
emphasized the readiness of all the principal European states to assist
the Ottomans in improving the circumstances of their Slavonic subjects, and expressed confidence in Ottoman preparedness to respond to
Europe's concern.[3] He seems to have paid as much attention to his
judicious foreign minister, Alexander Gorchakov, as he did to the
excitable Ignat'ev, and to have preferred negotiation rather than confrontation with Austria.[4] He tried to get Cherniaev to come home from
Serbia, and succeeded in preventing General Rostislav Fadeev from
joining him.[5] His censors took exception to the newspaper Cherniaev
had edited in St Petersburg on the grounds that, in their opinion, it
was trying to persuade the government to make war in the Balkans and
'have done with the Eastern Question once and for all'.[6] In May 1876
the British Foreign Secretary confided to his diary that 'The Czar dis-
likes war on principle.'[7]

By the end of October 1876, however, when Alexander addressed the
Moscow gentry on the subject of the Balkans, he was speaking of his
'firm intention to act independently' if he could not get his way by
international agreement.[8] By April 1877 he had provoked the Ottoman
Empire into declaring war on him. When his troops crossed the
Danube on their way south in June, he announced that 'Time and circumstances have not altered that sympathy which Russia has nurtured
towards her co-religionists in the East.'[9] On the twenty-third anniversary of his accession to the throne in early 1878 he allowed Ignat'ev to
impose the Treaty of San Stefano on the Ottoman Empire and brought
into being a large autonomous Bulgaria. He lost face when the Great
Powers required modification of the treaty at the subsequent Congress
of Berlin, but so far as the Slavs of the Balkans were concerned he
could take comfort from the fact that, at the end of the crisis,

Hercegovina and Bosnia had escaped the embrace of the Turks (if only for that of the Austrians); Montenegro, Serbia, and Romania had gained full independence from Istanbul; and a small autonomous Bulgaria had emerged whose orientation in foreign affairs might have been expected to be pro-Russian. Alexander could not be said to have pursued the interests of Balkan Slavs single-mindedly, but nor could he be said to have ignored them.

If, on the other hand, one tried to assess Alexander's attitude towards non-Russian Slavs in the mid-1870s on the basis of the way in which he dealt with ethnically conscious Ukrainians, one would be obliged to conclude that, in a crisis, he was likely to insist on maintaining their subordination.

The two main Ukrainian activists of the 1870s, Pavlo Chubyns'kyi and Mykhailo Drahomanov, had both been in trouble with the imperial authorities in the 1860s. Chubyns'kyi was exiled to the province of Archangel for unsettling Ukrainian peasants in 1862;[10] Drahomanov earned no plaudits for recommending the use of Ukrainian as the medium of instruction in Ukrainian primary schools in 1866.[11] At the end of the decade, however, and for a few years thereafter, the regime appeared almost to encourage Ukrainian attempts to delineate a specifically Ukrainian identity. Chubyns'kyi was given charge of an ethnographic survey of the south-western provinces of the empire which generated what is still an essential source for the study of Ukrainian customs.[12] Drahomanov earned his master's degree at the University of Kiev in 1870 and was promptly funded for foreign study to prepare himself for eventual appointment as a Kiev professor. In 1873 the authorities allowed Chubyns'kyi, Drahomanov, and other Ukrainophiles to set up a South-West Section of the Imperial Russian Geographical Society. For the first seven months of 1875 Drahomanov ran the *Kiev Telegraph* (*Kievskii telegraf*), a major Kiev newspaper. Briefly, the South-West Section and the newspaper enabled ethnically conscious Ukrainians to achieve a more substantial public profile than they had ever had previously in the Russian Empire.

The newspaper illustrates the use they made of their opportunities.[13] Their programmatic statement on taking charge of it cited a number of instances in the past in which the south-western region of the Russian Empire had provided the north with object lessons and went on to claim that the vitality of the region's local press might be on the point of supplying another.[14] An account of the work of the South-West Section argued that it was right to dwell on the culture of Ukrainian inhabitants of Ukraine rather than the cultures of Poles and Jews; that its activities were attracting attention both in the imperial capital and abroad; and that its ethnographic finds required the establishment of a permanent Ukrainian museum.[15] A pair of articles defended the South-West Section's wording of the language question in the Kiev city census of March 1874, which by preventing East Slav respondents from calling their language 'general Russian' (*obshcherusskii*) had obliged them to plump for Russian, Ukrainian, or Belarusian.[16] A review of Ukrainian scholarly activity detailed a wealth of books and other studies in the fields of Ukrainian ethnography and history and pointed out that many Ukraine-related papers had been read at the Empire's Third Archaeological Congress (which had taken place in Kiev in 1874).[17] News that Austria intended to open a university in Chernivtsi prompted an article on the ethnic composition of the Bukovyna, where Ukrainians were the largest single group.[18] On 1 June 1875 the newspaper devoted the whole of its front page to a discussion of Ukraine's greatest poet, Taras Shevchenko.

The newspaper and the activities and interests it chose to report provoked antipathy among non-Ukrainophile inhabitants of Ukraine. These tended either to be sympathetic to the idea of a strongly integrated Russian Empire or, in the case of Poles and Jews, to be ill-disposed towards Russians but positively hostile to ethnically conscious Ukrainians. In April 1875 Mikhail Iuzefovich, a well-connected Russophile, resigned from the South-West Section and despatched an anti-Ukrainophile diatribe to St Petersburg.[19] The imperial authorities had to decide whose side they were on. In August 1875 the tsar established a commission to advise him. The following year the commission recommended: (1) a ban on the importation into the Russian Empire of Ukrainian-language books published abroad; (2) a ban on the publication within the Russian Empire of most sorts of writing in Ukrainian; (3) a ban on theatrical productions and public readings in Ukrainian and musical publications with Ukrainian words; (4) the closure of the *Kiev Telegraph*; (5) increased monitoring of teachers in Ukrainian primary schools and exclusion from the libraries of Ukrainian primary and secondary schools of books and brochures whose dissemination and publication were to be halted under the first two recommendations; (6) the acquisition of information about the attitude towards Ukrainophilism of schoolteachers in Ukraine, the despatch of those who were unsound in this regard to non-Ukrainian provinces, and their replacement with Russians; (7) orders to the Minister of Internal Affairs to contact the relevant authority in respect of the activity and orientation of the South-West Section and to present a special report on two members of that Section, Chubyns'kyi and Drahomanov; and (8) an order to the head of the Russian Empire's secret police that he request a subsidy for *The Word* (*Slovo*), a newspaper published in Habsburg-ruled Galicia. By approving the commission's final report with only one significant emendation on 18 May 1876, the tsar turned its recommendations into law. His approval, usually called the 'Ems *ukaz*' (because Alexander was taking the waters at Ems near Koblenz), constituted the greatest misfortune to befall ethnically conscious Ukrainians in the course of the nineteenth century.[20]

Why then did the tsar assist the Slavs of the Balkans but repress ethnically conscious Ukrainian inhabitants of the Russian Empire? The following answers appear in what to me is an ascending order of likelihood.

Since the official file on the Ems *ukaz* barely referred to contemporary Balkan developments, it may be that the tsarist authorities simply saw no connection between their Ukrainian and Balkan problems. Although Nikolai Ignat'ev included Ukrainian autonomy among the 'serious dangers' that he thought could arise on the Russian Empire's western frontier if Austria established a 'Slavo-Catholic federation', he prefaced it with a 'perhaps' which indicated that the prospect worried him less than a reborn Poland and autonomy for Lithuania and the Baltic provinces.[21]

Yet educated inhabitants of Ukraine had been setting their country in the context of the wider Slavonic world since at least the beginning of the 1820s.[22] The most important document produced by the 'Kirillo-Methodian Society', a Kiev-based discussion group prosecuted in 1847 for supposedly subversive inclinations, was a summary history of the world whose principal argument was that Slavs in general (and Ukrainians in particular) had retained their primeval virtues when other peoples had lost them.[23] The 21 Ukrainian signatories of a letter from Kiev to a newspaper in Moscow in November 1862 justified the promotion of Ukraine's cultural identity partly on the grounds that everyone – so the signatories said – sympathized with the contemporary efforts of Bulgarians, Croatians, Slovenes, and Lusatian Sorbs to resurrect or develop their literatures. Why, the signatories asked, must the Ukrainians of the Russian Empire (*Rusiny russkie*) 'alone be denied a right granted to all other nationalities?'[24] In 1875 and 1876 popular support for the cause of the Balkan Slavs may have been greater in Russian-ruled Ukraine than it was in Russia.[25]

Could the imperial authorities really have been oblivious to the fact that, if the Balkans rose, Ukraine might follow? They had certainly worried about the possibility of interaction between Ukrainians and other subordinate Slavs when they closed down the Kirillo-Methodian Society in 1847, for they dubbed that circle the 'Ukraino-Slavonic Society' and looked, in the course of their investigations, not merely at Ukrainians whom they suspected of involvement in it but also at Russians whose interest lay in the general phenomenon of Slavonic culture.[26] Their failure explicitly to connect Ukrainians and other subordinate Slavs in the mid-1870s may have arisen not from their ignorance of a link between the two but from the fact that, by then, the connection was so obvious that it did not have to be spelt out.

The authorities would have been dim indeed if they had been unaware that Drahomanov, one of the Ukrainian activists who most troubled them, devoted even more time than most educated Ukrainians to locating his fellow-countrymen on the spectrum of subordinate Slavonic cultures. Drahomanov was sensitive to the fact that his own family was of Balkan provenance.[27] His activities in Ukraine in the mid-1870s could be regarded as the local application of a programme he had designed for Slavs beyond the frontier of the Russian Empire in 1868. '[H]istorical circumstances', he wrote at that time, 'have given the western Slavonic world three tasks at present: (1) the extension of education to the masses of the peoples, both for knowledge and the retention of their ethnic identity; (2) interaction, initially cultural, for mutual aid and the acquisition of political rights, and (3) influence on the educated world, historical activism like that displayed by other great tribes'.[28] That Drahomanov felt Ukraine belonged to the world in which the pursuit of such goals was appropriate is confirmed, up to a point, by his statement of 1870 that Russians ought to take Ukrainian culture more seriously because 'Geographically, ethnographically, and historically Little Russia [the contemporary Russian-language term for Ukraine] is a bridge [*perekhodnyi chlen*] between Russia and south-west Slavdom.'[29] In 1875 Drahomanov was responsible for the appearance in the *Kiev Telegraph* of articles on 'The Political and Cultural Strengths of the Southern Slavs', conflict among Czech national parties, Serbian domestic politics, and 'Hopes and Disappointments in Western Slavdom'.[30] He may have been the first inhabitant of the Russian Empire actually to pass money to the rebels of Hercegovina and Bosnia.[31] When he said in a private letter of 1876 that he made no distinction between politics inside and outside the Russian Empire,[32] he surely had in mind the fact that what to him was the principal political issue of the day, subordinate Slavdom, straddled the Empire's frontier. Immediately after learning of the Ems *ukaz*, he pointed out how remarkable it was that it had been issued 'at a time when so much is being said about Russia's Slavonic liberating mission'.[33] He maintained an interest in Bulgaria after 1878 and spent the last six years of his life as a professor there.[34] He was still writing about the relationship between the domestic and foreign policies of the tsarist regime in the 1890s.[35] Although almost all Ukrainian political thinkers of the later nineteenth and early twentieth centuries implied the need for the deconstruction of the Russian Empire,[36] not many of them thought as hard as Drahomanov about re-designing east Elbian Europe as a whole. Since Drahomanov's opinions were no secret and officials hounded him for them – he was dismissed from Kiev University at the end of the summer of 1875 and left the Russian Empire for Vienna several months before the promulgation of the Ems *ukaz*[37] – it seems unwise to suppose that the Russian authorities were unaware, when they suppressed Ukrainophilism, that they were also adopting a position on subordinate Slavs in general.

If it is unlikely, then, that the tsarist authorities simply saw no connection between their Ukrainian and Balkan problems, perhaps the different ways in which they treated them can be explained by a closer look at dates. A telegram at the end of the file on the Ems *ukaz* makes clear that it was being enacted at the very moment the tsar was trying to get Cherniaev back from Serbia.[38] The possibility therefore arises that at the time of the *ukaz* Russian policy was hostile to Slavonic causes both inside and outside the Russian Empire.

This argument may be countered, however, by pointing to the fact that the tsarist authorities continued to repress Ukrainians after their attitude to the Slavs of the Balkans had become more generous. The censors decided in February 1877, for example, that a brochure by Drahomanov entitled *On the Question of Little Russian Literature* had to be 'absolutely prohibited'.[39] The Governor of Kiev despatched an alarmist report to St Petersburg in April 1877 when he learned that a society of radical Ukrainophiles in Kiev was pretending to collect money for the Serbian cause but in fact sending it to Drahomanov in Geneva (whither he had moved from Vienna) to support the publication there and in L'viv of 'revolutionary books and journals'.[40] I have tried to show elsewhere that the authorities adhered rigorously to the policy enshrined in the Ems *ukaz* from the moment they conceived it until at least the revolution of 1905.[41]

This long-term anti-Ukrainophilism tends to undermine the further possibility that whereas the tsar's Balkan policy was carefully considered, his Ukrainian edict was a knee-jerk reaction to a sudden but passing shock. Superficially, distinguishing between the Balkan and Ukrainian policies along these lines has something to recommend it. Alexander took 22 months to commit himself to intervention in the Balkans (June 1875–April 1877). Although he seems also to have taken his time to decide upon the repression of Ukrainians (13 months, if one reckons from Iuzefovich's diatribe of April 1875 to the *ukaz* of May 1876), the appearance is deceptive because his bureaucrats did not convene for the purpose of drafting the anti-Ukrainian legislation until five weeks before it was ready for his signature.[42] Of government officials, only the censors contributed a significant memorandum to the file from which the *ukaz* emerged.[43] Provincial governors were not consulted.[44] Iuzefovich, who had followed up his original diatribe with a second paper, was very much the driving force.[45] Thus the anti-Ukrainian edict seems not to have been the product of mature reflection. The government could almost be said to have been 'bounced' (by Iuzefovich). But if lack of reflection on the part of officials sprang from the fact that all they wanted to do was eliminate a short-term difficulty, then considerations other than those operative in 1876 must have come into play to ensure the long-term operation of the edict; and it is hard to see what those considerations might have been.

It is far likelier, in fact, that the tsarist authorities did not feel the need to reflect widely on Ukrainian matters in 1876 because they knew where they stood on them and needed only to re-state their position. Indeed, an obvious way of explaining the difference between Russia's policies on the Balkans and Ukraine in the 1870s is to say that in both cases the tsarist authorities simply replicated the way in which they had acted when Balkan or Ukrainian developments had troubled them on earlier occasions. By the mid-1870s it was becoming conventional, in official Russian circles, to try to stay out of Balkan problems but eventually engage with them and to foster Ukrainian 'awakenings' but then condemn them. In respect of the Balkans one might compare Russia's hesitancy with regard to the Serbs and Bulgarians in the 1870s with her even greater hesitancy at the time of the Greek revolt of the 1820s.[46] In respect of Ukrainians one might compare the Russian authorities' non-obstruction of Ukrainophilia in the years 1869–75 with similar periods of non-obstruction in 1845–6 and 1859–62, both of which ended in proscription only a little less far-reaching than that of 1876.[47]

But the possibility that there was nothing new about the way in which the tsar responded to his Balkan and Ukrainian problems of the 1870s does not explain why his responses differed. On the contrary: far from resolving the paradox of support for one sort of non-Russian Slav and hostility to another, it deepens it.

Two explanations offer better prospects than any I have outlined so far. The first turns on Russian public opinion, which was strongly supportive of the Balkan Slavs but patronizing towards Ukrainians. The second abandons altogether the attempt to explain the imperial authorities' attitude to non-Russian Slavs in terms of Slavonic inter-relations, and claims instead that the tsar's different responses had in common the defence or promotion of the interests of the Russian state, whether or not those interests coincided with the interests of subordinate Slavs in either the Balkans or Ukraine. I shall devote the rest of my space to these approaches.

The contention that Russian public opinion was strongly supportive of the Balkan Slavs has been the theme of so many studies that it hardly needs developing.[48] I gave reasons at the beginning why many of the tsar's subjects believed he should help Serbia and Montenegro in their war with the Turks of June 1876. Perhaps the most notable of those who disagreed were the handful of revolutionaries who believed that socialism should come before nationalism or that involvement in the cause of the Balkan Slavs would distract radicals from work at home.[49] Even Russian peasants appear to have been excited by the cause.[50] Vronskii's departure for the Balkans at the end of *Anna Karenina* was a fiction taken from the life. For detailed confirmation of the fact that Russians tended to be enthusiastic proponents of intervention one has only to recall that just before the tsar declared at the end of October 1876 that he had a 'firm intention to act independently', pro-Slav sentiment among educated Russians had reached a peak. Serbia and Montenegro had performed badly in their war with the Turks. The tsar had helped them procure a truce, but many felt he ought to do more. Aleksei Suvorin, editor of the St Petersburg newspaper *New Time* (*Novoe vremia*), had become a war-monger.[51] In a speech at the Moscow Slavonic Beneficent Committee on 24 October, Ivan Aksakov suggested that

> the moment has finally come for the Russian people [*dlia russkoi zemli*] to hand over its business to the state – a business of state-level importance which until now, for so many months, with an incredible expenditure of effort, it has borne on its shoulders alone, without help or co-operation from its government. I mean by this not merely the care of sick, hungry, orphaned Bulgarians and Serbs of various kinds, not merely help in the form of money and cloth-

ing, but help in the form of blood, the intense work of liberation –
in a word the active involvement of the Russian people in the Serbs'
very war for Slavonic independence. The truce just signed by the
Porte does not yet guarantee that peace will follow ...[52]

It is easy to imagine, in the light of this speech, that when Alexander
began shifting towards a policy of military action in the Balkans he did
so at least in part because he could no longer resist pressure from
public opinion.

It is equally easy to argue that Alexander felt able to take strong
action against ethnically conscious Ukrainians because he knew that
few educated people would leap to their defence. I have mentioned
that, in nineteenth-century Russian, the term for 'Ukraine' was 'Little
Russia'. This usage did not admit of the possibility that Russians and
Ukrainians were fundamentally different from each other. Rather, it
implied something akin to the 'indissoluble brotherhood' of Russians
and Ukrainians of which so much was to be made in the Soviet period
of East Slavonic history. Hardly any nineteenth-century Russian intellectuals thought of Ukrainian culture as more than a local variant of
their own. Tchaikovsky had not fallen prey to Ukrainophilia when, in
1872, he based his Second Symphony, the 'Little Russian', on
Ukrainian folksongs. On the contrary, he was at the height of his
Russian nationalism.[53] When Ukrainians gave educated Russians the
impression that Ukrainian and Russian culture were separable, Russians
deplored the idea. Their disdain for the three concentrated manifesta-
tions of Ukrainophilism in the nineteenth-century Russian Empire may
be readily illustrated. In 1847 Aleksei Khomiakov, who is usually said
to have been enthusiastic about the development of Slavonic as
opposed to Western culture, condemned what the regime called the
'Ukraino-Slavonic Society' on the grounds that 'The time for politics is
past'; in 1863 the journalist Mikhail Katkov ridiculed the attempt of
ethnically conscious Ukrainians to promote the primary education of
their fellow-countrymen in Ukrainian rather than Russian; in 1876
Iuzefovich claimed simply that 'The tsarist principle is as sacred and
precious to the Little Russian people as it is to the Great Russian
people' and that 'Little Russians have never placed their birthplace
[*rodina*] above their fatherland [*otechestvo*]'.[54] Even the most liberal St
Petersburg newspaper of the 1870s expressed no more than conde-
scending toleration of what it called 'Ukrainian enthusiasms'.[55] A conservative Moscow quarterly condemned them.[56] Between the 1860s
and the 1890s the literary critic Alexander Pypin was perhaps the only

prominent Russian intellectual to express open sympathy for the aspirations of ethnically conscious Ukrainians.[57]

It looks, therefore, as if the weight of public opinion is a strong answer to the question why Alexander II treated his Balkan and Ukrainian problems differently. In this interpretation, the tsar acted as he did because educated Russians were well disposed to the non-Russian Slavs of the Balkans but unwilling to accept that there might be non-Russian Slavs (other than Poles) in Ukraine.

An answer based on the strength of Russian public opinion is unlikely to be complete, however, because imperial officials were not well known for taking public opinion seriously. Admittedly, the tsar's doveish foreign minister, Gorchakov, does seem to have noticed that public opinion on the Balkan question was at fever pitch in late October 1876, for in a letter of that date to the Russian Ambassador in London he made a vague connection between 'national and Christian senti-ment in Russia' and 'duties [in the Balkans] which His Majesty cannot disregard'.[58] As a whole, however, the letter expressed outrage at the thought that foreign powers could believe the Russian Empire's inten-tions were aggressive. As the regime moved closer to war, moreover, the tsar was careful to sideline the Slavonic Beneficent Committees which had played such a part in bringing the public to fever pitch in the first place.[59] Clamour for military action on his part, therefore, seems not to have been Alexander's primary reason for going to war in the Balkans. If, incidentally, his goal in making war was indeed to satisfy the Russian public, he came nowhere near achieving it.[60]

Public opinion may not have been the primary reason for the tsar's Ukrainian policy either. It is more likely that it simply made easier the pursuit of a policy Alexander would have adopted anyway. The censors began their memorandum in the file on the Ems *ukaz* by saying that one of their most important duties was 'to safeguard the state from such threats to its unity and existing structure as may arise in the sphere of the printed word'. Their conclusion, twenty pages later, was that if Ukrainophile writers, 'this ever-growing handful of people, are permitted to continue their separatist activity, then gradually there may emerge among the masses to whom they address themselves such thoughts and impulses as it will no longer be possible to cope with by censors' measures'. Although, on the way to this conclusion, the censors did everything they could to belittle Ukrainophilism (claiming, for example, that Ukrainophiles exaggerated the extent to which the Ukrainian language differed from Russian by spelling it oddly, and arguing that anyway the two languages were mutually comprehensible), the general tenor of their argument was that Ukraine was a country *in posse* whose emergence to statehood had to be prevented at all costs. This was to take the aspirations of Ukrainian intellectuals more seriously than they were taken by Khomiakov, Katkov, or Iuzefovich. Since many of the specific provisions of the Ems *ukaz* came from the censors' paper, the government's Ukrainian policy begins to look less reactive and more studied.[61]

Having boxed myself into a corner, therefore, so far as the importance of public opinion is concerned, I turn to the last of my possibilities: that the tsar's different responses to his Balkan and Ukrainian problems had in common the interests of the Russian state. This argument comes in two versions. First, the tsar believed reasons of state required him to prevent Austria–Hungary from pre-empting him in the Balkans or threatening him across the south-west frontier of his Empire. Second, and probably more important, Alexander was committed to a form of statism that involved insisting on his own authority. These variants of the statist imperative seem to me to provide the best way of explaining the conundrum I began with.

Nikolai Ignat'ev was not alone in feeling that the principal reason why Russia had to act in the Balkans was to prevent Austria from pre-empting her. Ivan Aksakov agreed with him. Although, in October 1876, Aksakov gave the impression at the Moscow Slavonic Beneficent Committee that the cause of 'Slavonic independence' was enough on its own to justify Russian action in the Balkans, in a private letter of July 1875 he had placed the emphasis elsewhere. After saying that he was 'very much occupied and troubled by the Slavonic movement in Turkey', he went on:

> To my mind there is not the least doubt that this is all Austria's doing, that, under cover of friendship with Russia, Austria is trying to lay hands on the East (or what goes by the name of the East in Europe). Austria has grasped, or Bismarck has explained to her, that it is incomparably more profitable to be close friends with Russia than to be openly at odds with her. Since this Triple Alliance of emperors came into being, roles in the Balkans have changed. Austrian policy has become active and aggressive, whereas we have become the thankless exponents of a policy of restraint, obstruction, and the pursuit of intolerable compromises.[62]

Thus the man who is usually held to be one of the greatest exponents of the positive case for Slavonic liberation seems to have been equally strongly motivated by the negative consideration that Russia had to act in the Balkans to prevent Austria forestalling her. Despite appearances to the contrary, Alexander II probably shared this position. Although he negotiated with Austria enthusiastically, in Balkan matters Russian rulers were well used to Austrian perfidy. By signing the Treaty of Carlowitz with the Ottomans in 1699 (and gaining the greater part of Hungary), Vienna had put an end to Peter the Great's dreams of an international crusade against Islam. Joseph II and Leopold II had been half-hearted in their support for Catherine the Great in the Russo-Turkish war of 1787–91. Alexander himself had been obliged to pull out of the Crimean War when Austria intimated that she might join the coalition against him. It is hard to believe, in the light of these considerations, that the tsar was wholehearted in his pursuit of agreement with Austria in 1876 and early 1877. He had assisted Napoleon III, after all, at the time of the Franco-Piedmontese campaign against Austria in north Italy in 1859. He had looked on complacently when Prussia drove Austria out of Germany in the second half of the 1860s. He certainly ignored his Austrian deals of 1876–7 in the brief period when he was in a position to do so, for, despite the fact that he had agreed not to create a large Slavonic state in the Balkans, he brought one into being at San Stefano. Two years after the Congress of Berlin he approved for distribution to his key diplomats a memorandum written by his War Minister which recommended that the Russian Empire ought to work towards the creation of a profoundly anti-Austrian confederation of Balkan states. It can be argued, then, that Alexander's main reason for intervening in the Balkans in 1877 was to put Austria in her place. In this interpretation his enthusiasm for Balkan Slavs was never more than a pretext and Academician Derzhavin was right when he said that the tsarist regime's attitude towards them would have been just the same if they had been Eskimos, Indians, or Persians.[63]

It is no less possible to treat Alexander's Ukrainian policy as a reaction to his mistrust of Austria, though in this case the reaction was not to Vienna's formal conduct of international relations but rather to what, in Russian eyes, were alarming developments in Galicia, the province on the north-eastern edge of the Dual Monarchy which contained roughly equal numbers of Ukrainians and Poles (and a substantial Jewish minority). Iuzefovich was thinking partly of Galicia when he claimed in his second submission to the tsar's Ukrainian commission that 'The political idea of Little Russian exceptionality is an invention of Austro-Polish intrigue.'[64] The censors said that one of the

reasons why the activities of Kievan Ukrainophiles had to be taken seriously was that 'they coincide with similar activity on the part of
Ukrainophiles in Galicia, who are constantly talking about a fifteen-
million-strong south Russian people as if it were something separate
from the other branches of the Russian trunk with a special fate ahead
of it'. 'This opinion', the censors went on, 'will sooner or later throw
the Galician Ukrainophiles, and then ours, into the arms of the Poles,
who are right to see in the Ukrainophiles' separatist aspirations a
movement which will be of the utmost use to them in the pursuit of
their own "Polish business".'[65] These judgements underpinned the provisions of the Ems *ukaz* which banned the importation into the
Russian Empire of Ukrainian-language books published abroad and
ordered a subsidy to *The Word*, a Galician newspaper whose orientation
the Russian authorities believed to be Russophile.

The views of Iuzefovich and the censors on the Polish–Ukrainian
relationship and Galicia were not very well informed. Although the
thought that ethnically conscious Ukrainians were tools of the
Poles occurred to Russians in all three periods of concentrated
Ukrainophilism in the nineteenth-century Russian Empire,[66] it was
largely a figment of their imagination. In 1863 the Ukrainian scholar
Mykola Kostomarov called it 'very funny, if it were not so offensive'.[67]
Drahomanov argued loudly with Poles in the pages of the *Kiev
Telegraph* in 1875 and later devoted an entire book to criticizing
Russian revolutionaries for thinking that, when the Russian Empire
eventually fell, Poland had to be re-created in its pre-partition
borders.[68] The censors showed greater subtlety than Iuzefovich when,
instead of arguing that Ukrainophiles' ideas were actually inspired by
Poles, they confined themselves to the view that Ukrainians and Poles
might eventually be driven to make common cause with each other. In
view, however, of the turbulent history of the Polish–Ukrainian relationship, even this was unlikely.[69] To believe that the Galician
Ukrainophiles of the 1870s were a significant threat on their own was
to be naive or paranoid. The lengthy studies of the activities of
Galician Ukrainians which Drahomanov published in a major St
Petersburg journal in 1873 could hardly have given an impartial
observer much cause to worry about them.[70] Although Galicia was later
to become known as the 'Ukrainian Piedmont' and is now the heartland of Ukrainian nationalism and the principal subject of study for
patriotically inclined investigators of the Ukrainian past,[71] between
1848 and the 1880s the majority of its educated Ukrainians were either
sympathetic to Russia or purely local in their political sympathies.[72]

Perhaps the real reason why the Russian authorities felt threatened by developments in Galicia was that, since they were in the habit of making trouble for Austria there, they expected trouble in return even when there were few real signs of it.[73]

But whether or not the Russian authorities faced a genuine threat from the Austrian province of Galicia, they thought that they did. Since they also worried about Austria's ambitions in the Balkans, pointing to their Austrian concerns may be the best way of explaining the duality of their policy towards subordinate Slavs. The one significant weakness of this approach is that it provides direct elucidation of only two of the eight points of the Ems *ukaz* (the ban on importing Ukrainian-language books from abroad and the subsidy to *The Word*). A final hypothesis may be worth canvassing in the hope of elucidating the entire *ukaz* without rendering Russia's Balkan policy inexplicable.

According to Roberto Vivarelli, paraphrasing Federico Chabod, German victory in the Franco-Prussian War played a major part in 'the emergence [in late nineteenth-century Europe] of a conception of the state that recognized no limit to its powers'.[74] Perhaps, in central and western Europe, it did. In the Russian Empire, however, the conception was a commonplace. The possibility that it was in abeyance there at the time of Alexander II's 'Great Reforms' does not stand up to scrutiny, for it is easy to demonstrate that the 'Tsar-Liberator' shared the authoritarianism of his predecessors and successors. One of the most significant features of the abolition of serfdom, after all, was the *ex cathedra* manner of its enactment. Convinced it was necessary, Alexander resisted all attempts on the part of conservative bureaucrats and the Russian gentry to deflect him from the idea.[75] After it had been promulgated, he was equally effective at the other end of the political spectrum in his resistance to the introduction of central representative institutions.[76] Alexander rarely listened even to the people who had his ear. He was not likely to welcome the empowerment of the unprivileged. Interpreting his Ukrainian and Balkan actions from the point of view of his authoritarian brand of statism may be helpful.

That Ukrainophiles were trying to empower the unprivileged may be readily demonstrated. Most nineteenth-century Ukrainians were peasants. Few of them had Drahomanov's opportunity, appetite, or capacity for accumulating degrees and professorships. Drahomanov's immediate goals for his fellow-countrymen were therefore the goals he urged on western Slavs in the four-part survey of 1868: mass education, interaction with other Slavonic minorities, and bringing the interests of the masses to the attention of people who had been educated already. His more long-term goals may be teased out of *Germany's Eastern Policy and Russification*, a book-length study he completed in Heidelberg in November 1871.[77] The thesis of this work was that Russian policy-makers were ill-advised to imagine that the challenge implied by the first part of the title could be met by the tactic identified in the second. In Drahomanov's opinion, trying to russify the western lands of the Russian Empire was a futile way of anticipating the possibility that a strong Germany might start coveting them. Russian policy-makers ought rather to pursue what in Drahomanov's opinion amounted to the opposite of russification: democracy, federalism, and local self-government. Only then, Drahomanov felt, might the ethnically non-Russian western edge of the Russian Empire respond willingly to edicts from St Petersburg. The creation of one newly integrated state did not warrant the closer integration of another. Two wrongs did not make a right. Political authority ought to be devolved, not concentrated.

When the Ukrainophiles of the Russian Empire controlled the *Kiev Telegraph* in 1875, their notions of empowerment reached the public domain. The newspaper's orientation was consistently pro-peasant. In March 1875, for example, it ran a two-part discussion of the efficacy of the law-courts set up for peasants at the time of the emancipation of the serfs; in May it called for the establishment of 'emigration agents' in Ukraine to help peasants take over land vacated by Tatars, the mountain peoples of the Caucasus, and Mennonites; in July Drahomanov informed his circle's Polish critics that 'what you call *khlopy* [a pejorative Polish term for peasants] we consider the foundation of our country, and from this flow all our conclusions on social, national, domestic, and international affairs!'[78]

By this time, moreover, Ukrainophiles had gone beyond talking. They were working hard to promote native-language primary education. Drahomanov was to express particular regret in 1877 that the Ems *ukaz* ended the dissemination of the tens of thousands of cheap booklets he and his colleagues had made available to Ukrainian peasants in 1874 and 1875.[79] The tsar established his commission of enquiry in August 1875 'in particular [because of] translations and the publication of textbooks and prayer-books in the Little Russian dialect'.[80] Iuzefovich deplored the fact that, by distributing their 'tendentious publications' at 'trifling prices', Ukrainophiles were reaching out beyond the ranks of the intelligentsia to the unsophisticated.[81] The input of the secret police into the work of the tsar's commission seems to have been based more or less entirely on information the police were collecting about a Ukrainophile activist who was giving away low-brow Ukrainian publications to peasants in the province of Volyn'.[82] The censors' memorandum urged that the government must 'in no way … permit the teaching of any subjects whatever in the Little Russian language in primary schools, to which Ukrainophiles aspire and which they hope to achieve'.[83] The Minister of Education accepted the insistence of other members of the tsar's commission on the need for 'the most careful and scrupulous selection of teachers' in the southern part of the empire and agreed with their view that teachers who had received their training in the Kiev, Kharkiv, and Odesa educational districts ought to be required to teach in provinces other than those in which they graduated.[84]

These official reactions make plain that the Ukrainophile belief in empowering peasants was wholly at odds with the political philosophy of the tsarist regime. Empowerment threatened to generate the very pressure 'from below' of whose dangers Alexander II had warned when he first committed himself to the state-led emancipation of the serfs in 1856.[85] Chubyns'kyi, Drahomanov, and their associates were likely to be able to work in the interest of Ukraine's unprivileged only so long as the tsar remained oblivious to their efforts. When he became aware of them, he was bound to respond vigorously. The wide-ranging nature of the Ems *ukaz* becomes comprehensible.

Can one discern the tsar's authoritarian brand of statism in his Balkan policy? Apparently not, for, in the sense that unprivileged Bulgarians stood to benefit from Russian intervention, one of the tsar's objectives in the Balkans appears to have been empowerment. The following case, however, can be made for the view that Russia's Balkan policy was indeed aimed, first and foremost, at the promotion of 'statist' rather than 'populist' interests: Alexander tried to get General Cherniaev back from Serbia and refused to associate himself with the Serbian–Turkish war of 1876 because he did not want to take sides in a war that he could not hope to direct; he was nevertheless prepared to contemplate a war in which he would be able to call the shots; he may positively have wanted the Serbs to lose their war with the Turks in order to make room for a war of his own making; and what he hoped to get out of that war was not Slavonic liberation but pliant Slav kingdoms and the two things he actually did get, restoration of the Russian toe-hold on the Danube and the inclusion in the Russian Empire of Kars in Anatolia. Disorder in the Balkans, in other words, was to be manipulated in order to provide the tsar with yet another opportunity of investing events with the mark of his authority; the empowerment of Bulgarians was a side-effect. Far from rendering Russia's Balkan policy inexplicable, an interpretation that relates it to the tsar's statism can be said to make it clearer.

This was certainly what Drahomanov thought. In 1875 and early 1876 he had been prepared to believe that good might come of Russian intervention in the Balkans.[86] In essays of October and November 1876, however, when Aksakov was calling upon the tsar to offer Serbs and Bulgarians 'help in the form of blood' and the tsar was announcing his 'firm intention to act independently', the exiled Ukrainophile excoriated St Petersburg for giving foreign adventure a higher priority than reform at home.[87] The suppression of Ukrainophilism had opened his eyes to the priorities of the Russian state. Far from contemplating the empowerment of subordinate Slavs, St Petersburg was determined to control them. In a letter of February 1878 Drahomanov insisted that he had always been 'the most fervent protagonist of war with Turkey to the point of the complete destruction of that state and the complete emancipation of all the peoples shackled by it'. But 'at the same time', he said, 'I was also a protagonist of the internal reform of Russia, holding, amongst other things, that this reform was an essential precondition of starting the war at the right time, conducting it successfully, ending it radically, and having the right attitude towards the peoples emancipated from Turkey'.[88] Perhaps, in the 1860s and early 1870s, Drahomanov had been hopeful that the empowerment of the unprivileged could be assisted by the state. No longer. By the end of the 1870s he had turned against statism in all its forms, even what he held to be the 'leftist' statism of the Russian revolutionaries who assassinated Alexander II.[89] He had divined that, from the point of view of the tsar, statism was a primary good whose pursuit could dictate different behaviour in apparently comparable circumstances. He did not like what he saw. Whether his dislike was reasonable is a topic too big to take on here.

Acknowledgements

I am grateful to my colleague David Moon for his comments on an earlier version of this essay, to Professor R. J. W. Evans for giving me the chance to discuss the subject at a seminar in Oxford, and to the British Academy for financial support. Dates are Old Style (twelve days behind Western Europe).

Notes

1. David MacKenzie, *The Lion of Tashkent: The Career of General M. G. Cherniaev* (Athens, Georgia, 1974), p. 124.
2. N. P. Ignat'ev, 'Zapiski', *Istoricheskii vestnik*, vol. 135, no. 1 (1914), p. 55.
3. S. S. Tatishchev, *Imperator Aleksandr II, ego zhizn' i tsarstvovanie*, 2 vols (St Petersburg, 1903, repr. Moscow, 1996), vol. II, pp. 275–7.
4. For the fact that the tsar listened to Gorchakov rather than Ignat'ev on the 'Andrassy Plan' of 1875 see David MacKenzie, *The Serbs and Russian Pan-Slavism 1875–1878* (Ithaca, 1967), p. 70; for the Austro-Russian Reichstadt agreement of 26 June 1876 see B. H. Sumner, *Russia and the Balkans, 1870–1880* (Oxford, 1937), pp. 172–6, 583–601; for the Austro-Russian Military Convention and Additional Convention of January and March 1877 see *The Great Powers and the Near East, 1774–1923*, ed. M. S. Anderson (London, 1970), pp. 94–6; for recent accounts of the Balkan crisis of 1875–8 as a whole see John P. LeDonne, *The Russian Empire and the World, 1700–1917: The Geopolitics of Expansion and Containment* (New York–Oxford, 1997), pp. 138–42, 266–70, 324–5, and *Istoriia vneshnei politiki Rossii: Vtoraia polovina XIX veka*, ed. V. M. Khevrolina *et al.* (Moscow, 1997), pp. 174–219.
5. *Osvobozhdenie Bolgarii ot turetskogo iga: Dokumenty*, 3 vols, ed. S. A. Nikitin *et al.* (Moscow, 1961–7), vol. 1, pp. 231, 237; Sumner, *Russia and the Balkans*, pp. 183–4, 70.
6. *Rossiiskii gosudarstvennyi istoricheskii arkhiv* (RGIA), f. 776, op. 2, d. 16, 1.209, minutes of the Council of the Main Censorship Administration, 5 July 1876.
7. *A Selection from the Diaries of Edward Henry Stanley, 15th Earl of Derby (1826–93) between September 1869 and March 1878*, ed. John Vincent (London, 1994), p. 301.
8. Tatishchev, *Imperator Aleksandr II*, vol. 2, p. 313.
9. L. M. Chichagov, *Dnevnik prebyvaniia Tsaria-Osvoboditelia v Dunaiskoi armii v 1877 godu* (St Petersburg, 1887, repr. 1995), p. 97. Despite the fact that much of the Ottoman Empire lay to the south-west of Russia, in official Russian parlance the whole of it belonged to 'the East' (which says something about the cultural orientation of Russia's rulers).
10. RGIA, f. 1282 (Chancery of the Minister of Internal Affairs), op. 1, d. 352, ll. 54–5 (from an untitled and unsigned official minute on Chubyns'kyi of 15 April 1876).
11. Uchitel' (M. P. Drahomanov), 'Pedagogicheskoe znachenie malorusskogo iazyka', *Sankt-Petersburgskie vedomosti*, 8 April 1866; M. P. Drahomanov, 'Avtobiograficheskaia zametka', in his *Literaturno-publitsystychni pratsi u dvokh tomakh*, 2 vols (Kiev, 1970), vol. 1, p. 48.
12. *Trudy etnografichesko-statisticheskoi ekspeditsii v zapadno-russkii krai*, 7 vols in 9 books, edited by P. P. Chubinskii (Chubyns'kyi) (St Petersburg, 1872–8).
13. A full account of their activities is to be found in Fedir Savchenko, *Zaborona ukrainstva 1876r.* (Kiev, 1930; repr. Munich, 1970).
14. *Kievskii telegraf* (*KT*), 1 January 1875.
15. *Ibid.*, 27 January 1875 (repr. in Savchenko, *Zaborona*, pp. 343–6).
16. *Ibid.*, 29 and 31 January 1875 (repr. in Savchenko, *Zaborona*, pp. 339–43).
17. *Ibid.*, 7 February 1875.
18. *Ibid.*, 23 March 1875.

19. *Ibid.*, 4 April 1875 (resignation); RGIA, f. 1282, op. 1, d. 352, ll. 47–52 (diatribe: repr. in Savchenko, *Zaborona*, pp. 368–72).
20. RGIA, f. 1282, op. 1, d. 352, l. 1, A. L. Potapov to A. E. Timashev, 28 August 1875 (establishment of the commission); *ibid.*, ll. 104–5, and Anon. (V. P. Naumenko), 'Do istorii ukaza 1876 roku pro zaboronu ukrains'koho pys'menstva', *Ukraina*, vol. 2, no. 5 (1907), pp. 149–50 (recommendations). The tsar turned recommendation (7) into an order for the immediate closure of the South-West Section.
21. Ignat'ev, 'Zapiski', p. 55.
22. David Saunders, *The Ukrainian Impact on Russian Culture, 1750–1850* (Edmonton, Alberta, 1985), pp. 227–30.
23. *Kyrylo-Mefodiivs'ke tovarystvo*, 3 vols, ed. P. S. Sokhan' *et al.* (Kiev, 1990), vol. 1, pp. 152–69.
24. Vladimir Antonovich *et al.*, 'Otzyv iz Kieva', *Russkii vestnik: Sovremennaia letopis'*, no. 46 (1862), pp. 3–6.
25. See, on the one hand, H. D. Desnitsa, 'Serbs'ko-turets'ka viina (1876r.) i ukrains'ka hromads'kist'', *Ukrains'kyi istorychnyi zhurnal*, no. 5 (1962), pp. 79–82, and M. Ia. Gol'berg, 'Balkanskie sobytiia 70-kh godov XIX v. i nekotorye voprosy razvitiia ukrainsko-serbskikh obshchestvenno-politicheskikh i kul'turnykh sviazei', in *Razvitie kapitalizma i natsional'nye dvizheniia v slavianskikh stranakh*, ed. V. I. Freidzon (Moscow, 1970), pp. 211–35; and, on the other, Z. M. Khanutin, 'Otnoshenie obshchestvennykh krugov Rossii k balkanskim sobytiiam v period serbo-turetskoi voiny 1876 goda', *Uchenye zapiski belorusskogo gosudarstvennogo universiteta*, vol. 16 (1953), pp. 299–328, and T. G. Snytko, 'Iz istorii narodnogo dvizheniia v Rossii v podderzhku bor'by iuzhnykh slavian za svoiu nezavisimost' v 1875–1876gg.', in *Obshchestvenno-politicheskie i kul'turnye sviazi narodov SSSR i Iugoslavii: Sbornik statei*, ed. S. A. Nikitin and L. B. Valeva (Moscow, 1957), pp. 78–106.
26. *Kyrylo-Mefodiivs'ke tovarystvo*, vol. 1, p. 20 (name of the society): vol. 3, pp. 211–57, 291–324 (investigations of Russians).
27. 'Z lystuvannia M. P. Drahomanova z O. S. Suvorinym', ed. D. I. Abramovych, *Ukraina*, no. 4 (1927), p. 139.
28. Slavianin (M. P. Drahomanov), 'Slavianskoe obozrenie', *Sankt-Peterburgskie vedomosti*, 7 June 1868.
29. P. T-ev (M. P. Drahomanov), 'Malorossiia v eë slovesnosti', in A. R. Mazurkevich, *I. G. Pryzhov: Iz istorii russko-ukrainskikh literaturnykh sviazei* (Kiev, 1958), p. 369.
30. *KT*, 7 February, 28 March and 25 April, 7 and 9 May, and 11 June 1875.
31. Drahomanov, 'Avtobiograficheskaia zametka', p. 62.
32. 'Z lystuvannia', p. 123.
33. M. P. Drahomanov, 'Po voprosu o malorusskoi literature', in his *Literaturno-publitsystychni pratsi*, vol. 1, p. 350.
34. See Petko Atanasov, 'Rol' M. P. Drahomanova u zmitsnenni ukrains'–kobolhars'kykh zviazkiv', *Ukrains'kyi istorychnyi zhurnal*, no. 9 (1965), pp. 26–39.
35. M. Dragomanov (Drahomanov), 'Russian Policy, Home and Foreign', *Free Russia*, vol. 2, no. 1 (1891), pp. 13–16; no. 2, pp. 12–13; no. 3, pp. 12–13; vol. 3, no. 6 (1892), pp. 10–12.

36. For an overview see Ivan L. Rudnytsky, 'The Fourth Universal and its Ideological Antecedents', in his *Essays in Modern Ukrainian History* (Edmonton, Alberta, 1987), pp. 389–416.

37. Drahomanov, 'Avtobiograficheskaia zametka', pp. 61–3; Ihnat Zhytets'kyi, 'Ostannii vyizd M. P. Drahomanova za kordon', *Ukraina*, no. 2–3 (1926), pp. 29–37.

38. RGIA, f. 1282, op. 1, d. 352, l. 132, S. S. Perfil'ev to L. S. Makov, Ems, 26 May 1876 ('Our news: ... an official summons has been issued to Cherniaev concerning his return to the Fatherland').

39. RGIA, f. 777 (St Petersburg Censorship Committee), op. 3, g. 1876, d. 10, ll. 53, 67.

40. RGIA, f. 1282, op. 3, d. 130, l. 383.

41. David Saunders, 'Russia's Ukrainian Policy (1847–1905): a Demographic Approach', *European History Quarterly*, vol. 25, no. 2 (1995), especially pp. 181–2, 201.

42. To judge by a pencil reference to a meeting of which no record was kept, the first session of the tsar's Ukrainian commission took place on 12 April 1876 (RGIA, f. 1282, op. 1, d. 352, l. 59).

43. Anon., 'O vrede literaturnoi deiatel'nosti Ukrainofilov i merakh k ego otvrashcheniiu', RGIA, f. 1282, op. 1, d. 352, ll. 23–32.

44. As M. I. Chertkov, the Governor-General of Kiev, Podillia, and Volyn', pointed out when trying to get the *ukaz* lifted in 1881 (anon., 'Naiblyzhchi vidhuky ukaz 1876 r. pro zaboronu ukrains'koho pys'menstva', *Ukraina*, vol. 2, no. 6 (1907), p. 251).

45. The file on the *ukaz* opens with a clerical copy of his second paper, 'O tak nazyvaemom ukrainofil'skom dvizhenii' (March 1876): RGIA, f. 1282, op. 1, d. 352, ll. 3–22 (published in Savchenko, *Zaborona*, pp. 372–81).

46. On Russia and the Greek revolt see, for example, LeDonne, *Russian Empire*, pp. 120–1.

47. On 1845–6 see Orest Pelech, 'Towards a Historical Sociology of the Ukrainian Ideologues in the Russian Empire of the 1830s and 1840s', unpublished doctoral dissertation, Princeton (1976), whose thesis is that until 1847 the Russian authorities positively encouraged 'patriotism, both national and local' (p. 141). On 1859–62 see David Saunders, 'Russia and Ukraine under Alexander II: the Valuev Edict of 1863', *International History Review*, vol. 17, no. 1 (1995), especially pp. 23–4, 32–4.

48. See, for example, Sumner, *Russia and the Balkans*, pp. 56–80; MacKenzie, *The Serbs and Russian Pan-Slavism*, and the references in n. 25, above.

49. These were mainly adherents of Peter Lavrov: Snytko, 'Iz istorii narodnogo dvizheniia', p. 86.

50. A. V. Buganov, *Russkaia istoriia v pamiati krest'ian XIX veka i natsional'noe samosoznanie* (Moscow, 1992), pp. 172–97 (I am indebted to David Moon for this reference).

51. See, for example, 'Russkoe obshchestvo i natsional'naia zadacha', anonymous leader in *Novoe vremia*, 17 October 1876, pp. 2–3.

52. I. S. Aksakov, *Slavianskii vopros, 1860–1886* (Moscow, 1886), p. 217.

53. David Brown, 'Tchaikovsky, Pyotr Il'yich', in *The New Grove Dictionary of Music and Musicians*, 20 vols, ed. Stanley Sadie (London, 1980), vol. 18, p. 611.

54. A. S. Khomiakov, 'Pis'ma', *Russkii arkhiv*, no. 11 (1879), p. 328; *Moskovskie vedomosti*, 22 June, 4 September 1863; Iuzefovich, 'O tak nazyvaemom', ll. 5 and 7 (slightly misprinted in Savchenko, *Zaborona*, p. 374).

55. 'Ukrainskie uvlecheniia', *Golos*, 28 September 1874.

56. Z, 'Sovremennoe ukrainofil'stvo', *Russkii vestnik*, vol. 115, no. 2 (1875), pp. 838–68.

57. See Alexis E. Pogorelskin, 'A. N. Pypin's Defence of Ukraine: Sources and Motivation', in *Ukrainian Past, Ukrainian Present*, ed. Bohdan Krawchenko (New York, 1993), pp. 35–54.

58. R. W. Seton-Watson, 'Russo-British Relations During the Eastern Crisis', *Slavonic Review*, vol. 4, no. 1 (1925–6), p. 195 (trans. in Anderson, *Great Powers*, p. 93).

59. S. A. Nikitin, *Slavianskie komitety v Rossii v 1858–1876 godakh* (Moscow, 1960), p. 342.

60. V. I. Ado, 'Berlinskii kongress 1878 g. i pomeshchich'e-burzhuaznoe obshchestvennoe mnenie Rossii', *Istoricheskie zapiski*, vol. 69 (1961), pp. 101–41.

61. Anon., 'O vrede', quotations from ll. 23 and 32, recommendations at ll. 29–31.

62. 'Perepiska I. S. Aksakova s kn. V. A. Cherkasskim (1875–1878)', ed. I. V. Koz'menko, in *Slavianskii sbornik: Slavianskii vopros i russkoe obshchestvo v 1867–1878 godakh*, ed. N. M. Druzhinin (Moscow, 1948), p. 142. The first *Dreikaiserbund* or 'League of the Three Emperors' (of Germany, Austria, and Russia) came into being in 1872–3 (LeDonne, *Russian Empire*, p. 265).

63. N. S. Derzhavin, 'Russkii absoliutizm i iuzhnoe slavianstvo', *Izvestiia leningradskogo gosudarstvennogo universiteta*, no. 1 (1928), p. 47. On Carlowitz, Joseph II, the Crimean War, north Italy, German unification, and the deals of 1876–7 see LeDonne, *Russian Empire*, pp. 90, 243–4, 126, 262, 138, 269. On the War Minister's proposal of 1880 for the creation of a Balkan confederation see S. D. Skazkin, *Konets avstro-russko-germanskogo soiuza*, 2nd edn (Moscow, 1974), pp. 164–8, and N. S. Kiniapina, 'Balkanskaia konfederatsiia v planakh voennogo ministra Rossii D. A. Miliutina', *Otechestvennaia istoriia*, no. 3 (1996), pp. 150–4.

64. Iuzefovich, 'O tak nazyvaemom', l. 8 (slightly misprinted in Savchenko, *Zaborona*, p. 375).

65. Anon., 'O vrede', ll. 26–7.

66. For 1847 see A. F. Orlov, 'Dopovid' Mykoli I pro diial'nist' kyrylo-mefodi-ivs'koho tovarystva', in *Kyrylo-Mefodiivs'ke tovarystvo*, vol. 1, p. 66 (deriva-tion of the central text of the Kirillo-Methodian Society from a work by Mickiewicz); for 1863 see David Saunders, 'Mikhail Katkov and Mykola Kostomarov: a Note on Pëtr A. Valuev's Anti-Ukrainian Edict of 1863', *Harvard Ukrainian Studies*, vol. 17, no. 3/4 (1996 for 1993), especially p. 371.

67. M. Kostomarov, *Naukovo-publitsystychni i polemichni pysannia* (Kiev, 1928), p. 160.

68. For examples of the press debate see *KT*, 2 May 1875 (leader entitled 'Pol'skomu bol'shinstvu galitskogo seima') and 18 June 1875 (leader entitled 'Pol'skii vopros v iugozapadnom krae'). The book was M. P. Dragomanov (Drahomanov), *Istoricheskaia Pol'sha i velikorusskaia demokratiia* (Geneva, 1882).

69. See Ivan L. Rudnytsky, 'Polish–Ukrainian Relations: the Burden of History', in his *Rethinking*, pp. 49–76.

70. M. P. Dragomanov (Drahomanov), 'Russkie v Galitsii' and 'Literaturnoe dvizhenie v Galitsii', both repr. in his *Politicheskie sochineniia*, ed. I. M. Grevs and B. A. Kistiakovskii, vol. 1 (Moscow, 1908), pp. 268–342, 343–417.

71. For the nickname see M. Grushevskii (Hrushevs'kyi), 'Ukrainskii P'emont', in his *Ukrainskii vopros* (Moscow, 1917), pp. 61–6; for the extent of the scholarly literature see Paul R. Magocsi, *Galicia: An Historical Survey and Bibliographic Guide* (Toronto, 1983).

72. For the former view see Ivan L. Rudnytsky, 'The Ukrainians in Galicia under Austrian Rule', in his *Rethinking*, pp. 329–33; for the latter, Paul R. Magocsi, 'Old Ruthenianism and Russophilism: a New Conceptual Framework for Analyzing National Ideologies in Late 19th-Century Eastern Galicia', in *American Contributions to the Ninth International Congress of Slavists*, vol. 2, ed. Paul Debreczeny (Columbus, Ohio, 1983), pp. 305–24.

73. For the irritation Russia caused Austria by annexing the Ternopil district of east Galicia in 1809 see LeDonne, *Russian Empire*, p. 251; for the Galician machinations of the chaplain at the Russian Embassy in Vienna in the reign of Alexander II see *Zarubezhnye slaviane i Rossiia: Dokumenty arkhiva M. F. Raevskogo*, ed. S. A. Nikitin *et al.* (Moscow, 1975), esp. pp. 26, 36, 158–60, 162–3, 240, 375.

74. Roberto Vivarelli, '1870 in European History and Historiography', *Journal of Modern History*, vol. 53, no. 2 (1981), p. 186.

75. See especially N. G. O. Pereira, 'Alexander II and the Decision to Emancipate the Russian Serfs, 1855–61', *Canadian Slavonic Papers*, vol. 22, no. 1 (1980), pp. 99–115.

76. V. G. Chernukha, *Vnutrenniaia politika tsarizma s serediny 50-kh do nachala 80-kh gg. XIX v.* (Leningrad, 1978), especially pp. 133–5.

77. M. P. Dragomanov (Drahomanov), 'Vostochnaia politika Germanii i obrusenie', repr. in his *Politicheskie sochineniia*, pp. 1–216 (first published in a St Petersburg journal in 1872).

78. *KT*, 2 and 3 March, 7 May, 30 July 1875.

79. M. Drahomanov, *Narodni shkoly na Ukraini sered zhyt't'a i pys'mennstva v Rossii* (Geneva 1877), pp. 54–5.

80. RGIA, f. 1282, op. 1, d. 352, l. 1.

81. Savchenko, *Zaborona*, p. 379.

82. RGIA, f. 1282, op. 1, d. 352, ll. 59–62, 71–8, 82–4, 95–6.

83. Anon., 'O vrede', l. 31.

84. RGIA, f. 1282, op. 1, d. 352, ll. 102–3; Anon., 'Do istorii ukaza', pp. 147–8.

85. 'It is better to start abolishing serfdom from above than to await the time when it starts spontaneously abolishing itself from below': quoted in Ia. A. Solov'ev, 'Zapiski o krest'ianskom dele', *Russkaia starina*, vol. 30 (1881), p. 228.

86. In 'Nadezhdy i razocharovaniia v zapadnom slavianstve', *KT*, 11 June 1875, he had implied that intervention would be worthwhile by regretting that it was unlikely in view of the currently friendly state of Russo-Austrian relations. The last paragraph of his *Pro ukrains'kykh kozakiv, tatar ta turkiv*, a brochure published in Kiev in the first half of 1876 (repr. in M. P. Drahomanov, *Vybrane* [Kiev, 1991], pp. 175–204) implied that, after freeing

the northern shore of the Black Sea from Muslims, Russia was well advised to think of moving on to the liberation of 'Serbs, Bulgarians, Moldavians, and Greeks'.

87. M. P. Dragomanov (Drahomanov), 'Chistoe delo trebuet chistykh ruk', *Molva*, 10 October 1876, and *Turki vnutrennie i vneshnie* (Geneva, 1876), both repr. in his *Sobranie politicheskikh sochinenii*, 2 vols, ed. P. B. Struve and B. A. Kistiakovskii (Paris, 1905–6), vol. 2, pp. 20–45, 46–73.

88. 'Z lystuvannia', p. 143.

89. M. P. Dragomanov (Drahomanov), '"Narodnaia Volia" o tsentralizatsii revoliutsionnoi bor'by v Rossii', in his *Sobranie politicheskikh sochinenii*, vol. 2, pp. 391–412.

6
The Russian Constitutional Monarchy in Comparative Perspective

Robert B. McKean

Among the many scholarly virtues of the dedicatee of this volume of essays has been an audacious willingness to place the Russian Revolution in a comparative perspective of time and space. To their discredit, historians of the Russian constitutional monarchy, for the most part, have been reluctant to emulate Paul Dukes's pioneering example. The debate on the fate of the monarchy, launched in the middle of the 1960s by Leopold Haimson and revived recently by the author of this essay, has been overwhelmingly Russian-centred.[1] Evaluation of the reformed monarchy's chances of survival after 1906 and of the prospects of political and social stability has occurred in terms of the particular conjuncture of domestic circumstances. There has been little effort to examine the Duma monarchy's chances in the light of the experience of other European constitutional monarchies in the nineteenth and early twentieth centuries. The purpose of this brief essay is to take the first tentative steps towards remedying this deficiency in the historical treatment of the 'renovated' political structure of the Russian autocracy in the brief period between Peter A. Stolypin's '*coup d'état*' of 3 June 1907 and the outbreak of the First World War in July 1914.[2] As a truly adequate survey of this theme would require the space afforded by a monograph, the author has consciously chosen to open what he hopes will become an on-going debate in the future by focusing his preliminary thoughts upon two aspects of the history of the Russian constitutional monarchy. In the first part of the essay attention will be directed to the 'constitution' itself, the Fundamental State Laws of April 1906. The second part will concern the implementation of this constitution in the eight years after its promulgation.

From the very moment of their publication on 23 April 1906 the characterization of the Fundamental State Laws has been a matter of profound disagreement among contemporary and subsequent commentators. In an essay published in the summer of 1906 the famous German pioneer of sociology, Max Weber, set the tone of much later debate by describing the new political structure as 'sham constitutionalism' (*scheinkonstitutionalismus*). He acidly referred to this 'caricature of the powerful idea of constitutionalism'.[3] It was a verdict with which Vladimir Il'ich Lenin concurred. For the Bolshevik leader, the Fundamental State Laws represented a deal between tsardom and the landowners and big bourgeoisie on the basis of minimal constitutional reforms in order to defeat the revolution. Lenin's analysis was dutifully echoed by Soviet historians until the demise of the Soviet Union itself. For example, one of the best Soviet textbooks on the last period of the monarchy, echoing Lenin, argued that the Fundamental State Laws transformed Russia into a dualistic monarchy which retained all executive and a significant part of the legislative power. '"There was a gulf between the rights of parliament"', Lenin (and the textbook) averred, '"and the prerogatives of the monarchy"'.[4] Western scholars, unlike their Soviet colleagues, have been less unanimous in their appraisal. Sidney Harcave's pioneering study of the 1905 revolution came to the conclusion that the changes of 1906 amounted to 'the beginnings of a constitutional parliamentary system'.[5] In the sole study in English devoted exclusively to the Fundamental State Laws, Marc Szeftel had no doubts that 'it would be false to call the Russian system *scheinkonstitutionalismus*'.[6] The most recent history of the 1905 revolution by Abraham Ascher concluded that the Fundamental State Laws amounted to a constitution, but a 'strikingly conservative constitution'.[7]

In attempting to place the Russian Fundamental State Laws of 1906 in a comparative perspective reference will be made in the analysis to the following constitutions: the French constitution of 1791; the French Charte of 1814 and as amended in 1830; the constitutions of Baden (1818), Bavaria (1818), and Württemberg (1819); the Prussian constitution of 1850; the Hungarian Law XII of 1867; the Austrian Fundamental Law, 1867; and the Imperial German constitution, 1871. A comparison between the Russian Fundamental State Laws and these constitutions needs to direct the reader's attention to specific constitutional provisions: the locus of sovereignty; the powers of the sovereign; the role of an Upper House in the legislature; the functions of the representative bodies; civil liberties; the electoral laws; the responsibilities of the executive or Cabinet.

The first point to be made about the Fundamental State Laws is that their enactment did not involve popular participation. They were the product of secret conferences of the tsar's ministers and high bureaucrats. The very fact that they were a revision of the Fundamental State Laws of the autocracy in their 1892 version, and were consciously issued on the eve of the convocation of the First State Duma, Russia's first popularly elected national representative assembly, indicated that they were a public denial of the doctrine of popular sovereignty. The Emperor and his advisors were determined to prevent the First State Duma from arrogating to itself the functions of a constituent assembly. This stood in stark contrast to the French Revolution where the Declaration of the Rights of Man and of the Citizen, 26 August 1789, inserted as the preamble of the constitution of 1791, stated bluntly that 'the source of all sovereignty resides essentially in the nation'.[8] Hence the Constituent Assembly had drafted the constitution without the participation of the king, Louis XVI.

On the other hand, Nicholas II's denial of popular sovereignty was in accord with all the other monarchical constitutions surveyed. When Louis XVIII returned to France in 1814, for example, the constitution he granted, the Charte, was 'voluntarily and by the free exercise of our power'.[9] The three South German constitutions of 1818–19 were issued by royal decree and made clear that sovereignty resided in the monarch. Frederick William IV of Prussia imposed the constitution of 1850. Although Emperor Franz Joseph permitted the participation of the German political leadership in the Reichsrat in the drafting of the Austrian Fundamental Law of 1867, he successfully prevented any notion that the constitution was based on popular sovereignty, as he did likewise with Hungary's Law XII of the same year. The case of the Imperial German constitution of 1871 is more complex as it was the product both of peace treaties between the North German Confederation and the South German states on their accession to the new Reich in 1870, and the scrutiny by the new national parliament, the Reichstag, of the draft constitution presented by the Chancellor, Bismarck. Formally sovereignty rested with the Federal Council or Bundesrat, which represented the princes. Although this was a fiction, it had the supreme merit of denying sovereignty to parliament.

The Russian Fundamental State Laws of 1906 created great confusion among contemporary observers, and succeeding generations of historians, on two accounts. Firstly, nowhere did the document use the noun 'constitution'. Secondly, article four resoundingly declared that 'To the All-Russian Emperor belongs the Supreme Autocratic Power'.[10] These developments were neither unconnected nor accidental. In the sessions of a conference held at Tsarskoe Selo in April 1906 to discuss the draft of the Fundamental State Laws, Nicholas II expressed a wish to retain in article four the epithet 'unlimited', as in the original 1892 definition of his power as 'autocratic and unlimited'. The tsar clung to a personalized and patriarchal conception of the monarchy. His mind conceived the October Manifesto of 1905, in which he had promised civil liberties and a true legislature, and autocracy as fully compatible. Although the majority of ministers and officials at the conference argued that the October Manifesto had limited the tsar's powers, an unspoken compromise was reached. Nicholas II reluctantly concurred in the omission of the adjective 'unlimited' in the final draft of article four, whilst his bureaucrats tacitly agreed to avoid the hated term 'constitution', with its dangerous, Western overtones, in the Fundamental State Laws and in public thereafter. Hence the clumsy term 'renovated state structure' came to be used as the official designation after 1906 for the changes introduced by the Fundamental State Laws.

In the refusal to describe the sum of the constitutional concessions as a 'constitution' and in clinging to the term 'autocracy', the Fundamental State Laws were indeed out of step with all the other constitutions mentioned above. For the French revolutionaries of 1789 the entire purpose of the revolution was to put paid for ever to royal absolutism. In 1814 Louis XVIII, unlike his brother the future Charles X, was wise enough to grasp that a return to absolutism was impossible, as was Frederick William IV of Prussia after the upheavals of 1848. After the February Patent of 1861 was rejected by the Hungarians and Poles and his army was defeated at Sadowa by Prussia in 1866, Franz Joseph understood that he could only preserve the essentials of his power, and restore Austria's great power status, by compromise with the German Liberals and the Hungarians. For Bismarck a key objective in 1870 was to deflect the energies of the liberal movement into safe channels by implementing some of its objectives, including a 'liberal' constitution, whilst preserving the existing authoritarian, monarchical state in Prussia.

The Russian Emperor's powers were defined in a sweeping fashion in chapter one of the Fundamental State Laws (articles 4 to 24). Marc Szeftel has written that Nicholas II had even greater powers reserved to him than to any other monarch in a European constitution. This claim requires closer scrutiny. It is certainly true that the Emperor's powers were far greater than those granted to Louis XVI in the constitution of 1791, but that was the case in fact regarding other European monarchs after 1813. The severely limited powers accorded the king in 1791 (the suspensive veto, the denial of the right of legislative initiative, the absence of effective royal control over the armed forces or foreign affairs) reflected the passions of the revolution and the revolutionaries' profound apprehensions of a return of royal despotism. It is also the case that article eight of the Fundamental State Laws – 'To our Sovereign the Emperor belongs the initiative in all matters of legislation'[11] – replicated a similar provision in some previous constitutions, although not all. Thus, under article 16 of the Charte of 1814, the French monarch enjoyed the sole right of legislative initiative, although after the overthrow of the Bourbon dynasty in the revolution of July 1830, the new Orleanist king, Louis Philippe, had to share legislative initiative with the chambers. In both the Austrian and Hungarian dispensations of 1867, the Emperor exercised the right of legislative initiative together with the respective parliaments. Article seven of the Fundamental State Laws – 'Our Sovereign Emperor exercises the legislative power in conjunction with the State Council and the State Duma'[12] – replicated almost exactly a similar provision in the Austrian and Hungarian constitutions, as well as the Prussian constitution of 1850. The Hungarian Law XII, for example, stated that the monarch must rule in agreement with parliament.

Furthermore, the Russian Emperor's power of absolute veto over laws approved by the legislature was shared by Emperor Franz Joseph in his Austrian lands after 1867, but not, technically at least, in his role as king of Hungary. On the other hand, the Imperial German constitution decreed that once a law was enacted by parliament the Emperor had to sanction it.

All the constitutions surveyed here accorded their monarchs the same privileges as did the Fundamental State Laws Nicholas II with respect to complete control over the executive and the armed forces, the conduct of foreign policy, war and peace. All sovereigns appointed and dismissed ministers and higher civil servants. For all monarchs these were powers they absolutely refused to concede to parliament. In the making of the *Ausgleich* of 1867, Franz Joseph, for example, was resolved to preserve his personal direction of the new joint Austro-Hungarian ministries of foreign affairs and war, as these determined the international strength and position of the monarchy, his main concern.

All sovereigns alike enjoyed the power to convoke, prorogue and dis-solve their respective assemblies. The emergency powers granted the Russian Emperor by article 87 of the Fundamental State Laws to imple-ment laws when the chambers were not in session were actually mod-elled on article 14 of the Austrian Fundamental Law of 1867. Although the post-Napoleonic constitutions of the South German states did not contain such a provision, the Imperial German constitution gave the Emperor the power to mount a *Staatsstreich*, a *coup* by the army to abolish the constitution.

The Russian legislature, whose powers were defined by the Fundamental State Laws, was bicameral, consisting of an Upper House, the State Council, and a Lower House, the State Duma. With the exception of the French constitution of 1791 and that of Kur-Hesse in 1831, both of which established a single chamber assembly, all other European constitutions embraced an Upper House. The purpose of this body was similar in all cases, including the Russian: the Upper House would act as a conservative counterweight to the popularly elected Lower House, which might possibly be radical and obstructive. Both the State Council and its counterparts elsewhere in Europe were accorded the same powers regarding legislation and the budget as the Lower Houses. The composition of the State Council, however, was *sui generis*. In other Upper Houses membership was restricted to hereditary nobles or nobles appointed by the Crown and to life members chosen by the monarch and drawn from senior bureaucrats and ministers. Baden alone had the distinction of an elected upper chamber. Half the State Council's membership was appointed by the tsar (generally senior or retired civil servants and ministers) and half elected by five separate corporations, namely the Orthodox Church, the provincial *zemstva*, the nobles' associations, the universities, and commercial and indus-trial organizations.

The State Council and the State Duma had to be summoned every year by the Emperor. Sessions were to be open to the press and public, with members of the legislature enjoying immunity and inviolability during sessions. By article 106 of the Fundamental State Laws, 'the State Council and the State Duma enjoy equal rights in matters of leg-islation'.[13] In the following articles their powers were defined essen-tially as encompassing the approval of laws and the annual budget. All bills, as well as the budget, had to be introduced first by the govern-ment into the State Duma; only if the latter gave its consent were they to be sent on to the State Council. These rights were replicated in the Charte, the Austrian, Hungarian, and Imperial German constitutions.

In the South German states alone did the assemblies lack control over the budget, although their assent was required for new taxes. Following similar provisions in the Austrian, Hungarian and Imperial German constitutions Russian deputies could interpellate ministers, requiring them to attend the house to justify their actions. However, unlike some, although not all, other European constitutional monarchies, the Russian legislature was denied the right to receive petitions and delegations from the public, or to impeach ministers. Due to the tsar's exclusive control over foreign affairs and the armed forces, the State Council and the State Duma exercised minimal influence, in theory at least, in these areas, a pattern found in other European legislatures.

A fundamental concern of Russian bureaucratic reformers from the 1860s had been the introduction of a *Rechtsstaat*, that is a state ruled by law. Thus, article 84 of the Fundamental State Laws boldly stated that 'the Russian Empire is ruled on the firm basis of laws'.[14] For the first time, too, the Fundamental State Laws included a section (articles 69 to 83) entitled 'Rights and Duties of Russian Subjects'. Articles 72 to 75 enshrined the due process of law in criminal justice and arrests, as well as the inviolability of the home. Article 76 bestowed the right of free choice of domicile, acquisition of property, and travel abroad. Articles 78 to 81 granted the freedoms to hold meetings, to express one's thoughts orally and in writing, to form societies and trade unions, and of religion. Nevertheless, this impressive catalogue was not all that it purported to be. Apart from the complete absence of any reference to specific rights for the Empire's non-Russian nationalities, each right was in fact restricted by generalized exemptions. As a later section in the essay will endeavour to show, the attitude of the authorities towards these rights after 1907 was ambivalent at best, and their willingness to enshrine them in subsequent laws dubious.

The inclusion of a bill of rights in the Fundamental State Laws had a long precedent in the history of European constitution-making, beginning with the Declaration of the Rights of Man and of the Citizen in 1789. The *Charte* (1814) recognized the fundamental principles of legal equality, personal liberty, property, freedom of the press and religion. Likewise so did the constitutions of the post-Napoleonic South German states, of Prussia (1850), and Austria (1867). Indeed the Austrian Fundamental Law was remarkable for its attitude to the nationalities. Article 19 proclaimed that 'all nationalities in the state enjoy equal rights'.[15] The Imperial German constitution alone failed to include a list of basic civil rights. However, many of these constitutions anticipated the Fundamental State Laws in qualifying the rights bestowed on citizens. The Bavarian constitution (1818), for example, proclaimed equality before the law, but also guaranteed patrimonial justice, as well as certain special prerogatives to the nobility. The Austrian Reichsrat, too, shrank from framing interpretative legislation which alone could realize the promises made to the nationalities by the aforementioned article 19.

The electoral law for the State Duma was not formally part of the Fundamental State Laws. There were in fact three electoral laws enacted in quick succession: the law of 6 August 1905, which was never implemented; of 1 December 1905, in use for the elections to the First (1906) and Second (1907) State Dumas; of 3 June 1907, in force to the collapse of the regime in February 1917. None of these instituted universal male, let alone female, suffrage. Under the second and third electoral systems, the franchise rested upon a complex mixture of estate- (*sosloviia*) and property-based requirements for males over the age of 24. Elections were indirect. The electorate was split into four curiae: landowners, communal peasants, cities and towns, industrial workers. The voters chose electors, who then met in provincial electoral assemblies to select the deputies. The 3 June electoral law established the Russian political nation within considerably narrower limits than those set by the law of 1 December 1905. Stolypin, President of the Council of Ministers, cut the peasants' share of provincial electors from 43 per cent to 22 per cent, whilst increasing the proportion of electors drawn from the nobility from 33 per cent to 50 per cent. The result was to make some 20,000 provincial landed nobles the dominant political force in the Third (1907–12) and Fourth (1912–17) State Dumas.

Neither indirect elections nor property-based franchises were in any way unique to Russia. Even the French constitution of 1791 had limited the vote to 'active' citizens, defined as males aged 25 or over, residing in the same locality for over a year, and paying the equivalent of three days' unskilled labour in taxes. The French Charte of 1814 ensured that the electorate to the Chamber of Deputies numbered a mere 110,000 males over the age of 30, the *'grands notables'*. The July revolution of 1830 merely raised the size of the electorate to 166,000 or 33 voters for every 10,000 inhabitants. The Austrian Fundamental Law of 1867 bestowed the vote to the Reichsrat on a mere 5.9 per cent of the population through a curial system. The nearest equivalent to the Duma electoral system was the Prussian three-class franchise of May 1849, on which the Russian law was in part consciously modelled. There were two exceptions to this general pattern among constitutional monarchies. The first was the Imperial German constitution, 1871, which retained for Reichstag elections the electoral law of the North German Confederation, established in 1867, whereby all males over 25 could vote. Bismarck had bestowed universal, equal, direct, and secret suffrage without any property qualifications in the calculation, mistaken as it turned out, that this would produce conservative majorities in the Reichstag due to the presumed loyalty of the politically inactive masses. The second, contemporaneous with Stolypin's electoral law, was the introduction by Franz Joseph in 1907 of the franchise for all males over 24 for elections to the Austrian parliament, though not for the Hungarian legislature.

One of the great deficiencies of the unreformed Russian autocracy was the absence of an effective, ministerial institutional mechanism which could both coordinate ministerial actions and act as a buffer to a tsar's inclination to personal rule. The decree of 19 October 1905, establishing a Council of Ministers with a President, which was incorporated in part into the Fundamental State Laws (articles 120–4), was intended to remedy this defect. By stating unambiguously that 'the President of the Council of Ministers, the Ministers and the Chief Administrators of separate agencies are responsible to our Sovereign the Emperor', article 123 abjured the doctrine of ministerial responsibility to parliament.[16] Ministers could not be removed by vote of parliament. Ministers, moreover, remained individually, not collectively, responsible to the Emperor and continued after 1905, as before, to report weekly to the monarch, although article 17 of the decree of 19 October 1905 laid down that all such reports of ministers to the sovereign had first to be brought to the attention of the President of the Council. The decree also did not expressly bar ministers from being members of the legislature.

The issue of ministerial responsibility was less clear cut in other constitutions. The Prussian constitution (1850) drew a distinction between ministers being accountable to the Landtag and responsible to it. Under the Austrian and Hungarian constitutions (1867) ministerial 'responsibility' was defined in a narrow, legalistic manner: ministers were 'responsible' to both assemblies for the legality of all measures enacted in their period of office. They were not bound, however, to obey the wishes of a parliamentary majority. The Imperial German Chancellor, the sole Reich minister, was unambiguously declared by the constitution to be responsible to the Kaiser alone.

A rounded assessment of how 'constitutional' the Russian constitutional monarchy was cannot be accomplished simply by a survey of the Fundamental State Laws. The manner in which the provisions of the 'constitution' were implemented in the eight years of peace left to the Romanov dynasty is of equal significance. In this second section of the essay the constitutional practices of Restoration France, Prussia after 1850, Austria and Hungary after 1867, and Imperial Germany after 1870 will be used for purposes of comparison.

Absolutely integral to the functioning of a constitutional monarchy is the sovereign's adherence to the spirit as well as the letter of the constitution. A fundamental sense of ambiguity was imparted to the 'renovated political structure' of tsarist Russia by the fact that after 1906 Nicholas II remained ambivalent about the new order. The Emperor distrusted the State Duma as a wall between tsar and people. He believed that he was still an autocrat. It is true that between 1906 and 1911 he acted the part of a legalistic, non-interventionist monarch. After Stolypin's murder in 1911, the tsar was increasingly determined to reassert his prerogatives as an autocrat. He refused to have any more powerful Presidents of the Council of Ministers, achieving this end by denying Stolypin's successors the post of Minister of Internal Affairs. He deliberately condoned dissent within the Council and ministerial intrigues. In 1913 and 1914 Nicholas II twice endeavoured to persuade his ministers to make the State Duma a purely consultative body. He leant his support to the contemporaneous attacks launched by the reactionary Minister of Internal Affairs, Nicholas A. Maklakov, against civil and political rights.

The part played by the sovereigns in other European constitutional monarchies reveals that Nicholas II's actions were not completely exceptional. In Restoration France, whilst Louis XVIII remained unconcerned with the details of politics and played the role of constitutional monarch, his brother Charles X adopted a prominent role from 1827 onwards, with disastrous consequences for the Bourbons. Louis Philippe, too, became increasingly active in politics after 1835. Whilst William I of Prussia was determined to rule constitutionally on his accession as Prince Regent in 1858, he soon found himself involved in a prolonged constitutional conflict with the Landtag over his army reforms. The clash became increasingly one between the monarch's prerogatives, which William was determined to uphold, and the principle of parliamentary government. As German Emperor after 1870 William was not interested in ruling personally and generally followed the lead of his Chancellor, Bismarck. His mercurial grandson, William II, wanted to use his powers to the full. Whether he did succeed in establishing his 'personal rule' by 1898 is a matter of continuing bitter disputes among historians of the Kaiserreich. Franz Joseph, on the other hand, felt constrained after 1867 to work within the Austrian and Hungarian constitutions, as the only way to keep Germans and Hungarians satisfied. When, however, the German liberals in the Reichsrat opposed the annexation of Bosnia-Herzegovina in 1878–9, the Emperor would brook no interference with his prerogative of foreign policy. He destroyed the German liberals' hegemony in Austria, replacing them with Count Taaffe as Minister–President, who was clearly the Emperor's man. Indeed, the breakdown of parliamentary government in Austria by 1895–7 left Franz Joseph as the sole source of authority, so enhancing his real power over domestic affairs.

The electoral practices, or more accurately malpractices, of Stolypin and his successor as Minister of Internal Affairs, A. A. Makarov, were certainly not at all unusual when comparison is made with other constitutional monarchies. Stolypin's revision in 1907 of the electoral law to the State Duma, devised to ensure a majority in parliament for 'trustworthy', well-to-do property owners and for Orthodox Great Russians, replicated, for example, Louis XVIII's introduction of the electoral law of 1817 in order to weaken the Ultra loyalists' domination of the Chamber of Deputies, or the Hungarian electoral law of 1874, designed to disenfranchise most of the national minorities. Premature dissolutions of legislative assemblies, whose legal timespan had not expired, was a standard device resorted to by monarchs against bodies considered troublesome. Nicholas II's dissolution of the First and Second State Dumas within the space of a year, 1906–7, was strikingly similar to William I's dissolution of the Prussian Landtag in 1862 and 1863, when it twice rejected the budget to finance his military reforms. In Imperial Germany Bismarck and his successors as Chancellor made almost a fine art of early dissolutions of the Reichstag as a weapon against the parliamentary opposition. Five of the thirteen Reichstags (from 1871–1918) came to an unexpected end in this fashion.

Governmental intervention in elections themselves to secure favourable majorities in national elected assemblies was likewise a skill mastered in many constitutional monarchies. The Bourbon and Orleanist dynasties in France between 1815 and 1848 were the first to perfect this art. The devices to which ministries resorted became routine: redrawing of constituency boundaries; shifting polling dates and stations; tampering with electoral registers; the prospect of employment or rewards; banning of opposition newspapers and meetings; harassment of party activists. In Hungary after 1867 the system of rigging elections reached an apogee under the Liberal Party and its leader, Kalman Tisza. It helped ensure that Magyars, a minority in the Hungarian kingdom, dominated the political system. Thus the Russian government's intervention in the elections to the Second, Third, and Fourth State Dumas was not at all unprecedented, although the mobilization of the clergy by the Holy Synod was rather excessive. In Imperial Germany and Austria, in stark contrast, elections were relatively free from blatant intervention by the authorities.

In many respects in its short span of existence the State Duma did function as a proper legislature. It emerged as a forum for political articulation, even if for a privileged minority, through its debates, interpellations and questions, all of which were published uncensored and normally verbatim in the press. It did discuss government bills and amend them. Opponents of government projects could and did use the Duma to block or distort them, as was the case, for example, with the provincial landed nobility's opposition to Stolypin's local government reforms, or the Orthodox Church's rejection of greater religious freedom for Old Believers and sectarians. It is true that the Duma's budgetary rights had been tightly circumscribed by the budget rules of 8 March 1906. The consequence was that in 1907 the legislature controlled only 53 per cent of the state budget. Parliament had no say at all in the budgets of the Imperial Household or His Majesty's Own Chancery, and no control over the government contingency fund. Nevertheless, the State Duma did make some progress as 66 per cent of the budget came under its purview by 1912. The greatest stride was made in parliamentary scrutiny of the budget of the Ministry of War. If, in 1907, a mere 13 per cent of military estimates came within the chambers' cognizance, by 1912 this had soared to 66 per cent, largely on account of extra appropriations for military reforms and arms programmes. The State Duma, furthermore, began to penetrate the executive's exclusive sphere of decision-making. The presentation of the annual estimates of the Ministries of War, the Navy, and Foreign Affairs allowed deputies to debate military and diplomatic issues, and express their views, often highly critical of the government's policies in these areas. The potentiality of interpellations for increasing ministerial accountability, however, was largely unrealized as over half of all interpellations were left unanswered by ministers. Worse still, from the perspective of liberals and bureaucratic reformers, the State Council did indeed fulfil the hopes of its creators. It constantly checked the 'excessive' reform measures from the Lower House.

A rather cursory survey of the actual practices of legislatures elsewhere in nineteenth- and early twentieth-century Europe would suggest that the successes and failures of Russia's new legislature were not out of alignment. In Austria and Hungary after 1867 the formal rules of parliamentary government were observed. Indeed the State Duma escaped the fate of the Austrian Reichsrat, which was reduced by the 1890s to an incoherent shambles by the explosive passions unleashed by the nationality struggles, in particular between Germans and Czechs in Bohemia and Moravia, and the parliamentary obstruction to which national representatives resorted. In the Prussian constitutional conflict in the early 1860s, the Diet four times rejected the budget. The Reichstag, too, was prepared to refuse assent to measures of which it disapproved, such as the state monopoly on tobacco or the Septennat army bill in 1887. Upper Houses elsewhere also acted as governments' generally trustworthy allies. Thus, in 1863, the Herrenhaus in Prussia threw out the Diet's bill on ministerial responsibility.

The Fundamental State Laws' promise of the establishment of a *Rechtsstaat*, a state ruled by law, was not realized after 1906 for several reasons. The chambers' limited powers of supervision over the bureaucracy and the lack of ministerial responsibility meant that the legislature was a very imperfect instrument for placing pressure on bureaucrats to obey the law. The retention of the 1881 emergency legislation gave great scope for abuse by civil servants and the police, especially in the provinces. The age-old habits of *proizvol*, of administrative arbitrariness, so ingrained in the bureaucracy, could not be easily or swiftly eradicated. In the years after 1906 the regime failed to enshrine in formal laws the rights granted in the Fundamental State Laws. Thus, the press, trade unions, public assemblies and associations all came under 'Temporary Regulations' which allowed the authorities wide scope for arbitrary actions. Indeed, police considerations predominated in the implementation of the 'Temporary Regulations'. There certainly was no improvement in the rights of the national minorities. Stolypin's proposed minor concessions to the Jews were vetoed by the tsar in 1906. Stolypin and his successors launched aggressive nationality policies, restricting the rights of Finland in 1910 and of the Poles in the western provinces by the Western *Zemstva* bill in 1911. The revolutionary parties and even the liberal Kadets were denied legalization. Nevertheless, despite all these restrictions, a flourishing and relatively free press did emerge after 1905. Newspapers could and did criticize government policies harshly. Many public congresses and conferences were held. Economic and social pressure groups were allowed to form. Even the illegal revolutionary parties were permitted to participate in elections to the legislature and their deputies to take up their seats.

In this respect 'renovated Russia's' record in civil rights stands up less well when comparison is made with other European constitutional monarchies. In Austria, France, Hungary and Imperial Germany the rule of law, including civil rights for Jews, was established over time. But even in such states the authorities were prepared to ignore the rule of law when the occasion arose. In France, for example, after the murder of the Duc de Berry in 1820, the government introduced emergency laws on press censorship and detention without trial. Similar laws were passed after an assassination attempt on Louis Philippe in 1834. All workers' organizations remained illegal in France until 1864, punishable by the penal code. In Imperial Germany, despite the constitutional sanctioning of the equality of all faiths, the *Kulturkampf* in the 1870s witnessed a raft of legislation against Roman Catholics. In Prussia's eastern provinces, too, the Poles endured many restrictions, such as making German the language of instruction in all primary schools in 1873. In Hungary, the liberal Nationalities Law of 1867 paradoxically became the main instrument of magyarization in the succeeding decades. Thus, the Education Acts of 1879, 1883 and 1891 made the teaching of Magyar compulsory in schools. Most famously in Germany the Anti-Socialist Laws of 1878, and their Austrian equivalent in 1886, endeavoured to proscribe the nascent Social Democratic parties and trade unions. In practice, however, the laws were applied rather half-heartedly and were repealed in 1890 and 1891 respectively.

All the constitutional monarchies had Councils of Ministers headed by a Minister–President. The function of these councils was to co-ordinate governmental policy making and the prime concern of the chief ministers was to secure the assent of the new legislatures for government bills and financial measures. In this respect in 'renovated Russia' the new Council of Ministers was no exception. Despite, or rather because of, the predominance of the provincial landed nobility in the Third and Fourth State Dumas, Stolypin and his successors found it impossible to fashion a secure and reliable majority for their legislation. Both State Dumas lacked a majority either for reform or for counter-revolution between 1907 and 1914. The moderate liberal Octobrist party, on whom Stolypin relied between 1907 and 1909, as well as the moderate right Nationalist party, to whom he turned after 1909, fell well short of a majority of deputies. Stolypin, and his successors, could not rely on a single political or social group to support all of their programmes.

A similar pattern may be discerned in the case of Imperial Germany and Austria after 1867. Whilst Bismarck as Imperial Chancellor was able to rely upon the National Liberals to furnish him with a majority in parliament in the 1870s, in the crisis of 1879, the so-called 'refounding of the Reich', he decisively broke with them. Thereafter, he and his successors lacked a reliable majority in the Reichstag. Chancellors could only campaign in elections for parties likely to stand by them. After elections, any pro-government alliance in the Reichstag was precarious and had to be propped up with *ad hoc* concessions. The pro-government coalition, the Kartell, for example, formed for the parliamentary elections of 1887, broke down within three years. In Austria an identical pattern may be observed. In the 1870s the German Liberals' predominance in the Reichsrat ensured parliamentary ministries. After Franz Joseph broke with the German Liberals in 1879, as recounted above, Count Taaffe ruled through an unsteady coalition of heterogeneous clerical and national parties with concessions to each. He turned Austrian politics into a trade of support for favours. The unravelling of his system in the 1890s, due above all to the German–Czech quarrel in Bohemia and Moravia and the continuous obstruction of the Reichsrat by the constant filibustering of the opposition parties, led to the permanent breakdown of parliamentary government in Austria after 1897.

The harsh criticisms made of the Russian constitutional monarchy, many of which cannot be denied, and the common depiction of it as 'sham constitutionalism', like similar criticisms of the Imperial German constitution, are based on two basic misconceptions. In the first place, most critics forget to compare the Fundamental State Laws and their implementation in practice after 1906 with what preceded them in tsarist Russia. The plain fact is that in 1906 the Romanov monarchy ceased to be an unlimited autocracy, a development even the usually impercipient Nicholas II did grasp. Article four notwithstanding, in legal terms the Russian monarch was no longer an autocrat, the sole source of all legislative, juridical and administrative power. The rights of the tsar were now restricted by the functions of a nationally elected legislature and by the Council of Ministers. The civil freedoms enshrined in the Fundamental State Laws marked a definite advance. Before 1905, most of these freedoms simply did not exist. The grant of the right of veto to the State Duma did make the government dependent for the first time upon the support of a parliament, and hence of society (*obshchestvo*), or at least its educated, privileged members. However hedged about these new rights were, they opened up at least the possibility of further constitutional advance in a peaceful, legal manner: such an opportunity was not there before 1906.

In the second place, when comparisons are made with the constitutions of other European monarchies, 'renovated Russia' was a genuine constitutional monarchy. No historian denies that France after 1791 and 1814, Prussia after 1850, Austria and Hungary after 1867 were no longer legally absolute monarchies. Despite the ambiguity imparted by article four to the Fundamental State Laws, neither was Russia. The fact that the word 'constitution' was not used signifies little. Neither did the Charte of 1814 or the Austrian Fundamental Law of 1867 specifically embrace the term, yet scholars rightly describe these countries' political systems as constitutional monarchies. When one compares both the provisions of the Fundamental State Laws and their implementation before 1914 with those of other European constitutional monarchies, the Russian constitutional monarchy stands up well. The powers of the tsar and of the new legislature were not out of alignment with other constitutions. Nicholas II's clinging to the outdated myth of a patriarchal absolutism did not result in dire consequences before 1914. The fact was that a majority of his ministers blocked his plans for a veiled *coup d'état* against the State Duma in 1913 and 1914. The examples of Charles X and William II show that other constitutional monarchies harboured sovereigns with similar delusions, and neither of them succeeded in realizing their fantasies of 'personal rule'. The successes and failures of the State Duma paralleled those of other European legislatures, as did the electoral malpractices of the Council of Ministers those of other constitutional governments. Arguably the major area where the generally favourable comparison breaks down concerns the institution of a *Rechtsstaat*. Even here the record is distinctly mixed. Other states condoned temporary suspensions of civil freedoms or qualified legal rights by exemptions. In particular, it should be remembered that the Russian constitutional monarchy had a mere eight years of peace in which to develop respect for the rule of law. It had taken decades in other European constitutional monarchies to develop a proper *Rechtsstaat*.

The writer is aware that, in the comparatively short space of an essay, he has only been able to scratch the surface of this topic. Many of the comparisons have not been developed in depth. Others have had to be omitted. In particular the question of the development of civil society as a fundamental foundation of a *Rechtsstaat* has been deliberately ignored, in part because the author has touched upon it elsewhere as it relates to 'renovated Russia' after 1906.[17] Nevertheless, in the light of the detailed comparisons made above with other

European constitutional monarchies, the conclusion must be that 'renovated Russia' after 1906 was indeed a proper constitutional monarchy.

Notes

1. Leopold H. Haimson, 'The Problem of Social Stability in Urban Russia, 1905–1917,' Parts 1 and 2, *Slavic Review*, vol. 23, no. 4 (1964), pp. 619–42 and vol. 24, no. 1 (1965), pp. 1–22; Robert B. McKean, 'Constitutional Russia', *Revolutionary Russia*, vol. 9, no. 1 (1996), pp. 33–42; *idem, Between the Revolutions: Russia 1905 to 1917* (London, 1998).
2. Throughout this essay dates are referred to in the style of the time and country concerned. Thus dates referring to Russian events are rendered in the 'Old Style' of the pre-revolutionary calendar.
3. Max Weber, *The Russian Revolutions* (Cambridge, 1997), p. 184.
4. *Krizis samoderzhaviia v Rossii 1895–1917* (Leningrad, 1984), p. 343.
5. Sidney Harcave, *First Blood: The Russian Revolution of 1905* (London, 1964), p. 250.
6. Marc Szeftel, *The Russian Constitution of 23 April 1906: Political Institutions of the Constitutional Monarchy* (Brussels, 1976), p. 261.
7. Abraham Ascher, *The Revolution of 1905: Authority Restored* (Stanford, Cal., 1992), p. 70.
8. Keith M. Baker, *The Old Regime and the Revolution* (Chicago, Ill., 1987), p. 238.
9. Robert Tombs, *France, 1814–1914* (London, 1996), p. 332.
10. Szeftel, *The Russian Constitution*, p. 84. Szeftel usefully includes an English translation of the full text of the Fundamental State Laws: chapter 2, pp. 84–109.
11. Szeftel, *The Russian Constitution*, p. 85.
12. *Ibid.*, p. 85.
13. *Ibid.*, p. 102.
14. *Ibid.*, p. 99.
15. Arthur J. May, *The Hapsburg Monarchy, 1867–1914* (Cambridge, Mass., 1965), p. 43.
16. Szeftel, *The Russian Constitution*, p. 104.
17. Robert B. McKean, 'The Constitutional Monarchy in Russia, 1906–17', in *Regime and Society in Twentieth-Century Russia*, ed. Ian Thatcher (London, 1998); McKean, 'Constitutional Russia'; David Moon, 'Peasants into Russian Citizens? A Comparative Perspective', *Revolutionary Russia*, vol. 9, no. 1 (1996), pp. 43–81; Peter Gatrell, '"Constitutional Russia": a Response', *Revolutionary Russia*, vol. 9, no. 1 (1996), pp. 82–94.

7
Red Internationalists on the March: the Military Dimension, 1918–22

John Erickson

The vast consuming tragedies of the First World War brought a tidal wave of humanity flooding into Russia: refugees from Poland, the Baltic states and Rumania, unskilled labourers from Persia, China and Korea, skilled workers from Belgium, Italy, Finland and Canada and a huge multi-ethnic train of wretched prisoners of war. By 1917 the figure of the displaced, the dispossessed and the detained had climbed to 5 million, prisoners of war representing almost half that total. Between 1914 and 1916 the tally of prisoners rose from 100,000 to 1 million. In September 1917 the Russian General Staff recorded a total of 1,961,331 prisoners of war, but investigations conducted throughout 1918–19 by the Soviet agency for war prisoners and refugees (*Tsentroplenbezh*) and the International Red Cross produced figures of 2,112,646 and 2,343,378 respectively for prisoners of war in Russia.

Confusion over numbers had its counterpart in the bewildering kaleidoscope of nationalities involved, reflecting the multi-national composition of the armies of the Central Powers. The Austro-Hungarian Army embraced Austrians, Hungarians, Czechs, Slovaks, Serbs, Croats, Galician Ukrainians and Italians. The German Army had its complement of 100,000 Poles, the Turkish Army fielded contingents of Kurds and Armenians, and a few hundred Bulgarians. Rank-and-file soldiers made up the mass of the prisoners of war; officers a mere 4 per cent.[1]

As labour shortages began to bite in wartime Russia the War Ministry turned increasingly to the prison camps as a source of man-power for farms, factories and mines, but earlier in the war the bulk of prisoners of war were located largely in non-European Russia, in Siberia, in the Irkutsk Military District and in Turkestan. To bring this labour force nearer to the mines, factories and railway construction sites inevitably meant transporting prisoners of war from these easterly reaches for relocation in central and southern Russia. By the beginning of 1917 1,330,000 prisoners of war, working for 30 kopeks a day, exchanged the hunger, squalor and mortality of the prison camps for what was little better than slave labour. These conditions triggered the first prisoner-strikes as early as 1915 and subsequently stimulated anti-war and revolutionary agitation. Refugee and unskilled immigrant labour, earning starvation wages, fared equally miserably. Chinese and Korean contract workers, paid a bare minimum, were for all practical purposes regarded as 'civilian prisoners' condemned to forced labour.

Not all prisoners of war languished in camps or toiled in the mines. Miniature 'national armies' had begun to spring up before 1917, manned by volunteers and prisoners. The Czechoslovak Army Corps had its origins with Czechs living in Russia who volunteered in 1914 to fight against the Central Powers, creating a small military unit, the *Družina,* its losses replaced in 1915 with Czech prisoners of war. By October 1917 the Czechoslovak Army Corps consisted of two divisions and was assigned to the Russian 11th Army on the South Western Front.[2] The Serb Volunteer Corps drew its manpower from prisoners of war, authorized and financed by the Russian government in consultation with the Serb Minister in Petrograd, though fierce differences over adherence to the cause of 'Greater Serbia' or alternatively 'Yugoslav federation' undermined the cohesion of the Corps.

The Poles in search of independence faced a cruel dilemma whether to support or oppose Russia. Piłsudski, adamant that Russia was the prime enemy, chose co-operation with Austria. Early in the war the tsarist regime set its face against organizing separate Polish units from Poles serving in the Russian Army, a situation which changed abruptly in 1917 with the Provisional Government's proclamation on Poland, revoking previous false promises, denouncing the treachery of the Central Powers and recognizing the right of the 'fraternal Polish people' freely to decide their own fate.[3] One result of this was the emergence of the Polish 1st Army Corps, a bad compromise modelled on the tsarist army, its commander Jozef Dowbór-Muśnicki lacking vision and insight, an enterprise aimed at an independent Polish army which ended in defeat and finally the demise of all three Polish corps.[4]

The February Revolution ignited a huge powder keg of passion, frustration and anticipation. The disintegration of the Russian Imperial Army had begun. Agitation at the front and in the rear combined with popular excitement from which neither foreign workers nor prisoners of war were immune. In March 1917 Finnish workers in Petrograd set up the armed Finnish Workers' Militia. Refugees and immigrant workers also set about organizing themselves. Writing in *Pravda* in June 1917 Alexandra Kollontai trained a searchlight on the problem and the plight of prisoners of war, recommending improvement in the conditions of 'our prisoner comrades' and regular distribution of 'socialist literature' amongst them.[5] The Provisional Government also eyed the prisoner colonies, momentarily favouring the idea of strong national military formations, a design encouraged by the Allies and applauded by General Denikin.

The Bolshevik seizure of power in October 1917 blew these plans apart. The 'democratization' of the Russian army was designed to neutralize the internal threat to the new regime. Radicalizing the prison camps and mobilizing refugee and immigrant 'socialist-internationalists' generated political support for the Bolsheviks across the length of Russia. 'Prisoner of war-internationalists' also stiffened and supported the Red Guard, battling to install Bolshevik control. In distant Omsk in October 1917 Josip Broz Tito, taken prisoner on the Carpathian Front in 1915, joined the Red Guard at the same time continuing his 'revolutionary work' among prisoners of war.[6]

The vast pool of war prisoners presented both problems and opportunities. Freed from the dreadful camps, prisoners presented a huge welfare problem, one compounded by the arrival of yet more refugees, but negotiations at Brest-Litovsk held out the prospect of peace with the Central Powers and the repatriation of prisoners of war. Lenin viewed this as an unrivalled opportunity, an exchange of prisoners would mean Bolshevik Russia hurling into Germany 'a huge mass of men who had seen our revolution in action, learned from it', men able to work all the better to awaken revolution in Germany.[7]

The 'political enlightenment' of repatriated prisoners thus assumed major importance, but as civil war loomed large a second vital undertaking was to organize direct armed support for Russia's 'proletarian revolution'. To meet that urgent need the All-Russian Conference of Prisoners of War decided in April 1918, in closed session, to set up the 'Central Collegium for the Formation of the International Proletarian Army' (*Tsentral'naia kollegiia dlia formirovaniia internatsional'noi proletarskoi armii*).[8] But the real driving force proved to be the Central

Federation of Foreign Groups of the Russian Communist Party (*Tsentral'naia federatsiia inostrannykh grupp RKP(b)* – TsFIG in its short-ened form). Formed in May 1918 from the leadership of five 'foreign communist groups', Hungarian, Rumanian, German, Czechoslovak and Yugoslav, and the Communist Party Central Committee, the Federation developed close contacts with local Party committees and local groups of foreign communists stretching from Petrograd to Khabarovsk.[9] Presided over by Bela Kun until his departure for Hungary in November 1918, the Federation worked assiduously to influence prisoners of war and to raise 'international units' for the Red Army, setting up its own body to implement this programme, the *Komissiia po sozdaniiu internatsional'nykh grupp Krasnoi Armii*. In the spring of 1919 it was reorganized as a formal administration (*Upravlenie po formirovaniiu chastei internatsional'noi Krasnoi Armii*) and charged with establishing the 'International Red Army'.[10]

The Imperial Russian Army, demoralized, 'democratized' and demo-bilized, had vanished from the scene.[11] The infant Red Army remained a military weakling in the spring of 1918, 'a conglomeration of occasional, improvised detachments [*otriady*], not held together by any command organization'.[12] The call for volunteers produced only negligible results, producing few fighting troops. Four Latvian Rifle Regiments, dour, drilled and tested troops, provided the basic capabil-ity of the embattled Soviet regime but they were spread dangerously thin.[13] The Red Army was desperate, not only for men, but above all for trained men who could organize and who were also politically reli-able. 'Social-democratic prisoner of war internationalists' fitted the bill perfectly, trained soldiers, the 'revolutionary reserve of the Soviet Republic, able to take up stations in the front-line of the struggle against 'counter-revolution and Intervention'.[14]

Bolshevik arming of prisoners of war excited great alarm abroad. The Allies evidently were fearful that this might mean a German seizure of Siberia. The German and Austro-Hungarian governments expressed outrage at the enlistment of their men in the Red Army. Reports of an 'International Legion 1918' only increased this foreboding and height-ened suspicions over Bolshevik aims. Recruiting for the International Legion of the Red Army (*Internatsional'nyi Legion Raboche-Krest'ianskoi Krasnoi Armii*) had indeed begun in Petrograd in February 1918, a bizarre enterprise offering either 'active membership' for a minimum of six months or rudimentary military training. The appeal for volunteers went out in Russian and English. Albert Williams, an American, was put in charge of recruiting. Transferred to Moscow in March, with

A. Ebengoltz appointed commander, the Legion attracted Englishmen, Americans, Finns, Germans, Chinese, Russians and Poles, ending up as part of the 41st Moscow Soviet Regiment.[15]

The explosion, when it came in May 1918, was triggered by the Czech Corps' revolt against the Bolsheviks. Moving from the Ukraine into Siberia, aiming for Vladivostok and ultimately France, the Czechs, fearful of German plans to take over Siberia, were increasingly convinced of German–Bolshevik collusion. Conspiracy theories were given added weight by the Bolshevik arming of prisoners of war in Siberia. The Bolsheviks, trusting neither the Allies nor the Central Powers, intensified their appeal to Allied citizens and the drive to recruit German and Austro-Hungarian prisoners of war. If the Allies aimed to destroy the Soviet regime, soldiers of the Central Powers were presumably not averse to engaging their long-standing enemy. Repatriated, proselytized German soldiers might well weaken the German Army, introducing the incubus of 'revolutionary consciousness' within its ranks. While this was one component in the defensive struggle against *Weltkapital*, the commitment to world revolution suggested a present and future call to arms. In that offensive phase the 'internationalist instrument' of the proletarian revolution, armed, ready and waiting, could well serve as a vanguard.

As civil war flared in the summer of 1918 and intervention loomed, 'international regiments' fought alongside the Red Army. Tibor Samuely (Szamuely) organized the 1st Communist International Detachment, San Fu-Yan a Chinese battalion, Yaroslav Hašek, prisoner of war, communist activist and author of *The Good Soldier Schweik*, raised international units in Samara.[16] A Czech unit was formed in Astrakhan, another Chinese battalion was assembled in Tula and a Polish company was mustered in Irkutsk. Hašek's Czech Detachment, a breakaway group from the Czechoslovak Legion, began to assemble on 15 April 1918 and grew to 120 men (80 Czechoslovaks and 40 Serbs), the first step in raising the Czechoslovak Red Battalion. The Serb Volunteer Corps had split and disintegrated, with 'revolutionary elements' separating to form the Yugoslav Revolutionary Detachment and the Yugoslav Revolutionary Union in Kiev. Evacuated from Kiev, the Yugoslav detachment wound up in Samara. At the end of May 1918 the Inspector of Infantry for Samara province reviewed Hašek's detachment, the Chinese Detachment, the 1st Socialist Revolutionary

Yugoslav Detachment and Yugoslavs manning the Samara guard troop (1,339 men and 500 rifles).[17] The manpower of the Chinese Red battalions, organized in Samara and Siberia, was drawn exclusively from the poor, workers and miners; merchants and dealers were barred.[18]

In the early summer of 1918 the Red Army abandoned the volunteer system and introduced compulsory military service for the working class. Erstwhile military radicals such as Podvoiskii underwent a change of heart with respect to military organization. Miasnikov, commander of the embattled Volga Front, demanded the amalgamation of units, an end to flimsy, unconnected 'detachments', the imposition of firm discipline and the creation of 'a powerful, well-equipped, manoeuvrable regular army'.[19] The early military utopianism, preferences for a militia as opposed to a regular army, voluntary service and elective command were inexorably sacrificed in the interests of battlefield effectiveness, professionalism and centralization, enabling the Red Army not only to fight but to win. Between June and August 1918 worker mobilization plus a special mobilization of former NCOs netted the Red Army 540,123 men and 17,800 NCOs.[20]

Red Army international units could not escape the process of amalgamation and attempts at tighter control. Detachments turned into battalions and some into regiments, though establishments varied widely and wildly. Designations 'battalion' and 'regiment' were often indistinguishable or interchangeable, the manpower in most cases minuscule. The 1st Astrakhan International Communist Regiment began life as a battalion in March 1918, attaining the status of a regiment in December. The several Polish 'national corps' had already disintegrated. Polish 'internationalists' in Belorussia had organized 'Polish revolutionary detachments' in November 1917 and a Polish revolutionary battalion in Minsk. The Polish Belgorod Regiment, 12,000 strong, proved to be 'the most revolutionary'.[21] Withdrawn to Moscow, the Belgorod Regiment in March 1918 formed the basis of a new Red Army unit, the 1st Revolutionary 'Red Warsaw' Regiment. Two Polish 'revolutionary battalions' were also organized, one of them manned by soldiers who had served with the 1st Polish Corps.[22]

A kaleidoscopic array of 'international' units sprang up. The 2nd International Rifle Regiment was organized in Tambov in May 1918 from a Czechoslovak detachment and assigned to the Red Army's 16th Rifle Division, only to be virtually wiped out in the late winter of 1919. The survivors were assigned to the 3rd Battalion of the 138th Rifle Regiment, which was then designated the 'Special International Battalion'. The amalgamation of three Finnish detachments at the end of 1918 created the 3rd Finnish Communist Regiment which moved first from Perm to Petrograd and subsequently to Karelia where the unit was incorporated into the 6th Finnish Rifle Regiment. The Saratov International Rifle Regiment combined Czechoslovak, Polish, Serb and Hungarian detachments into a single unit, though its life span was relatively brief, lasting only from August to December 1918.

The 225th Chinese Rifle Regiment, commanded by Zhen Fu Chen, was also an amalgamation in 1918 of detachments already fighting with the 3rd Brigade of the Red Army's 29th Rifle Division on the Eastern Front. Raising more Chinese units became the responsibility of a special staff, *Shtab po formirovaniiu kitaiskikh boevykh otriadov*, set up in Moscow in August 1918. At its head was Shen Chen-ho, commander of a Chinese Red Guard detachment at the end of 1917. Representatives of the staff sought recruits from centres of Chinese population throughout the country, a task eventually handed over in 1920 to the Central Organizational Bureau of Chinese Communists in Russia.[23]

Some prisoners of war were returned home, others stayed to fight. By the late autumn of 1918, 101,000 German prisoners of war, 675,719 men of the Austro-Hungarian Army and 25,000 Turks had been repatriated, a grand total of 801,719, of whom some 300,000 were deemed to have been former members of 'revolutionary organizations'.[24] At the same time the Organization of Foreign Workers and Peasants (*Organizatsiia innostrannykh rabochikh i krest'ian*) reported that about 50,000 'internationalists' were serving with the Red Army.[25] A plethora of central and local bodies, multiple committees and commissions involved themselves in raising men for international units: the Staff of International Revolutionary Troops, the Staff of the International Red Army, the Staff of Foreign Detachments with the Russian Red Army, the military sections of the Czechoslovak and Yugoslav departments of the Nationalities Commissariat (Narkomnats) plus the Polish Commissariat.

In an effort to reduce duplication and confusion the Military and Naval Commissariat (*Narkomvoenmor*) entered the fray in June 1918, taking up TsFIG's proposal to create a Commission for the Formation of International Groups in the Red Army. The Commission proceeded to set out the procedures for inducting recruits into international units: *Instruktsiia o priëme i rabote v chastiakh internatsional'noi Krasnoi Armii*. In particular, the recruitment of former prisoners of war required that they take up Soviet citizenship, submit a recommendation from the committee of foreign internationalists, undergo an oral examination to ascertain their political complexion and sign a written solemn promise of devotion to the Soviet cause.[26]

The 'internationalists' had yet to overcome the 'national communists', elements within the foreign groups of the Party and the separate nationality departments within the Commissariat for Nationalities itself, all bent on raising single-nationality military units. To raise and organize a distinctive Czechoslovak Red Army in its own right the military section of the Czechoslovak department of the Nationalities Commissariat set up its own separate staff in July 1918, the 'Staff for the formation of Czechoslovak companies of the Red Army'.[27]

Political objections apart, the task of bringing together small units or even individuals scattered across the vastness of Russia would have been well nigh impossible, given the prevailing chaos in transportation. Narkomnats took the view that national units should only be set up within the territory of given nationalities, for example in the Ukraine and in Armenia. As for military units formed from refugees, emigrants and former prisoners, the Nationalities Commissariat took a very wary view, stipulating that there would have to be cast-iron guarantees from the Commissariat itself and from the relevant communist organizations about political reliability to ensure that such units did not fall victim to 'nationalists and the bourgeoisie'.[28]

TsFIG, the Central Federation, vigorously opposed the idea of forming national units.[29] The best course was to consolidate international units up to battalion level, thus paving the way for larger units, possibly divisions. Internally, international units were free to organize sub-units, companies and sections, from men of one nationality or men using a common language, largely to facilitate training, political education and command in battle.[30]

At the end of December 1918 the disorderly state of international units, their recruitment, organization and deployment inevitably provoked a reaction from Vatsetis, the irascible Soviet Commander-in-Chief. At his prompting the chief of staff of the Soviet Republic's highest military authority, the Revolutionary Military Council of the Republic (*Revvoensovet respubliki* or RVSR in shortened form),[31] informed the chief of staff of the All-Russian Supreme Staff (*Vserosglavshtab*) that international units must form battalions corresponding to Red Army formal establishments prior to their incorporation into Red Army regiments and brigades. Subject to agreement, the head of the Commission for the Formation of International Units should assign two or three of his men to *Vserosglavshtab* itself in order to regularize contact with international units. Any unit unfit for action must be disbanded.[32]

Vast distances, sprawling battle fronts and chaotic local conditions militated against central control and co-ordination. The Red Army itself suffered from 'guerrilla-ism' (*partizanshchina*), which tended to produce military anarchy and which War Commissar Trotskii was determined to suppress. The jigsaw pattern of the geographic locations of the prisoners of war exerted a major influence on the manner in which they were drawn or not drawn into 'international units'. In Turkestan the prisoner of war population numbered 41,285. The majority came from the Austro-Hungarian Army, 3,565 Germans, a few Turks and Bulgarians. Prisoner resistance to Bolshevik propaganda and blandishments was evidently considerable, but by September 1918 some had volunteered to serve with the Turkestan Red Army and by October there were enough men to form the 1st Internationalists' Training Regiment, a recruiting and training unit for war prisoners volunteering to serve. Towards the end of 1918, 2,500 Germans, Austrians, Hungarians, Czechs, Slovaks and Poles had joined Russians and native Turkestanis in Red Army units operating on the Transcaspian, Orenburg and Fergana Fronts.[33]

The Kazan Military District held a much greater concentration of prisoners of war: 285,376 officers and men. Kazan itself was the scene, in August 1918, of fellow-nationals fighting each other, anti-Bolshevik nationalist Serbo-Croat officers killing Serb and Croat 'internationalists'. Kazan was also the scene of the Red Army's recovery from near catastrophe on the Eastern Front.[34] International and national units, a Hungarian cavalry detachment, the Karl Marx Regiment, the Polish Mazovian Regiment of Red Ulans and the Tartar-Bashkir Battalion fought alongside the 2nd and 5th Red Armies to recover Kazan in September 1918. The Tartar-Bashkir Battalion had been reinforced with a company of former Turkish prisoners of war raised initially in Moscow under the auspices of the Central Moslem Military Collegium (*Tsentral'naia musul'manskaia voennaia kollegiia*) and subsequently transferred to Kazan.[35]

The Moslem Collegium laboured not only to raise Moslem military units but also to influence Turkish prisoners of war. In September 1918 Turkish communists in Kazan, led by Mustafa Subkhi, one of the founders of the Turkish Socialist–Communist Party, met to establish their own organization, to choose a commissar for the Turkish company and to intensify work among Turkish prisoners of war in the region.[36] The former Turkish prisoners of war assigned to the Tartar-

Bashkir Battalion fought alongside the 1st Kazan Regiment, itself manned by Turks, Uzbeks, Tadzhiks, Persians and Kirghiz. The 'foreign communist group' also set up its own 'commission for the struggle against counter-revolution' to counter anti-Soviet propaganda conducted by officers and 'various foreign missions' among prisoners of war.[37]

Local conditions almost invariably dictated both the form and the function of 'international units'. In eastern Siberia German and Hungarian former prisoners intermingled with 'Red partisans' fighting against Kolchak's White regime, the *Kolchakovshchina*.[38] Mixed nationalities made up fighting detachments, reflecting camp conditions where different nationalities had lived for long periods cheek by jowl. The self-styled Irkutsk International Division was a particular example, manned predominantly by Germans and Hungarians, joined by Czechs, Slovaks, Russians, Serbs, Italians, Chinese, Koreans, Buriats, Turks, Bulgars, Rumanians and Poles, 'even a few French, one Scot and one huge black man [*gigant-negr*]'.[39] The savage fighting in the area surrounding Lake Baikal involved 12 'international units', among them 250 Russians, Germans and Hungarians of the internationalist 'anarchist detachment'.[40] The available artillery was commanded by an Austrian senior lieutenant, but the associated Chinese detachment did not survive, wiped out to a man.

At the beginning of 1919 the position of the Soviet Republic had improved substantially. Reviewing the general situation Trotskii was eager to complete the investment of the Ukraine and exploit the opportunity created by the collapse of German power. Lenin was preoccupied with the situation in the northern Caucasus and the region of the Don, anxious to prevent it becoming a White base. In the spring Soviet forces were able to mount offensive operations in the Ukraine, bringing the Red Army westwards, encouraging militant communists to think in terms of internationalizing the revolution. Bolshevism had already been 'exported' to Hungary and Austria by repatriated prisoners of war, but no 'serious revolutionary leadership' was provided in either case. This applied particularly to Hungary and Bela Kun, the 'frightened tyrant', who proclaimed the establishment of the Hungarian Soviet Republic in March 1919.[41]

The prospect of direct assistance from the Red Army diminished almost by the hour. Threatened by Denikin and Petliura in the

Ukraine, Soviet troops were now forced back from the westerly frontiers to Kiev. In May the appeals from the Hungarian Soviet Republic for Russian help became more urgent.[42] Lenin himself urged the Red Army command to concentrate on two tasks, to aid the Don region and to form 'solid connections by rail with Hungary', but the arrangements to maintain contact between the Hungarian Red Army and the Soviet armies of the Ukraine broke down, evidently sabotaged by officers who found Bela Kun's policies 'not sufficiently revolutionary' and plotted against him.[43]

Orders went out to transfer international units from the Eastern Front to the Ukraine and the western military district. The 1st International Soviet Division was being hurriedly assembled at Odessa. In May the RVSR instructed international units to concentrate at Kiev and Nizhnii Novgorod. With the establishment of a 'comradely relationship' between the Hungarian Soviet Republic and Moscow, the status of Hungarian prisoners of war in Russia changed overnight. They were now legally citizens of a fraternal Soviet Republic. On 8 May 1919 Bela Kun, with Moscow's agreement, announced the 'mobilization of all Hungarians in Russia and the Ukraine aged between 18 and 45 (save for those already serving in the Red Army)'.[44]

Some of this manpower was used to organize the 'Independent International Brigade (Division) for Special Assignment' subordinated to Antonov-Ovseenko, commander of the Ukrainian Red Army. On 8 May 1919 Podvoiskii reported from Kiev on measures to assemble the 4th and 6th Ukrainian Divisions, the 'International Division' and a Bessarabian division for operations in both Hungary and Bessarabia.[45] Time, however, was running out for the Hungarian Soviet Republic. The prospects for its survival had already dimmed by the beginning of June. Bela Kun's hopes of enlarging his republic were dashed when a planned communist *coup* in Vienna fizzled out. The Allies demanded that the Hungarian Soviet Republic evacuate its recent conquest, Slovakia, in return for which Rumanian troops would relinquish the Hungarian territory they held. Kun accepted, abandoning Slovakia. Proclaimed on 20 June 1919, the Slovak Soviet Republic and the Slovak Red Army enjoyed only a brief life, a momentary rally snuffed out by Kun's submission to Allied demands. Withdrawal from Slovakia enraged Hungarian nationalists who had earlier supported Kun's dictatorship. The leading military commander, Wilhelm Boehm, resigned, as did his chief of staff Colonel Aurel Stromfeld. The middle classes and the workers deserted the regime. The surrender of Slovakia proved to be fruitless as Rumanian troops did not relinquish their gains. In mid-July Kun sent a desperate telegram to Chicherin, Soviet Commissar for Foreign Affairs, pleading for a powerful Soviet thrust through Galicia, now a matter of life or death for the Hungarians.[46] Harried now by Denikin's rapid advance, the Red Army had neither the available strength nor the operational freedom to respond to Kun's plea.

On 1 August 1919 Bela Kun resigned, seeking diplomatic protection and reserving a private train to take himself, his family and friends to Vienna. Tibor Szamuely, who had earlier drenched the counter-revolution in blood, shot himself. White terror now replaced its Red predecessor. Bolshevism was driven out of Hungary and with it Kun's government, leaving it to Hungarian communists in Moscow, on 6 August, to set up the Hungarian Revolutionary Committee in Exile, *Revkom Vengrii*, the refugee Bela Kun included among its membership. The Hungarian newspaper in Kiev, *Vörös Ujság* (Red News), printed a militant manifesto from the Hungarian communists and 'Red Army-internationalists' to the proletariat of the erstwhile Hungarian Soviet Republic. The text of the radiogram sent to Budapest urged the Hungarian proletariat not to lay down their arms, promising 'from the free land of the Russian and Ukrainian Soviet Republic' to continue the struggle for the world proletarian revolution assisted by the Red Army and the proletariat of the west.[47]

The defiant rhetoric belied the actual situation of the *internatsionalisty*. On 17 April 1919, under RVSR Order No. 730 and *Vserosglavshtab's* secret Order No. 122, all existing agencies concerned with forming international units were wound up, transferring them and their personnel to the Administration for the Formation of the International Red Army. Recruitment was to be confined solely to men who were not of Russian nationality before July 1914. Responsibility for the new Administration was assigned to the Czech Slavoyar Častek, a former prisoner of war, presently commander of the 1st International Regiment. The aim was to establish an international brigade with three rifle regiments, two cavalry units and a light artillery battery. The 1st Regiment was to be formed from international units already in the rear, with Nizhnii Novgorod the designated assembly point, to which an international reserve battalion and the Administration itself was to be transferred from Moscow.[48]

In May 1919 the field staff of the RVSR put the strength of 'all registered international units serving with the Red Army' at 15,000–18,000; 10,000 were registered with Častek's 'commission' on the Eastern Front, and 5,200 men and two guns with the 6th Orenburg

International Battery.[49] The revolutionary events in Hungary had certainly stimulated a rush to mobilize international units. Words were free and flamboyant, and the vision almost apocalyptic: 'The Red front in support of proletarian Hungary has been opened', the Hungarians had 'taken the first step on the road home', two Red fronts, Soviet Russian and Hungarian, would unite, together turn westwards and take the offensive in the cause of the proletarian revolution.[50] Mustering effective strength was another matter, the manner of its use was even more problematical. The frustrations of Hungarian–Rumanian 'internationalists' was reflected in an appeal from Rakovskii, President of the Ukraine Sovnarkom, in mid-May, urging both Hungarians and Rumanians to join efforts to suppress Ataman Grigor'ev's insurrection in the Ukraine: 'I know what you want. You want to lend speedy aid to your brothers in Rumania and Hungary. ... That is what I [Rakovskii] want.' However, the way home at that moment, the only direct route, lay over Grigor'ev's corpse.[51]

On 12 June 1919 the 'Administration for the Formation of International Units of the Ukrainian Red Army' in Kiev reported available strength of international units at 4,932 men.[52] The first attempt to assemble the 1st International Soviet Division in the Odessa region collapsed due largely to lack of weapons and poor organization. This was followed by fresh instructions for raising an 'international division' on 20 June. Divisional staff in Odessa and the staffs of 1st and 2nd Brigades were moved to Kiev, units already raised were ordered to Cherkassy. Divisional command was assigned to Bashkovich, that of 1st Brigade to Častek, who had been released from his administrative post. Formation of 1st Brigade was to be completed by 1 July, the 2nd was to be raised simultaneously but not at the expense of the 1st Brigade's readiness.[53] The RVSR confirmed those orders on 22 June with instructions to raise a reserve battalion and to subordinate Častek's 1st International Brigade to the 12th Red Army.[54]

The planned 1st International Division never materialized. Both international brigades, 1st and 2nd, were committed to the heavy fighting to counter General Denikin's offensive in the south, his 'Moscow drive', with its mounting danger to the Soviet Republic. Disorder, demoralization and battle casualties also took their toll. The collapse of the Hungarian Soviet Republic had dealt a savage blow to the morale of the *internatsionalisty*. According to a report of 8 September 1919 the demoralization following the *débâcle* in Hungary was such that:

> the further participation of the international brigade (*interbrigada*) in the civil war in Russia must be ended. ... According to them, the

instructions of the *Revkom Vengrii* are no longer binding, since Soviet Hungary is no more, and so it must rescind its mobilization orders and the international brigade remain composed only of volunteers.[55]

Since its inception on 6 August 1919 the *Revkom Vengrii* had acted as the main agency organizing international units. On 25 August the Administration for the Formation of the International Red Army, which had been wound up in July, was reconstituted under the Hungarian communist I. Kovacs. One month later, after negotiations between TsFIG and the RVSR the Administration for the International Red Army, in Serpukhov, was wound up once more and the organization of international units assigned to the Military Commission of TsFIG, replacing the former Military Section. Each national group, Hungarian, Czechoslovak, Rumanian, Yugoslav and German, was represented on the Commission.

The TsFIG Military Commission's report dated 18 November 1919 made alarming reading. The condition of the International Brigade, *Interbrigada*, operating with the 12th Red Army at the front, was extremely bad. Any idea of raising an international corps at Serpukhov was abandoned.[56] The immediate task was to save the international brigade from 'shameful disintegration'. One immediate measure to restore the situation had involved assembling all commanders and political workers at Serpukhov into an international reinforcement battalion, dispatching it to the front at the end of October with orders to 'rescue the brigade'.[57]

In spite of attempts to mobilize all available foreign communists for assignment to the 12th Red Army to replace unsuitable personnel in the *Interbrigada*, very little had been achieved. Old habits among the *Interbrigada* commanders had led to slackness and failure to obey orders. The international reinforcement battalion evidently failed in its 'rescue mission' since it was not correctly deployed. There was desertion: 170–180 deserters had been identified and returned to their units. In the absence of timely help for the international brigade, it had been disarmed and the remnants sent to Kazan for re-organization. A special three-man commission was also dispatched to Kazan, its task to purge the *Interbrigada* of 'harmful elements'. The 'purified' residual force would then be formed into small artillery, cavalry and infantry units, retrained and made 'politically conscious'.[58]

One-week training courses were mandated for commanders and political workers, the competent sent to units and the less than competent assigned for more training. This was designed to furnish the Soviet Republic with 'true and politically conscious fighters for the liberation of the world proletariat from the yoke of world capitalism'.[59]

At the end of 1919 all international units deployed with the Red Army's Southern Front were pulled back to Kazan. Under TsFIG's revised instructions international units would be manned by volunteers, unit organization and establishments would conform with those of 'the Russian Red Army'. All new volunteers would be at the disposal of, and subordinated to, the command of the Reserve Army located in Kazan since 1919. The unnamed 'guilty men' of the *Interbrigada* were handed over to the Reserve Army for trial and undisclosed punishment. In March 1920 Častek, prisoner of war, communist and *Interbrigada* commander, died of typhus in Penza, the town in which, two years earlier, he had first raised an international detachment.

In the spring of 1920 the Soviet Republic experienced a short 'breathing space' (*peredyshka*), before the onset of the Soviet–Polish war. The civil war had been effectively won and the Red Army began to demobilize, simultaneously releasing those of the 'internationalist volunteers' who were Soviet citizens. Though providing only a fraction of the strength of the multi-million-man Red Army, the 12 nationalities of the *Internatsional'nye formirovaniia Krasnoi Armii* had generated a kaleidoscopic, far-flung order of battle deployed across great stretches of the Soviet Republic, from Petrograd to Irkutsk and further east.

Over time, and spread over hugely dispersed battlefronts, the *internatsionalisty* had raised numerous self-styled divisions, among them the 1st International Division in the Ukraine, the Polish Western Division, the Special International Division, the 1st Czechoslovak Division, the 1st 'Third International' Division and the Irkutsk International Division. The *Interbrigada* came increasingly to the fore during the civil war, though its fortunes were mixed. A complete order of battle runs to inordinate length, but a summary list of unit documentation below division and brigade identifies 59 regiments, 40 battalions (3 Chinese and 1 Korean), 27 companies and 3 legions (1st Red Army International Legion, 3rd International Legion of the 1st Red Army's Orenburg Division and the Smolensk International Legion).[60]

Detachments ran into the hundreds, many dating back to association with the Red Guard, many hurriedly improvised like the Chinese detachment mobilized in the defence of Petrograd in 1919, or expanded like the singular Independent Persian International Detachment which also included a company of Turks. Raised on the Turkestan Front in April 1920 within three months, the detachment was reconstituted as the Independent Persian Rifle Regiment.[61]

With infantry, cavalry, artillery and engineer units, however minuscule the scale, the *internatsionalisty* embraced a useful range of arms and services. International cavalry units served with Budënnyi's famous 1st Cavalry Army and several Red Army cavalry divisions. The Independent International Cavalry Brigade, formed in October 1920 and attached to the Southern Front's 4th Red Army, fought in the spectacular and speedy offensive to destroy Wrangel's White forces in the Crimea. It was then employed in the operations to eliminate Makhno's peasant-anarchist Revolutionary Insurgent Army. The attack on Wrangel also provided the occasion for the re-emergence of Bela Kun, returned once more to Soviet Russia and a leading commissar in this final phase of the civil war. His baleful reputation was further sullied by adding the massacre of captured White officers to his repertoire. These vile atrocities ignited even Lenin's fury.[62]

Elsewhere, in distant Siberia, *internatsionalisty* rendered the Soviet Republic a signal service of a different order. Istvan Varga's 1st International Regiment ('Third International' Division) guarded the 13 American railway wagons loaded with the Russian gold reserves seized from Kolchak during the transfer from Irkutsk to the vaults in the bank in Kazan.[63]

Red Army demobilization inevitably affected international units. In May 1920 the Military Commission of the TsFIG was disbanded and responsibility for the *internatsionalisty* transferred to the All-Russian Supreme Staff (*Vserosglavshtab*), which set up a special body to deal with these units (the 9th Section in the Organization–Administration's department responsible for structure and troop training). This arrangement lasted until the end of the year and the onset of full-scale demobilization.

War with Poland violently reversed this process. In April 1920 Polish troops drove into the Ukraine, occupying Kiev on 6 May. Chauvinism, patriotism and communist enthusiasm seized the Soviet Republic, to which Trotskii responded by warning against political fancies that revolution in Poland would automatically clear the way for the Red Army. 'Wild prophecies' hardly matched the forces which the Comintern could command beyond Russia's borders. Bolshevism had been bludgeoned in Hungary and only marginal support existed in Austria and Germany.[64]

The Red Army concentrated for the counter-attack in the west and the south-west. On 4 July the Western Front commanded by Tukhachevskii launched a major operation, striking deep into Belorussia along a line of advance pointed directly at Warsaw. The talk was of 'revolutionary war', war as a means of spreading revolution, a doctrine to which Tukhachevskii enthusiastically adhered. On 18 July 1920 he addressed a letter to Zinov'ev on the occasion of the world congress of the Comintern, propounding 'the strategy of class, that is civil, war', war concluded only 'with the coming to power of the universal dictatorship of the proletariat'. The Comintern 'must prepare the proletariat with a military point of view for the moment of the world attack with all the armed forces of the proletariat on world armed capital'. Given the inevitability of world civil war 'we must now set up the General Staff of the Third Comintern'.[65]

During the heady Soviet advance on Warsaw the 'Polish bureau' in Moscow (*Pol'biuro pri TsK*), on 21 July, discussed the question of organizing Polish military units in the Red Army. On 6 August Feliks Dzerzhinskii, president of *Pol'biuro*, telegraphed Lenin: 'We consider organizing the Polish Red Army the most important task, with adequate organization we expect to create a proletarian army quickly.'[66] The first step involved the formation of an all-volunteer Polish Soviet regiment in Bialystok. To build the Polish Red Army meant utilizing the 52nd Polish Rifle Division which had been deployed on the Southern Front since November 1919. In August Poles joined the training courses for 'Red commanders' but everything shuddered to a halt when Tukhachevskii's armies were driven back in mid-August from the immediate approaches to Warsaw, retreating in disorder.[67] The 'export of revolution' on bayonets had failed. The Polish Red Army was hurriedly re-designated 'Polish Red units', changed quickly to 'Red communards units', emerging finally in July 1921 as the 'Red communards' rifle brigade' of the Red Army.

The rate of demobilization in the Red Army increased in 1920. It was accompanied by the disbanding of Red Army international units and the discharge of their personnel. Fresh contingents of 'agitators' returned home to central and eastern Europe, exciting fears over the appearance of more 'rabid Bolsheviks', indoctrinated war prisoners and ex-soldiers. Prisoner-of-war camps still provided convenient locations in the quest for men, either their persons or their potential political persuasions. In February 1920 TsFIG reported that the numbers of war prisoners were dwindling, none the less insisting that 'the main task at the moment [is] to educate and propagandize [*spropagandirovat'*] the remaining groups of prisoners of war in Soviet Russia'.[68]

With respect to international units the aim now was to re-organize the International Brigade in Kazan, 'establish a cadre of well trained political workers and command staff' and bring all the scattered units, including those in Turkestan, under the authority of the TsFIG Military Commission. By its own reckoning the Military Commission could account for a total of 4,155 men, 1,155 serving with the Red Army in Russia and 3,000 in Turkestan. To create that special cadre efforts were under way to identify former officers of 'the old foreign armies (Austro-Hungarian) and the volunteer corps (Serb, Czechoslovak and Rumanian)' in order to assign them, after careful screening and training, to international units.[69]

Though officially dissolved in May 1920 the TsFIG Military Commission appeared on the scene in November 1920, drafting fresh instructions on Red Army international units.[70] In view of 'past foul experience' in raising units, leading to disorder and indiscipline, the Commission recognized that large units were out of the question, owing to the lack of trained commanders and political officers to run them properly. The RVSR should issue strict orders that the Military Commission alone was responsible for organizing international units; it was vital to eliminate the anarchic methods: 'persons unknown to us have used, without any kind of selection, undesirable elements in forming units, leading to disorders, to indiscipline producing the complete disintegration of units'. Men of a special section should be posted temporarily to certain units to 'root out all illegal acts, theft and fraud, all kinds of illegality'.[71]

This attempt to re-organize and replenish the *internatsionalisty* coincided with a new phase in the civil war and foreign intervention in the Far East. The Red Army had advanced from the Urals to Lake Baikal, but Japanese troops held the coastal provinces and the Transbaikal, supporting Ataman Semënov's Buriat Mongol Republic and shielding what remained of Kolchak's army. Over the protests of those demanding the outright sovietization of the Far East, Lenin and Trotskii chose the strategy of the 'buffer state', formally 'recognizing' the new-found Far Eastern Republic (*Dal'nevostochnaia respublika* or DVR), on 14 May 1920. In the summer of 1920 the All-Russian Staff for the Formation of Chinese Internationalist Detachments moved from Moscow to Irkutsk, at a time when strenuous efforts were afoot to rein in turbulent rebellious partisans and incorporate them into the People's Revolutionary Army (NRA), the DVR's own local 'Red Army'.[72]

Freshly raised mixed Chinese–Korean units, together with Chinese and Korean partisans, operated across eastern Siberia and the Far East. In 1921 some 5,060 Koreans, including the Korean Independent Rifle Battalion, were in action 'on the territory of the Russian Far East'. On the Chinese–Korean border, fighting the Japanese, 'Korean revolutionary troops' were organized into four regiments and subordinated to the command of the NRA.[73] The direction of Chinese Communist activity in Russia was centralized with the establishment in 1920 of the Central Organizational Bureau of Chinese Communists. In the autumn of 1920 this body, like its affiliate for organizing Chinese internationalist units, left Moscow for the east, establishing itself in Chita, capital of the DVR. The Bureau did not confine its work to Soviet Russia. Seeking contacts with national revolutionary movements in China, an emissary from the Central Organizational Bureau was dispatched in 1920 to seek out Sun Yat-sen. The following year Liu Shao-chi paid his first 'study visit' to Russia.[74]

Moscow and the DVR nevertheless acted with great circumspection. It was no part of Moscow's policy that the Far Eastern 'buffer state' should provoke China or precipitate outright war with Japan. One urgent task involved the reduction of the *belopovstantsy*, the White remnants and survivors including Ungern-Sternberg, commander of the Asiatic Cavalry Corps, installed in Mongolia. Vasilii Bliukher, famous for his civil war achievements, now occupied the position of DVR War Minister and commander of the NRA, a force he drastically re-shaped and re-organized. His orders to NRA troops introduced into Mongolia to eliminate 'the Ungern gang' specified 'correct behaviour' towards the Chinese authorities and Chinese troops and 'full agreement and contact' with the Mongolian National Revolutionary Army under Sukhe-Bator and 'Red Mongolian partisan detachments'.[75]

Chinese communists in the DVR were expressly forbidden to form partisan units to operate in China proper, in spite of overtures to do precisely that, and tight control was exercised over any blatant 'export of Bolshevik propaganda'. *Realpolitik* overrode revolutionary zeal, plus the calculation that the Chinese Communist Party, newly formed in 1921, was presently too weak and inexperienced to direct armed units in any 'national-liberation struggle'.[76] That day had yet to come, but there was immediate triumph in which the *internatsionalisty* shared, the Korean–Chinese Regiment, the Korean Rifle Battalion, and every Chinese and Korean partisan. On 25 May 1922 the NRA finally entered Vladivostok. The Japanese had sailed away. The Whites had been effectively routed.

Neither in numbers of actual fighting effectives manning brigades, regiments and detachments, nor in their battle-field contribution were the *internatsionalisty* especially significant. The question of their numbers remains controversial, understandably so given the chaotic conditions of civil war, the vast geographical dispersal, the swarming of refugees and the continuous migrations of prisoners of war. Red Army staff recorded a figure of 18,000 in Red Army international units. 'Other data', never actually specified, mentioned a total of 35,000–40,000 men. A recent compilation referred to 500 international units, an assortment of detachments, companies, 'legions' and brigades, a force involving no less than 200,000 men, possibly more.[77] That figure is as suspect as it is improbable, if only because no full-strength international division was ever raised, much less an 'International Red Army', in spite of this multitude reportedly willing to serve.

Brigade, regiment and battalion designations flitted like will o' the wisps throughout the Red Army order of battle. The 'Special International Division' began life in November 1918 as the 2nd Moscow Workers Division, raised as a reserve division of the Moscow City Military Commissariat. On 28 November the 2nd Division was re-designated the Special Red Militia Division, one month later it emerged as the Special International Rifle Division with its two Worker Regiments (39th and 47th), a force of 1,923 men with a howitzer battery. The division, 'in great heart, anxious to be at the front', was assigned to 'Army Group Latvia', forerunner of the Army of Soviet Latvia, itself subsequently absorbed into the Western Front in 1919. Such droplets of manpower with over-inflated designations have long complicated the problem of establishing the true order of overall field strengths. Numbers apart, TsFIG reports clearly indicated the prevalence of disorder, indiscipline, desertion and widespread anarchy in raising units within geographically dispersed and operationally disparate fronts and sectors.

The reputation of the *internatsionalisty* has varied, over-idealization, denigration, denunciation and even contrived oblivion, this last at Stalin's command. The charge of 'mercenary' (*naëmnik*) was undermined by the fact that the majority of the men were not in Russia of their own volition, least of all lured to serve by the promise of 'Bolshevik gold'. Nor, for all the accusations levelled over 'Latvian rifles and Magyar pistols', did the *internatsionalisty* constitute a force which foisted and fastened an alien revolution on a hapless Russia. Such a feat was beyond their strength, steadily diminished by repatriation and increasingly dwarfed by the massive 'Russian Red Army'.[78] This is not to say that 'Red internationalism' and 'Proletarian international solidarity' were either empty slogans or instruments of 'foreign occupation'. The contemporary agonies and savageries were perceived by thousands as a prelude to proletarian triumph in the coming global civil war, though the reality proved otherwise, leading to disillusionment and bouts of despair. Equally 'internationalism' never eradicated or concealed national enmities, rivalries and internal class divisions. The Polish and Yugoslav corps splintered from such causes. The Czechoslovak Legion affirmed the objective of national independence above all else, immune to any seduction or other persuasion. That sense of separate national identity also prevailed in the opposite camp, manifesting itself in the moves to establish an autonomous 'Czechoslovak Red Army'.

If internationalism waned among the masses, diluted by repatriation, disillusioned by defeat in Hungary and the reversal before Warsaw, it fired the imagination of the communist political and military leadership. In spite of the Warsaw *débâcle* and Trotskii's ridiculing the idea of an 'International General Staff' attached to the Comintern, Tukhachevskii's enthusiasm for the internationalist cause was, if anything, strengthened, proclaiming the Red Army 'the buttress for the socialist revolution in Europe'.[79] The programme of the 'International Military School', training Red Army officers and foreign communists, bore witness to Tukhachevskii's assertion in 1928 that the Red Army continued to be educated 'in the spirit of internationalism'.[80] The military section of the Comintern prepared shadow German and Polish units. Vatsetis, former Red Army Commander-in-Chief, was reported in the late 1920s as having proposed a Red Foreign Legion, formed from foreign volunteers of 'proletarian origin' to serve the revolution. However, Red Army 'internationalists' misread not only the temper of the times but also that of their new master. Stalin's move to 'national defensivism' henceforth required the Red Army to rely solely on 'the sinews of its own strength'.[81]

For a brief period the Spanish Civil War dramatically breathed new life into 'internationalism'. The International Brigades were advertised as living proof of the 'international solidarity of the anti-Fascist front', drawing in 40,000 men organized into seven brigades from 54 nations.[82] Many of the *internatsionalisty* of the Russian Civil War became the *interbrigadovtsy* of the 1930s. 'General Kleber', leader of the International Brigade, was in reality Manfred Stern, a former Austro-Hungarian prisoner of war in Krasnoiarsk, who fought with the Red Army in the Civil War.[83] 'General Walter', the *nom de guerre* of Karol

Świerczewski, commander of the 14th Brigade, was himself a 'Polish internationalist' who had joined the Red Guard in 1917 and fought with the Red Army.[84] The Hungarian Mate Zalka, one of the escorts transferring the Russian gold reserve in 1920, was killed in action with the 12th Brigade. From Paris Tito organized the 'underground' transit of Yugoslav volunteers to the brigades.

Stalin kept a watchful eye on this brand of internationalism, placing an iron curtain between it and the Red Army personnel he sent to Spain. In the Soviet Union he mercilessly erased any trace of 'Red internationalism'. The purges eliminated foreign communists in the Comintern apparatus. German, Italian and Finnish communists were shot. The Polish Communist Party was virtually annihilated. Leaders of the 1919 Hungarian revolution were systematically 'liquidated'. Bela Kun was taunted, tortured and finally shot.[85] Vlada Ćopić, Yugoslav 'internationalist' in 1918 and commander of the 15th Lincoln International Brigade in 1937, was shot on his return from Spain.[86] 'General Kleber' died miserably in the Gulag.[87] The Red Army itself did not escape. Ian Berzin, otherwise 'General Grishin' in Spain, effectively the Soviet head of the Republican armies, was shot once he was back in the Soviet Union. This fate was meted out to others of the Soviet military contingent. Malinovskii feared for his life.[88]

Stalin aimed to wipe out the *internatsionalisty* physically and obliterate them politically. He never fully succeeded in either attempt, but inflicted fatal damage. The historical record was distorted, the idealism maligned and the notion of international class solidarity first caricatured and finally usurped by crude Stalinist monolithism, chauvinism and brute imperialism.

Notes

1. For data on prisoners of war, foreign labour and refugees, see *Internatsionalisty Trudiashchiesia zarubezhnykh stran – uchastniki bor'by za vlast' sovetov*, ed. A. Ia. Manusevich *et al.* (Moscow, 1967), pp. 14–46; specifically on prisoners of war A. Kh. Klevanskii, 'Voennoplennye Tsentral'nykh derzhav v tsarskoi i revoliutsionnoi Rossii (1914–1918 gg.)', in *Internatsionalisty v boiakh za vlast' Sovetov*, ed. M. A. Birman *et al.* (Moscow, 1965), pp. 21–62.
2. John Bradley, 'The Czechoslovak Revolt against the Bolsheviks', *Soviet Studies*, vol. XV, no. 2 (1963), pp. 125–6.
3. For text see Robert P. Browder and Alexander F. Kerensky, *The Russian Provisional Government 1917: Documents*, vol. 1 (Stanford, 1961), pp. 322–3.

4. Piotr S. Wandycz, *Soviet–Polish Relations, 1917–1921* (Cambridge, Mass., 1969), pp. 55–8.

5. *Pravda*, 3 (16) June 1917, reproduced in *Uchastie iugoslavskikh trudiashchikhsia v Oktiabr'skoi revoliutsii i grazhdanskoi voine v SSSR: Sbornik dokumentov i materialov*, ed. I. A. Khrenov *et al.* (Moscow, 1966), pp. 41–3.

6. I. D. Ochak, *Iugoslavianskie internatsionalisty v bor'be za pobedu Sovetskoi vlasti v Rossii (1917–1921 gody)* (Moscow, 1966), pp. 161–2.

7. V. I. Lenin, *Polnoe sobranie sochinenii*, vol. 35 (5th edn., Moscow, 1961), pp. 318–9. Speech to the Central Committee, 19 January 1918.

8. Birman, *Internatsionalisty v boiakh*, p. 62.

9. Details of TsFIG organization and personalities are in Manusevich, *Internatsionalisty*, pp. 176–228: see also documentary collection in 'Internatsional'nye gruppy RKP(b) i voinskie formirovaniia v Sovetskoi Rossii (1918–1920)', *Istoricheskii Arkhiv*, no. 4 (1957), pp. 3–37.

10. See *Boevoe sodruzhestvo trudiashchikhsia zarubezhnykh stran s narodami Sovetskoi Rossii (1917–1922)*, ed. G. V. Shumeiko (Moscow, 1957), p. 13. This invaluable collection of documents from Red Army archives evidently formed *Sbornik 1* of what was presumably intended to be a serial documentary publication under the rubric *Iz istorii mezhdunarodnoi proletarskoi solidarnosti* (Moscow, 1957). For details of the archive holding, *RGVA* (*TsGASA*) see *Putevoditel'*, vol. 1 (Minnesota, 1991), p. 104.

11. See Allan K. Wildman, *The Road to Soviet Power and Peace*, vol. II of *The End of the Russian Imperial Army* (Princeton, 1987), *passim*.

12. Cited in John Erickson, 'The Origins of the Red Army', *Revolutionary Russia*, ed. Richard Pipes (Harvard, 1968), p. 240.

13. The single most comprehensive work on the Latvian riflemen is *Istoriia Latyshskikh strelkov (1915–1920)*, ed. Ia. P. Krastyn (Riga, 1972): also Ia. Kaimin, *Latyshskie strelki v bor'be za pobedu Oktiabr'skoi revoliutsii 1917–1918* (Riga, 1961); T. Ia. Draudin, *Boevoi put' latyshskoi strelkovoi divizii v dni oktiabria i v gody grazhdanskoi voiny (1917–1920)* (Riga, 1960); and Uldris Germanis, *Oberst Vacietis und die lettischen Schützen im Weltkrieg und in der Oktoberrevolution* (Stockholm, 1974).

14. Manusevich, *Internatsionalisty*, p. 194.

15. On reaction on the part of the Allies and the Central Powers to the recruitment of prisoners of war see John Bradley, *Allied Intervention in Russia, 1917–1920* (London, 1968), pp. 54–7. In August 1918 the 'International Legion' had a reported strength of 231 men.

16. See N. Elanskii, *Iaroslav Gashek v revoliutsionnoi Rossii (1915–1920 gg.)* (Moscow, 1960); also B. S. Sanzhiev, *Iaroslav Gashek v vostochnoi Sibiri* (Irkutsk, 1961).

17. See document no. 46 (31 May 1918) in Shumeiko, *Boevoe sodruzhestvo*, pp. 77–9.

18. On Chinese units see *Kitaiskie dobrovol'tsy v boiakh za Sovetskuiu vlast' (1918–1922 gg.)*, ed. Liu Iun-An' (Moscow, 1961), placing the strength of 'Chinese volunteers in the Red Army' at 40,000–50,000.

19. On Miasnikov see Erickson, 'Origins', p. 247.

20. Figures in *ibid.*, p. 248. For figures see also S. M. Kliatskin, *Na zashchite Oktiabria. Organizatsiia reguliarnoi armii i militsionnoe stroitel'stvo v sovetskoi respublike, 1917–1920* (Moscow, 1965), p. 201, using *Vserosglavshtab* data.

For a recent discussion of these data and the discrepancies see M. A. Molodtsygin, *Krasnaia Armiia, Rozhdenie i Stanovlenie, 1917–1920 gg.* (Moscow, 1997), pp. 117–22.

21. Alexander Zatorski, *Dzieje pułku Biełgorodzkiego. 1 Polskiego pułku Rewolucyjnego w Rosji* (Warsaw, 1960), pp. 235–56.

22. Manusevich, *Internatsionalisty*, pp. 235–42.

23. Details in N. A. Popov, 'Kitaiskie internatsional'nye chastei', *Voprosy istorii*, no. 10 (1957), pp. 104–24: quotes *Shenboa*, 22 May 1919, that 30,000–40,000 Chinese were currently serving with the Red Army. Nineteen Chinese were evidently attached in April 1918 to the 1st Company of the 1st Revolutionary 'Red Warsaw' Regiment.

24. For repatriation figures see Klevanskii in Birman, *Internatsionalisty v boiakh*, note to pp. 63–4.

25. See *ibid.*, note to p. 65.

26. Text in Manusevich, *Internatsionalisty*, p. 575.

27. A. Kh. Klevanskii, *Chekhoslovatskie internatsionalisty i prodannyi korpus* (Moscow, 1965), p. 240.

28. Manusevich, *Internatsionalisty*, p. 566.

29. 'Internatsional'nye gruppy RKP(b)', *Istoricheskii Arkhiv*, no. 4 (1957), p. 14.

30. Shumeiko, *Boevoe sodruzhestvo*, document no. 139, pp. 164–5; also document no. 140, 'Spisok voiskovykh chastei organizovannykh Komissiei po sozdaniiu Internatsional'noi Krasnoi Armii', pp. 165–6; also document no. 156 'Spisok internatsional'nykh chastei Krasnoi Armii' (24 April 1919), pp. 178–9.

31. See *Revvoensovet Respubliki (6 sent. 1918 g.–28 avg. 1923 g.)*, ed. A. P. Nenarokov (Moscow, 1991).

32. Shumeiko, *Boevoe sodruzhestvo*, document no. 133, p. 150.

33. See *ibid.*, 'Internatsional'nye formirovaniia na territorii Turkestana', documents nos 385–407, pp. 319–415; also *Inostrannaia voennaia interventsiia i grazhdanskaia voina v Srednei Azii i Kazakhstane. Dokumenty i materialy*, ed. Kh. Sh. Inoiatov *et al.*, vol. I (Alma-Ata, 1963) and vol. II (Alma-Ata, 1964).

34. See A. P. Nenarokov, *Vostochnyi front 1918* (Moscow, 1969); also David Footman, *Civil War in Russia* (London, 1961), pp. 145–50.

35. See I. G. Gizzatullin, *Zashchishchaia zavoevania Oktiabria. Tsentral'naia musul'manskaia voennaia kollegiia 1918–1920* (Moscow, 1979) on the 'Moslem Worker–Peasant Red Army' (*Musul'manskaia Raboche-Krest'ianskaia Armiia*), the Tartar-Bashkir Battalion, the Moslem Rifle Brigade, pp. 21–74.

36. On Subki and the Turkish Communist Party, the Central Bureau of Moslem Communist Organizations (renamed the Central Bureau of Communist Organizations of the Peoples of the East), Manusevich, *Internatsionalisty*, pp. 222–4. Subki was first imprisoned and then drowned with 14 of his associates in January 1921, on his return to Turkey.

37. Manusevich, *Internatsionalisty*, p. 225. POWs also had to be protected against 'the putrid influence of social-chauvinism, reformism and nationalism'.

38. On the Siberian partisans Ia. Zhigalin, 'Partizanskoe dvizhenie v Zapadnoi Sibiri', *Proletarskaia Revoliutsiia*, no. 106 (1930), pp. 98–114; also M. I. Stishov, *Bolshevistsoe podpol'e i partizanskoe dvizhenie v Sibiri v gody grazhdanskoi voiny (1918–1920 gg.)* (Moscow, 1962); on the *Kolchakovshchina*,

Jonathan D. Smele, *Civil War in Siberia. The Anti-Bolshevik Government of Admiral Kolchak 1918–1920* (Cambridge, 1996).

39. Details of the 'Irkutsk International Division' in V. A. Kondrat'ev, 'Iz istorii bor'by nemetskikh voennoplennykh internatsionalistov za ustanovlenie Sovetskoi vlasti v Sibiri i na Dal'nem Vostoke v 1917–1920 gg.', in *Noiabr'skaia revoliutsiia v Germanii. Sbornik statei i materialov*, ed. V. D. Kul'bakin *et al.* (Moscow, 1960), pp. 470–1.

40. On the bitter ideological struggle between the Bolsheviks, 'petty bourgeois parties' and the anarchists see N. S. Lar'kov, 'Iz istorii ideino-politicheskoi bor'by v anti-kolchakovskom partizanskom dvizhenii v Sibiri', in *Iz istorii interventsii i grazhdanskoi voiny v Sibiri i na Dal'nem Vostoke 1917–1922 gg.*, ed. Iu. I. Korablev and Iu. I. Shishkin (Novosibirsk, 1985), pp. 134–41.

41. Franz Borkenau, *World Communism. A History of the Communist International*, intro. Raymond Aron (Ann Arbor, 1962), pp. 113–15.

42. Chief of the General Staff of the Hungarian Red Army, Aurel Shtrom'feld (Stromfeld) to Bela Kun, document no. 320 (11 May 1919) in *Vengerskie internatsionalisty v Oktiabr'skoi revoliutsii i grazhdanskoi voine v SSSR. Sbornik dokumentov*, ed. P. A. Zhilin *et al.*, vol. II (Moscow, 1968), p. 63.

43. Franz Borkenau, *World Communism*, p. 115.

44. *Vengerskie internatsionalisty*, vol. II, document no. 316, p. 60.

45. *Ibid.*, document no. 317, pp. 60–1.

46. *Ibid.*, document no. 335 (14 July 1919), p. 81.

47. Text, document no. 161, *Vengerskie internatsionalisty*, vol. 1, pp. 242–3.

48. RVSR order no. 730 (17 April 1919), document no. 153 in Shumeiko, *Boevoe sodruzhestvo*, pp. 176–7.

49. Listing of international units at the front and in the rear, 24 April 1919, *Boevoe sodruzhestvo*, document no. 156, pp. 178–9; Field Staff RVSR report, May 1919, report on Red Army international units in *Vengerskie internatsionalisty*, vol. II, document no. 326, p. 69.

50. See, for example, document no. 323, pp. 66–8 in *Vengerskie internatsionalisty*, vol. II.

51. Shumeiko, *Boevoe sodruzhestvo*, document no. 440 (13 May 1919), pp. 451–2, 'No teper' mozhno idti na Rumyniiu tol'ko cherez trup Grigor'eva'.

52. Table in Shumeiko, *Boevoe sodruzhestvo*, document no. 449, Kiev (12 June 1919), pp. 462–3; see also notes to document no. 449, p. 464.

53. *Ibid.*, document no. 451 (20 June 1919), pp. 465–7; note to p. 466 on the slow progress forming the International Division, only 1,337 rifles of various types available.

54. *Ibid.*, document no. 452, pp. 467–8, signed by Sklianskii, Vatsetis, Aralov and Okulov.

55. This report (8 September 1919) is cited as note to document no. 340 in *Vengerskie internatsionalisty*, vol. II, p. 88.

56. See document no. 337, 15 September 1919, under paragraph 5 in *Vengerskie internatsionalisty*, vol. II, p. 84, para 5: 2nd International Rifle Regiment to be considered part of establishing the '1st division of the international corps'. See also document no. 340, p. 87.

57. Document no. 340, *Vengerskie internatsionalisty*, vol. II, p. 87.

58. Details on desertion and re-organization in document no. 340, *Vengerskie internatsionalisty*, here p. 88.

59. Text, 'Doklad Voennoi komissii v Federatsiiu inostrannykh grupp RKP(b).', 18 November 1919, document no. 340 in *Vengerskie internatsionalisty*, vol. II, pp. 87–9.

60. To compile a complete and accurate order of battle of international units presents formidable difficulties, partly from lack of data and partly from the bewildering sequence of changes in unit designations. One listing is provided in *Grazhdanskaia voina i voennaia interventsiia v SSSR. Entsiklopediia*, ed. S. S. Khromov *et al.* (Moscow, 1987) under 'Internatsional'nye formirovaniia Krasnoi Armii', pp. 235–8; it is possible to search the huge strength tabulations, order of battle and military–statistical material in *Direktivy komandovaniia frontov Krasnoi Armii (1917–1922 gg.). Sbornik dokumentov v 4-kh tomakh*, ed N. N. Azovtsev *et al.*, here vol. IV 'Materialy, ukazateli' (Moscow, 1978).

61. Shumeiko, *Boevoe sodruzhestvo*, document no. 403, pp. 412–13.

62. Robert Conquest, *The Great Terror* (London, 1968), p. 80.

63. *Vengerskie internatsionalisty*, vol. II, document no. 659 'Akt o priniatii okhrany zolotogo zapasa RSFSR dlia dostavki ego iz Sibiri v Kazan' (12 April 1920), pp. 395–7.

64. Borkenau, *World Communism*, on the Comintern, pp. 165–9.

65. Text in M. N. Tukhachevskii, *Voina klassov* (Moscow, 1921), pp. 138–40.

66. Birman, *Internatsionalisty*, pp. 581–2.

67. Recounted in two famous studies combined in one recent reprint, *M. Tukhachevskii. Pokhod na Vislu – Iu. Pilsudskii. Voina 1920 goda* (Moscow, 1992).

68. Shumeiko, *Boevoe sodruzhestvo*, document no. 206 (Pt IV, Zakliuchenie), p. 229. The Federation announced this as its swan-song, its work in this form done, but its significance as the first example of implementing practical internationalism (*prakticheskii internatsionalizm*) would endure.

69. Shumeiko, *Boevoe sodruzhestvo*, document no. 207, pp. 230–1.

70. The business of formally dissolving the Commission proceeded so slowly that it simply continued to function.

71. Shumeiko, *Boevoe sodruzhestvo*, document no. 272, 'Proekt voennoi komissii pri TsFIG o formirovanii internatsional'nykh chastei Krasnoi Armii (12 November 1920)', pp. 286–8.

72. John J. Stephan, *The Russian Far East: A History* (Stanford, 1994), on the Far Eastern Republic, pp. 141–55; also *Geroicheskie gody bor'by i pobed. Dal'nii Vostok v ogne grazhdanskoi voiny*, ed. F. I. Petrov *et al.* (Moscow, 1968), on the re-organization of the NRA, pp. 231–41; also B. M. Shereshevskii, *V bitvakh za Dal'nii Vostok (1920–1922 gg.)* (Novosibirsk, 1974), on re-organizing the NRA, pp. 81–92.

73. Shumeiko, *Boevoe sodruzhestvo*, 'Kitaiskie i koreiskie partizanskie otriady v Sibiri i na Dal'nem Vostoke', documents nos 367–74, pp. 384–90.

74. M. A. Persits, *Dal'nevostochnaia Respublika i Kitai. Rol' DVR v bor'be Sovetskoi vlasti za druzhbu s Kitaem v 1920–1922 gg.* (Moscow, 1962), pp. 262–3.

75. Shumeiko, *Boevoe sodruzhestvo*, documents nos 376–7, pp. 391–4.

76. Persits, *Dal'nevostochnaia Respublika i Kitai*, pp. 198–9.

77. Figures in *Grazhdanskaia voina i voennaia interventsiia v SSSR. Entsiklopediia*, p. 236.

78. Discussed in Marc Jansen, 'International Class Solidarity or Foreign Intervention? Internationalists and Latvian Rifles in the Russian Revolution and the Civil War', *International Review of Social History*, vol. XXXI, pt 1, pp. 68–79.
79. See Erich Wollenberg, *The Red Army* (London, 1938, here 1978 repr.), p. 202.
80. Lembert Pern, *V vikhre voennykh let. Vospominaniia* (Tallin, 1969), pp. 22–30.
81. John Erickson, *The Soviet High Command: A Military–Political History 1918–1941* (London, 1962; repr. Boulder, Col., 1984), p. 298.
82. Figures in *Sovetskaia voennaiia entsiklopediia*, vol. 3 (Moscow, 1977), p. 567, under 'Internatsional'nye brigady v Ispanii'.
83. Burnett Bolloten, *The Spanish Revolution. The Left and the Struggle for Power during the Civil War* (Chapel Hill, 1979), p. 282 on Manfred Zalmanovich Stern.
84. On 'Walter', *Hispańska wojna narodowrewolucyjna 1936–1939 i udział w niej Polaków* (Supplement to *Wojskowy Przegląd Historyczny*, no. 3, 1986) (Warsaw, 1986), pp. 41–3. After 1945 he became Polish Deputy Defence Minister and was assassinated in 1947.
85. Details in Robert Conquest, *The Great Terror*, p. 433.
86. Ochak, *Iugoslavianskie internatsionalisty*, note to p. 105, 'the victim of unjustified oppression'.
87. Bolloten, *The Spanish Revolution*, p. 286, 'unjustly accused and convicted, died in a labour camp, posthumously rehabilitated'.
88. R. Ia. Malinovskii (Marshal Malinovskii), 'Gnevnye vikhri Ispanii' in *Pod znamenem Ispanskoi respubliki 1936–1939*, ed. N. N. Voronov *et al.* (Moscow, 1965), here p. 190 on the implications of being identified as a 'non-returner'.

8

Paths to World Socialist Revolution: West and East

Boris A. Starkov

Translated by Josephine Forsyth

When the Bolshevik party seized political power in October 1917, acquiring the responsibilities of a governing party, among the tasks it had to tackle were those of formulating its own domestic and foreign policies. The Bolshevik leaders set up a harsh dictatorship at home, while banking on the mistaken assumption that socialist revolution would very soon triumph in the rest of the world. The political and economic situation in the countries of Eastern and Western Europe supported their illusions, encouraging them to believe that their hopes were about to be realized. In 1919 an acute political crisis flared up in the countries of the former Triple Alliance, Germany and Austria–Hungary, which resulted in the emergence of Soviet republics in Hungary, Bavaria and Slovakia. The Bolshevik leadership tried to organize military and political support for these republics by sending them Red Army troops, weapons and propaganda material. Their efforts met with powerful opposition on the part of the Entente. General Haller's 70,000-strong Polish corps was dispatched from France to Galicia in a remarkably short time. Haller routed the forces of the West-Ukrainian People's Republic and pinned down units of the 1st Ukrainian Soviet Army. At the same time General Denikin's White forces began an offensive against Ukraine. A planned advance by the 3rd Ukrainian Soviet Army was abandoned because of the defection of the divisional commander, N. A. Grigor'ev.

A second attempt to set off world socialist revolution was made during the Soviet–Polish war of 1920, but again the impetus for revolution was thwarted. The unsuccessful campaign to take Warsaw and subsequent defeat of Red Army forces indicated to the Bolsheviks that their assessment of the actual economic and political situation abroad was inadequate. Military intelligence was not in a position to provide them with an accurate appraisal of the political situation in Western Europe. It was necessary to set up a special office within the state security apparatus which would be in charge of gathering foreign intelligence.

On 20 December 1920 the Cheka (*Vserossiiskaia Chrezvychainaia Komissiia*) chairman Feliks Dzerzhinskii signed Order No. 169.[1] This order disbanded the existing Foreign Sub-Section of the Cheka and set up a new one with full Section status. The first head was Ia. Kh. Davtian, who was at that time also in charge of the Baltic and Polish sections of the People's Commissariat for Foreign Affairs (NKID). The staff of the new Foreign Section of the Cheka were highly qualified specialists from the better-off ranks of the population. They had enjoyed a good all-round education and were competent linguists. The Foreign Section occupied a privileged position among the other departments of the Cheka (later OGPU). Its staff frequently worked abroad, and the section head was usually one of the deputy chairmen of the Cheka or OGPU. In the 1920s and 1930s a network of Soviet intelligence agents existed in practically every country in the world.

Besides the Cheka and the NKID, a third institution was involved with foreign relations. The Comintern, or Third International, had been founded by Lenin, Trotskii and Zinov'ev in 1919 with the task of bringing about world revolution. It is necessary to elucidate the roles of these three bodies. The NKID conducted foreign policy for the Soviet government and in the early 1920s its trade and diplomatic missions often provided cover for Comintern agents. The Comintern had military training as one of its top priorities and worked in close co-operation with Soviet security forces under the command of the Red Army Intelligence Directorate, and with the Foreign Section of the Cheka. The Cheka was responsible for state security in the Soviet regime. It had been created as a special force to combat counter-revolution in December 1917, but after the Soviet–Polish war foreign intelligence became one of its major concerns. During the early 1920s all these bodies focused their activity on preparation for world revolution.

In the first half of the 1920s the leaders of the USSR and the Comintern were still evolving policies aimed at initiating world socialist revolution. Until recently relevant documents were not available to researchers – they were kept strictly secret in the state archives of the former USSR. Today the situation has changed and historians are in a better position to establish what actually happened at that time.

Germany or the Balkans?

Defeat at the gates of Warsaw in 1920 did not at first cast a shadow on the prospect of world socialist revolution. Documents show that the leadership of Soviet Russia continued to support political activity by the working class in Europe. Bolshevik foreign policy was still dominated by the belief that socialist revolutions would occur around the world. This policy is seen most clearly in attempts to start a 'German October' in the autumn of 1923, and also to initiate revolution in the Balkans.

In the spring of 1922 the Foreign Section of OGPU prepared a special report for the Politburo of the Russian Communist Party.[2] The report summarized information collected by the Registration Directorate of the Red Army (military intelligence), the Comintern, the NKID and the Section's own agency, on the prospects for socialist revolution in Western Europe. The report was strictly confidential, prepared in the first place for the leaders of the Soviet delegation to the Genoa conference. The likelihood of revolution was connected to events taking place in Germany, Poland and Italy.[3] It was proposed that workers, peasants and radical members of the intelligentsia should be used as the shock troops of revolution. Special emphasis was placed on 'young people keen to take action'. It was proposed to infiltrate reliable military and political personnel into these countries. Their job was to build up stocks of armaments, train military units and spread propaganda among the population. It is interesting that the Foreign Section's proposals to OGPU suggested that the 'dissenting Galician element' should be used for military activity in Poland.[4] In Italy anarchists were seen as the potential leaders of revolution, and the Foreign Section went so far as to propose that OGPU should free some of them who were locked up in Moscow's Butyrki prison. After a 'necessary explanatory briefing' they could be sent to work in Italy.[5]

Germany had a special place in plans for the world socialist revolution, and a whole section was devoted to it in the report. The crisis in the German economy after defeat in the First World War was described, and special emphasis placed on relationships between the government and political parties. The report's main conclusion was that these three countries were the potential vanguard of revolution in Europe.

In the summer of 1923 the political situation in Western Europe became much more unstable. A parliamentary crisis in Germany placed the country on the brink of a new revolutionary upheaval. A delegation of the German Communist Party arrived in Moscow in August for talks and political consultations with the Executive Committee of the Comintern and the USSR leadership. A two-week conference of representatives of the communist parties of Germany, France, Czechoslovakia and Poland began on 21 August, under the auspices of the Comintern. The purpose of the meeting was to discuss the organization of a cordon around Germany in the event of intervention by the Entente.[6]

On 23 August 1923 a 'Commission on the International Situation' was set up at a Politburo meeting. The commission's main task was the conduct and co-ordination of events in Germany. Its members were G. Zinov'ev, L. Trotskii, I. Stalin, K. Radek and G. Chicherin. They were later joined by L. Kamenev, F. Dzerzhinskii, Iu. Piatakov and G. Sokol'nikov. On 27 September the commission was declared to be in permanent session.

On the personal instructions of the People's Commissar for the Army and Navy, Lev Trotskii, the operations section of the Military Revolutionary Council drew up a timetable for the German revolution: a series of armed uprisings in the cities and regions of Germany.[7] On 4 October at a Politburo meeting a date, 9 November, was fixed for an armed rebellion in Berlin, and the Russian Communist Party (Bolshevik) delegation to be sent to Germany was named.[8] The delegation included Iu. Piatakov, K. Radek, V. Kuibyshev and Ia. Rudzutak. (The two latter were later replaced by V. Shmidt and N. Krestinskii.) The German revolution was allocated 400,000 US dollars in financial aid. M. Rakoshi, S. Lozovskii, L. Shatskin, E. Tseitlin, A. Stetskii and others entered Germany illegally. Graduates and senior students of the Special Faculty of the Military Academy of the Red Army were also sent to Germany. They knew the country and were trained in intelligence and diversionary work. Among them were M. Shtern, V. Karpov, I. Klochko, S. F. Anulov, M. Rybakov and V. Balk. They built up stocks of weapons and acted as instructors in the military units being formed at that time.

In September I. Unshlikht, deputy chairman both of OGPU and the Military Revolutionary Council of the Republic, was in Germany, together with M. Trilisser, head of OGPU's Foreign Section and Ia. Berzin, deputy head of the Registration Directorate of the Red Army. Others who played an active part were the Consul-General in

Hamburg, G. Shklovskii, the Russian Press Agency correspondent, G. Kaminskii, and also staff from the West-European Secretariat of the Comintern, Ia. Reikh, E. Stasov, S. Osinskaia-Unshlikht, B. Idel'son and M. Grol'man. A Comintern representative, A. Gural'skii (Klein), was appointed to the Central Committee of the German Communist Party (CPG) and took up the post of secretary. By October 1923 the CPG had 350,000 members, 900 'proletarian companies' (130,000 men), 330 groups of partisans and 5,000 men who had attended Red Commanders courses. The stock of weapons consisted of 11,000 rifles, 2,000 revolvers and 150 machine-guns.[9]

The military wing of the CPG was a powerful organization, consisting of 90 officials, 11 secret army training establishments, and 18 laboratories and workshops for arms production. The organization was divided into five sections: training, weapons, intelligence, *Abwehr* (infiltrating judicial institutions, intelligence and counter-intelligence, police, exposing *agents provocateurs* and spies) and a section for subversive activity which itself had five sub-sections. These controlled work in the trade unions, fascist organizations, the police, army, industrial and press circles. The Soviet organization, called the 'Soviet Instruction Unit', was accommodated in the Soviet Embassy on Unter den Linden. The Unit was headed by a professional Soviet intelligence officer, Stefan Zhbikovskii. The German organization was headed by a Latvian, the Red Army divisional commander Vol'demar Roze. After Roze's arrest another intelligence officer S. Firin took over at the start of 1924. The whole intelligence operation was directed by a Russified German, Werner Rakov, better known as the Comintern official Feliks Vol'f.

The Soviet military and political leadership took steps designed to support the embryonic revolution. Trotskii, as president of the Military Revolutionary Council of the Republic, ordered cavalry units of the Red Army to start moving to the Western frontiers of the USSR, in order to be ready to move to help the German proletariat as soon as an order was given, and to start advancing into Western Europe. Many of the officials involved already imagined the red flag flying on the Eiffel Tower and Red Army tents in London's Hyde Park.[10]

At the same time Evgenii Berens, Trotskii's personal envoy, started talks with the 'Guchkov Circle', a group of military and political experts drawn from the Russian émigré community, about the possibility of unhindered passage across Poland by troops of the Red Army on their way to assist the German proletariat.[11] In September 1923 demonstrations by workers began in Kraków – clashes were already taking place at barricades. Then workers in Lithuania and Estonia also started protest meetings. It seemed as though all the hopes and predictions of the Kremlin were coming true.

However, events overturned the plans of the Soviet leadership. The High Command of the Entente were well briefed by French intelligence about the Kremlin's plans. Additional contingents of occupying forces were sent to the Ruhr and Silesia, and the British government undertook a diplomatic *démarche* against the USSR. White émigré military units on the Western frontiers of the USSR were mobilized, numbering 50,000 men. To lead these units General P. N. Wrangel, Commander-in-Chief of the (White) Russian Army, sent 50 generals and senior officers from the Kingdom of Serbs, Croats and Slovenes.[12] At the same time reports were received in Moscow about a planned uprising in the Far East. Talks with the Guchkov Circle were broken off. Trotskii sent Berens a letter in code in which he proposed that the talks should be represented as a personal initiative by Berens himself.[13] French counter-intelligence had succeeded in neutralizing the military leadership of the CPG.

Faced with this situation the Executive Committee of the Comintern, and above all the Chairman, Zinov'ev, showed hesitation and indecisiveness. Contradictory directives and orders were sent to Germany. This most obviously affected the organization of the armed uprising in Hamburg. Serious disagreements arose in the Commission on the International Situation. Trotskii wanted decisive action, but the others wavered. This eventually led to a serious leadership crisis.

In the final analysis the defeat of the German revolution in the autumn of 1923 was the consequence of a number of factors, among which the indecision of the Comintern leadership and the Soviet government played a very significant part. The West was also seriously underestimated. Intelligence reports sent from abroad usually gave an objective assessment, but the leaders of Soviet Russia already by that time completely ignored all information which did not fit in with their preconceived ideas. Moreover intelligence officers abroad frequently concentrated on matters of secondary importance. Trotskii wrote the following in his 'Letter to the Politburo' on 29 December 1923: 'The German Communist Party leaders cannot be unaware of the fact that the majority of members of the Politburo do not have an opportunity to follow events in Germany closely, and obviously need information from German comrades themselves. We need to reconsider seriously the question of revolution and information as a whole.'[14]

In the mid-1920s the start of world socialist revolution was still expected in Europe. The Soviet leaders were closely watching the

Balkans. In Karl Radek's graphic expression the Balkan states were a 'powder keg, the explosion of which would scatter the sparks of socialist revolution around the whole of Europe'.[15] As early as 1921 a Soviet intelligence officer, Dr Gol'denshtadt, had been sent to Bulgaria. Gol'denshtadt very quickly managed to create a highly efficient intelligence service in the Balkans. He helped in the successful expulsion from Bulgaria of the remaining troops of the Russian Army under Wrangel. Bulgarian communists even made an attempt to seize power by an armed uprising. In 1922 a Comintern official, I. A. Piatnitskii, arrived in Varna by illegal channels. The former tsarist general Komissarov accompanied him as a military adviser, and the two were based in a monastery near Varna. Weapons and detachments of communist troops were sent to the Balkans from Odessa via the Black Sea. The Soviet government counted on revolution succeeding in the Balkans without any special efforts. However the attempted revolution in September 1923 ended in failure.[16]

Defeat of left-wing forces did not discourage hotheads in the Comintern and Soviet leadership. In 1924 further attempts at revolutionary uprisings were made in the Balkans. In early 1924 the new head of the Soviet Intelligence Service in the Balkans, V. S. Nesterovich-Iaroslavskii, arrived in Vienna. He had been a professional soldier and had fought in the First World War. He had graduated from the Infantry Academy in 1916, and by 1917 was already a staff-captain. Nesterovich joined the Bolshevik party in 1917, volunteered to serve in the Red Army in 1918 and was given command of the 1st Moscow regiment, followed by a brigade, then the 42nd Rifle Division and the 9th Cavalry Division. His cavalry fought distinguished battles against Makhno's insurgents. Nesterovich was awarded the Order of the Military Red Banner for personal bravery in 1919, followed in 1921 by a Revolutionary Weapon of Honour, the highest award in the Soviet forces. From 1922 to 1923 he was an instructor in the Red Army Military Academy, and subsequently was sent abroad on subversive intelligence duties.

At the beginning of 1925 Nesterovich proposed that Pan-Slavist ideas could be used to start world socialist revolution. In a detailed memorandum addressed to the Politburo and the Presidium of the Soviet Union, he described the Pan-Slavist movement in the countries of Eastern and Western Europe, and proposed ways of taking advantage of the various political, cultural and educational organizations of the Slavonic countries. He strongly recommended co-operation with the Macedonian Military–Revolutionary Organization. According to

Nesterovich revolution should start in Bulgaria and in the Kingdom of Serbs, Croats and Slovenes, and then spread across Austria into Western Europe.[17]

Under the heading 'Paths to revolution in the Balkans', the memorandum gave a detailed description of the countries of Western Europe from the point of view of the prospects for socialist revolution. The most likely candidates were the countries of the Little Entente, and also Austria and Germany. Nesterovich said that France was the main enemy of Soviet Russia. He came to this conclusion because French governmental, financial and industrial circles were actively supporting the Russian emigration. On a copy of the memorandum, preserved in Stalin's archive, there is a note in the margin: 'Correct'.[18] It can be surmised that this document was studied very carefully by the leaders, despite the fact that sometimes the style and content reveal it to be a rather hackneyed piece of political writing.[19]

An attempt to put the plan into practice was made in 1925. On 18 April an explosion occurred during the funeral service in St Sofia's Cathedral for the murdered governor of Sofia, General Georgiev. This was to be the signal for an armed uprising by communist groups throughout the country. The Military Centre, an organization set up by the Bulgarian Communist Party and dedicated to the preparation and carrying out of just such an event, was responsible for this uprising, but for many years it was believed to be the work of anarchists and activists of the Macedonian Military–Revolutionary Organization.

The political leadership of the USSR were involved in the uprising, but the Bulgarian police were informed in good time about the plan and only a few hours after the explosion Sofia was literally flooded by thousands of police and soldiers. Police raids started in the workers' districts, and martial law was declared in the country. It turned out that the Bulgarian police had prepared 'blacklists' in advance, and during the night of 18–19 April a massacre began. In the provinces the authorities, without even explaining that they were hunting criminals, dragged people out onto the street and shot them without trial.[20]

This venture ended in defeat not only of the communists but also of all the democratic forces in Bulgaria, Romania and the Kingdom of Serbs, Croats and Slovenes. Mass terror was directed not only at radical organizations but also to a considerable extent against Slavonic cultural organizations in Europe. Anti-Slav sentiments increased considerably. In a number of right-wing newspapers in Western Europe articles appeared about the racial inferiority of the Slavs, who were said to be only capable of destroying state institutions.

It is clear that Nesterovich-Iaroslavskii was very distressed by these events. At first he organized help for Bulgarian and Yugoslav political refugees, but then became deeply depressed. At that time he thought it was possible to resign from the Soviet secret service, and he wrote to OGPU and the Communist Party about his wish to leave the service, explaining that he wanted to live as a private citizen. However M. A. Trilisser, on behalf of the Foreign Section, decided that the resignation of such a well-informed agent could not be permitted. The German communist Golke was instructed to meet Nesterovich, and during discussions in a café in Mainz, Nesterovich was poisoned. According to the official version of events released to employees of the Foreign Section of OGPU, Nesterovich had been recruited by the British agent Sidney Reilly in Moscow as early as 1918.[21] However, few people believed this. The defector G. Besedovskii wrote in his memoirs that the real reason for the death of Nesterovich was his attempt to leave the secret service, and his detailed knowledge of the Kremlin's plan for Western Europe.[22]

World Islamic revolution

The colonial countries of the East were another potentially important location for socialist revolution. Here the Bolsheviks were putting their faith in national-liberation movements. As hopes for victorious revolution in the West faded, ever more expectations were focused on China, India and Afghanistan. In 1919 the Bolsheviks began to take the idea of revolution starting in the East seriously. This view was encouraged by the delayed revolution in the West. Among the Soviet leadership one of the most zealous supporters of action in the East was Trotskii. He wrote: 'our Red Army will make a fairly modest contribution to both attack and defence in the European sphere of politics ... the situation will be otherwise if we face East. ... At the present moment the road to India may turn out to be shorter and less strewn with obstacles than the road to Soviet Hungary ...'.[23]

In order to achieve their aims the Bolsheviks resorted to the most unprincipled deals and alliances. In the struggle with imperialism they tried to exploit not only national-liberation movements, but also the religious fanaticism of the people of the East and such transnational doctrines as Pan-Islamism and Pan-Turkism, Buddhism and the mystical teachings of the East. On 14 July 1919 the chairman of the Kalmyk Central Executive Committee, A. Chapchaev, proposed to Lenin that Buddhism should be used in the struggle against the British in India.[24]

His letter was sent immediately to the People's Commissariat for Foreign Affairs so that steps could be taken to put the proposal into practice. Around the same time another idea emerged, namely the use of Pan-Islamism to start the world socialist revolution. This suggestion came about in the following way.

An armed uprising by the communist-inspired group 'Spartak' took place in Berlin during the summer of 1919. Karl Radek, secretary of the Executive Committee of the Comintern, played a very active and direct part in its organization. He was arrested for his role in the uprising by the German police and incarcerated in Berlin's Moabit prison. While still in prison he was appointed ambassador of the Ukrainian Soviet Republic to Germany. Radek's prison cell became an unusual kind of political salon. It was here that contacts were established with military and political leaders and ideas about the future reconstruction of the whole world were worked out, which in many ways were to determine the course of world history in the twentieth century.[25]

One of these outstanding politicians undoubtedly was the acknowledged leader of Pan-Turkism, the former Minister of War in the Young Turks' government, Enver Pasha. One of the leaders of the Young Turk revolution, he was a most popular figure in political circles in the East. He had come to the notice of Russian military intelligence in the years before the First World War. As a fervent russophobe and supporter of the German–Turkish alliance, Enver Pasha did a lot to involve Turkey in the First World War on the side of the Triple Alliance. Under his leadership the Turkish army achieved some success and inflicted a serious defeat on the British Expeditionary Force. Enver Pasha was hailed as a national hero and his authority was extremely high in Islamic political circles. After Turkey's defeat in the war, the forced resignation of the Young Turk government and the signing of the Mudros armistice, he was declared to be a war criminal, condemned to death and put in prison. He managed to escape to Germany. Here, in the summer of 1919, with the help of the leading German secret agent Niedermaier, he met and made contact with Karl Radek. After the necessary political briefing Radek gave Enver a personal invitation from Lenin to visit Soviet Russia.[26]

Talks took place in Moscow between Lenin, Stalin and Trotskii on the one side and Enver Pasha on the other in conditions of strict secrecy.[27] Mustafa Subkhi, leader of the Turkish communists and the Volga Tatar Mirsaid Sultan-Galiev, a prominent member of the national-liberation movement, acted as intermediaries. The latter was chairman of the Muslim military college, run by the People's

Commissariat for the Army and Navy, and also head of the Eastern section of the Political Directorate of the Red Army. Sultan-Galiev had a number of discussions with Lenin and Stalin about the Bolshevik leaders' underestimation of the growing desire of the Eastern peoples for self-determination. Evidently the concept of a world Islamic revolution grew out of these conversations.[28]

This was in fact the subject of the talks with Enver. The Bolshevik leaders considered the Islamic revolution to be an integral part of the world socialist revolution. Enver himself did not share these goals, and was pursuing his own aim of creating 'Great Turan'.[29] However at this stage he actively supported co-operation with the communists and even put forward a plan for the start of revolution in the East. He believed that Russia's main opponent was Britain. He proposed starting with the sovietization of Central Asia, India, China and Afghanistan. The main attacking force was to be made up of Muslim military units combined with the support of communist groups in these countries. Enver proposed that the military formations should be commanded by Turkish officers who were in Soviet Russia as prisoners of war from the First World War.

These ideas generally accorded with the views of the Bolshevik leaders about the development of the world revolutionary movement. After a resolution by the leadership of Soviet Russia a start was made on practical measures to implement these plans. On Trotskii's suggestion the formation of three Muslim cavalry corps was begun in the southern Urals. It was intended that they should subsequently be sent to India and China to 'stimulate' revolutionary processes in the East. By that date the military and political leadership of Soviet Russia had already acquired some experience in forming army units from non-Russian ethnic groups. The Red Army had Bashkir, Tatar, Kalmyk and other units serving in its ranks.

Steps were taken to set up a Soviet strategic military base in Turkestan. On 16 October 1919, Lenin sent a letter to Sh. Eliava, chairman of the special temporary commission of the RSFSR Sovnarkom on Turkestan affairs. In particular Lenin wrote: 'It is essential to set up quickly in Turkestan an independent base, even if it is small. Make cartridges (we'll send machines), repair military equipment, get coal, oil, iron. ... Get weapons, links with America and Europe, give aid to people of the East in the struggle with imperialism.'[30] By a resolution of the Politburo and Sovnarkom the Turkestan Commission of the All-Russian Central Executive Committee and the Sovnarkom of the RSFSR was created with Sh. Eliava as chairman.[31] In the summer of 1920 the

Turkbiuro of the Central Committee was set up, headed by
G. Sokol'nikov.[32]

Party members responsible for preparing revolution in the East were
trained at the Eastern Faculty of the Red Army Military Academy. The
head of the faculty from 1919 to 1921 was the former General
A. Snesarev, a well-known Russian agent and a specialist on Eastern
affairs. He considered that 'Russian Turkestan' could serve as 'a base for
preliminary operations in the conquest of India'. Snesarev proposed
two routes for military campaigns with the aim of getting through to
the southern oceans: through Afghanistan, or directly to India via the
Hindu Kush, Tibet and the Himalayas.[33] Apart from preparing Red
Army campaigns it was planned that aid should be given to revolutionaries. On 20 September 1920, the question of giving arms to India was
discussed at a plenum of the Central Committee of the Russian
Communist Party. The following resolution was adopted: 'To accept
the necessity in principle of giving arms and gold, the amount and
timescale to be agreed after consultation with corresponding agencies.
The Turkestan Commission will be responsible for carrying out the
resolution.'[34]

Action taken by the Bolsheviks included more than setting up a military base. Besides this they began to train military and political personnel on Red Commanders courses. Tashkent became the training
centre. Army units were being formed from the native populations in
Central Asia. Ironically it was these units and not the irregular rebel
units which made up the main troops of the Basmachi movement, the
national movement directed against the sovietization of the Central
Asian republics.[35]

It would be a mistake to think that Bolshevik leaders were beginning
to lose interest in initiating revolutionary processes in Central Asia by
the end of 1920. The Bolsheviks were certainly forced to take British
diplomatic pressure into account, and the signature on 16 March 1921
of a provisional Anglo-Soviet agreement marking the political recognition of Soviet Russia required a measure of political compromise from
both sides.

The Bolshevik leaders made a political error in identifying the key
figure in the East. When tested by events, Enver Pasha turned out to be
a purely national Islamic leader. Information gathered by secret agents
of the Special Section of the Cheka, who were keeping him under sur-
veillance, revealed that the Muslim units, armed and equipped in
Soviet Russia, could at any moment turn their weapons against the
Bolsheviks. At this time the newly created Eastern Section of the

Cheka, headed by Ia. Kh. Peters, started an intelligence operation named the 'Second Parliament' directed against all nationalist Muslim leaders, including members of the Central Committee of the Party and the Executive Committee of the Sovnarkom. Subsequent events confirmed that the Bolshevik leaders deceived themselves in their hopes for a world Islamic revolution, and events in Central Asia took an unexpectedly dangerous turn.[36]

In 1920, after an unsuccessful attempt to enter Turkey clandestinely and lead a struggle there against Kemal Atatürk's government, Enver was ordered to go to Bukhara by the Soviet leadership. There he was appointed military *nazir* (minister) in the government formed after the collapse of the emirate. Turkish officers went to Bukhara with him, and they occupied key posts in military units of the Bukhara republic. The Soviet leadership received intelligence reports that the British secret service was showing a keen interest in Enver. Enver's correspondence with the Afghan minister of war was intercepted. This gave evidence of his intentions regarding the creation of Great Turan. At the same time agents of the Eastern Section of the Cheka reported that an illegal 'Committee of national unification' had been formed under Enver's leadership. In addition he openly expressed his dislike of the policy of sovietization which the emissaries of Moscow were carrying out. Because of this the Soviet government, on the instigation of the Cheka, passed a secret resolution to hand Enver Pasha over to the Turkish government as a war criminal. Enver found out about this resolution and fled to Eastern Bukhara where he tried to lead all the Basmachi units. Once he had received weapons and ammunition from Afghanistan, Enver demanded in an ultimatum to the Soviet government that Red Army troops be withdrawn from Central Asia and the policy of sovietization halted. At the start of 1922 his forces began a campaign of liberation and occupied Dushanbe. However, Enver suffered defeat in battle at Bukhara. On 4 August 1922 he was surrounded by special operations units of the Red Army and killed in an attempt to break out.[37]

The Soviet leadership refused to use Pan-Islamism as a catalyst of global socialist revolution for a long time afterwards. In conversation with Sultan-Galiev, Stalin said in early 1923 that it had after all been decided to initiate revolution in the West.[38] It is worth noting that Trotskii again brought up the idea of using Red Army cavalry for a campaign into India, Nepal and Afghanistan after the failure of the German revolution.

The defeat of revolutionary uprisings in the countries of Western and Eastern Europe, as well as the unsuccessful attempts to 'sovietize'

Eastern countries, in the final analysis postponed the prospect of a world socialist revolution for an indefinite period. There were no further serious and open attempts to start a world socialist revolution and eventually the Bolshevik leadership put forward the slogan of 'socialism in one country'. Inside the ruling Communist Party itself, a split took place which led to a permanent inner-party struggle for political leadership, and for power in the party and the state. Huge material and human resources intended to spark off world revolution had been expended in vain. The struggle with the Basmachi in Central Asia ended only in the early 1930s. In the USSR a new society was being built by means of forced industrialization and collectivization of agriculture, a harsh transformation which was called the Stalinist revolution 'from above'. Faith in the possibility of setting up a just and humane society expressed itself in the real enthusiasm and hard work of millions of Soviet citizens, and in international support for the USSR.

The political situation abroad changed in the second half of the 1930s. The socio-economic crisis in Europe, which had been a consequence of the First World War, gave way to a process of stabilization. After the failure of an attempted communist revolution in China in 1927, the Comintern lost its significance as the leader of world socialist revolution. Plans to export revolution from now on were put into practice by Soviet foreign policy. Soviet participation in the Spanish Civil War was an example of this, as were the formation of the 'socialist bloc' after the Second World War, and the offer of 'fraternal help' to any country where there was even the slightest chance of it developing socialism according to the Soviet model. All these are topics for further investigation.

Notes

1. Text in *Ocherki istorii Rossiiskoi vneshnei razvedki*, vol. 2 (Moscow, 1998), p. 177.
2. B. A. Starkov, 'Zapad glazami sotrudnikov OGPU', in *Rossiia i Zapad* (St Petersburg, 1996), p. 189.
3. For a detailed account see *ibid.*, p. 189.
4. *Ibid.*, p. 189.
5. *Ibid.*, p. 189.
6. 'Naznachit' revoliutsiiu v Germanii na 9 noiabria: Dokumenty Politbiuro TsK RKP (b)', *Istochnik*, no. 5, 1995, pp. 115–39.
7. *Ibid.*

8. *Ibid.*
9. *Ibid.*
10. *Gosudarstvennyi arkhiv rossiiskoi federatsii* (GARF), f. 374, op. 27, d. 7, ll. 161–3.
11. GARF, f. 5955, op. 1, d. 12, l. 223.
12. GARF, f. 5955, op. 1, d. 4, ll. 13–17, 43.
13. GARF, f. 374, op. 27, d. 1245, l. 21.
14. GARF, f. 374, op. 27, d. 7, l. 181.
15. *Kommunisticheskii Internatsional*, 1920, vol. 2, p. 6.
16. See I. Ts. Vinarov, *Boitsy nevidimogo fronta. Zapiski sovetskogo razvedchika* (Sofia, 1987), pp. 72–102.
17. *Tsentral'nyi arkhiv federal'noi sluzhby bezopasnosti* (TsAFSB): Arkhivnoe delo Nesterovicha-Iaroslavskogo, ll. 52–5.
18. *Arkhiv prezidenta rossiiskoi federatsii* (APRF), f. 5, op. 1, d. 49, l. 138.
19. *Ibid.*
20. Vinarov, *Boitsy nevidimogo fronta*, p. 38.
21. *VChK-GPU: Sbornik dokumentov* (Benson, 1989), pp. 196–7.
22. G. Z. Besedovskii, *Na putiakh k termidoru* (Paris, 1931), pp. 76–7.
23. Quoted from *Rassekrechennyi Lenin* (Moscow, 1996), p. 195.
24. *Ibid.*, pp. 191–4
25. TsAFSB: Arkhivno-sledstvennoe delo Feiergardta, ll. 29–31.
26. B. A. Starkov, 'Panislamism v Sovetskoi Rossii i avantiura Envera-Pashi', in *Islam, Balkany i Velikie derzhavy* (Belgrade, 1997), pp. 431–2.
27. *Ibid.*
28. See B. Sultanbekov, *Mirsaid Sultan-Galiev* (Kazan, 1992), pp. 16–17.
29. Great Turan was the state which early twentieth-century Pan-Turkists hoped to create by uniting all the Turkic-speaking peoples from the Crimea to Iakutia. The term harks back to the time when the Turkic–Mongolian peoples (Huns, Mongols and Tatars) emerged from Inner Asia and the Persians named their realm 'Turan'.
30. *Rossiiskii tsentr khraneniia i izucheniia dokumentov noveishei istorii* (RTsKhIDNI), f. 2, op. 2, d. 202, l. 21.
31. *Grazhdanskaia voina i voennaia interventsiia v SSSR. Entsiklopediia* (Moscow, 1983), pp. 601–2.
32. *Ibid.*
33. TsAFSB: Arkhivno-sledstvennoe delo Snesareva A. E., ll. 36–7.
34. RTsKhIDNI, f. 17, op. 2, d. 126, ll. 18–20.
35. For a detailed account see Starkov, 'Panislamism v Sovetskoi Rossii', pp. 427–43.
36. TsAFSB: Agenturno-operativnaia razrabotka '2 Parliament'.
37. Starkov, 'Panislamism v Sovetskoi Rossii', pp. 427–43.
38. Sultanbekov, *Mirsaid Sultan-Galiev*, p. 21.

9

Soviet Perceptions of the Allies during the Great Patriotic War

Sarah Davies

Until 1941, official Soviet propaganda portrayed Britain, and, to a somewhat lesser extent, the United States, in a critical light. If the intensity and nature of this criticism varied over the course of 1917–41, throughout the period both countries were regarded as epitomizing all the evils of capitalism and as fundamentally hostile to the USSR. Britain in addition was portrayed as an imperialist power ruled by a tiny, corrupt elite with a two-faced and unprincipled foreign policy; in the second half of the 1930s it curried favour with the fascists, while after September 1939 it was a rapacious aggressor.

Following Hitler's attack on the Soviet Union in June 1941, the propagandists were required to accomplish something of a *volte-face*, adjusting the official image of the United States and Britain to accommodate their alliance with the USSR. Such sudden *volte-faces* were nothing new, a similar transformation from foe to friend had accompanied the Nazi-Soviet pact.[1] It was simple enough for the regime to make these adjustments. But how did Soviet citizens, large numbers of whom 'had been conditioned to be anti-British',[2] respond to the new situation? The present essay will address this question by focusing on continuity and change in popular Soviet perceptions of the Allies, particularly of the United States and Britain, through the different phases of the war.

The role of propaganda and public opinion in the Soviet Union in wartime has received little attention, while the question of the Soviet public's response to the new propaganda during the war raises other related issues.[3] Although the USSR had no 'public opinion' in the Western sense of opinion capable of exerting pressure on governments,

168

various currents of non-official opinion always existed in the Soviet Union. The term 'popular opinion' might be a more appropriate term to categorize this phenomenon. In wartime popular opinion mattered. It was related to the state of public morale and the latter was crucial in determining the outcome of the war. The NKVD and Communist Party devoted huge resources to ascertaining the state of public morale and it is their secret reports which form the main basis of this study.[4] Memoirs, diaries and eye-witness accounts have also been used.

All of these sources provide evidence of the actual discourse of Soviet citizens. The relationship between this non-official discourse and official propaganda is a question worth exploring. People relied almost entirely on official sources for information about international affairs, and government propaganda clearly made an impact. However there was considerable variety in the way official information was interpreted. The role of rumour also should not be underestimated. Rumours proliferate in all countries in wartime and the Soviet Union was no exception. Indeed the Soviet people, fed an unremitting diet of often incredible Stalinist propaganda, had developed a strong culture of rumour well before the war.

Popular discourse reveals recurring themes and stereotypes about Britain and the United States naturally absent in the regime's own bland propaganda which was designed not to alienate the Allies. For example, stereotypes about the British which were propagandized in the pre-war period remained an intrinsic part of popular opinion in wartime.[5] These included the notion that the British were deceitful, perfidious and prone to manipulation and intrigue: all these stereotypes provided a ready-made framework for interpreting Allied delays in opening a second front. Rarely was it suggested that the Allies might have sound tactical reasons for doing this – it was more convenient just to attribute the action to facets of the 'British character'. Likewise, the British, as stereotypical 'capitalist imperialists', were bound to desire the downfall of the socialist Soviet Union and have aggressive designs on other territories. Regardless of whether or not there were elements of truth in these stereotypes, what is significant is the way they limited popular thinking and foreclosed alternative perspectives.

Although many of the non-official stereotypes recorded in the sources were negative, some had more positive connotations. For example, there were recurring references to the prosperity of Britain and America (in implicit or explicit contrast to the poverty and backwardness of the USSR). Clearly there was a certain ambivalence in popular perceptions.

It is impossible to gauge how widely such stereotypes were shared by the Soviet people as a whole. NKVD and Communist Party reports record what people said, not what they did not say. For every individual who held views, positive or negative, on the Allies, there were doubtless many others who were apathetic about the whole issue, which was of relatively minor importance compared with the business of day-to-day survival. There is remarkably little mention of the Allies in memoirs, for example. Many, although by no means all, of the comments recorded in the reports were made by members of the Soviet intelligentsia. Ordinary workers and peasants *tended* to express an interest only when the issue was related to more immediate problems such as material questions. The lack of interest in the Allies, compared with the great curiosity about and admiration for Russia in Britain, reflects perhaps the absence of official Soviet propaganda setting out to popularize the Allies, and the whole nature of the Soviet war, which was above all 'patriotic'.

Before the war

Prior to the German attack on the Soviet Union in 1941, the United States and Britain were portrayed in rather different ways. The United States had never represented a major strategic threat to Russia, unlike Britain. America had also been a victim of British imperial rule and had thrown this off in a revolution which gave her a certain ideological cachet. Her efficiency (*delovitost'*) was much admired in the Soviet Union and significant economic links developed between the two countries in the 1920s. The resumption of Soviet–American diplomatic relations in 1933 was accorded great importance within the USSR, and in 1939 there were high hopes for co-operation between what one propaganda publication termed 'the two strongest states'.[6] However, by 1940 the tone was changing, with America increasingly being accused of imperialist intentions, and described as 'the heir to England in the imperial question'.[7]

The official perception of Britain was almost uniformly negative. As Stafford Cripps pointed out to Eden on 15 November 1941: 'there is a long and unfortunate history of bad relationship between the two countries leading up to the present time'.[8] Russian–British relations in the nineteenth century had been constantly antagonistic. British intervention in the Civil War, the war scare of 1927 and the Metro-Vickers incident had all combined to sour relations with the new Soviet state. Despite some encouraging signs in the mid-1930s (including Eden's visit to Moscow in 1935), apprehension persisted about Britain's intentions, particularly in regard to Germany. *Dvoistvennost'* (duplicity) was the word frequently used to characterize British foreign policy.[9]

It was often claimed that the English 'imperialists' were intrinsically hostile to the USSR and possessed a 'class sympathy' for fascism.[10] The events of 1938 exacerbated this suspicion. Following the *Anschluss* it was argued that 'British imperialism does not wish to co-operate with the forces of peace because the forces of peace are mainly the forces of democracy fighting against fascism and war with the country of socialism – the USSR – at its head' and 'British imperialism hates the Soviet Union and dreams of weakening or, if it can, of destroying her'.[11] British colonial interests were highlighted: 'British imperialism is prepared to make any concessions to the aggressors, to allow them complete freedom of action so long as they don't take a nibble at her stolen wealth.'[12] Munich represented the ultimate in treachery, 'a clear example of the capitulationist treacherous policy of the British government'.[13]

This venomous tone was moderated during the three-power negotiations of 1939. Britain, along with France and the United States, were now termed 'non-aggressive' and 'democratic' states. With the failure of negotiations, the conclusion of the Nazi–Soviet pact in August and the outbreak of war at the beginning of September, this line changed dramatically.

Reactions to the Nazi–Soviet pact indicate some popular antipathy towards Britain (and France) in this period. It was felt that the treaty was a well-deserved 'slap-in-the-face' for Britain. 'That's the Stalin method of work, fast, good and strong. They've scored off Britain and France.' The language used by people indicates that official stereotypes about Britain had popular resonance. Britain had tried to 'deceive' the Soviet Union; it was right for the USSR to conclude a pact with Germany rather than with France and Britain, 'since Britain has long been known as a country with a mercenary and ambiguous policy'.[14]

Britain and France were reviled as 'instigators of war' and 'aggressors', especially given their reactions to the Finnish War and the exclusion of the Soviet Union from the League of Nations in December 1939.[15] In 1940 the war was explained as a result of a clash of economic interests. Britain and France wanted to dismember Germany. The war was thus a continuation of Britain's traditional aggressive imperialist policies.[16] The motif of 'theft' featured prominently in propaganda phrases such as 'Anglo-French imperialist plunderers'.[17] Parasitic images also proliferated: the British Empire was 'a huge machine for sucking the blood and sweat from a hundred million colonial slaves, serfs, share-croppers, workers', the British were identified as 'accustomed to fighting for new positions and maintaining their old ones with other people's blood' and Britain was said to demand 'tribute and blood from her dominions'.[18]

Barbarossa and the first months of war

Given the general background of suspicion, how did official and popular perceptions alter following the German invasion on 22 June 1941? On the day of the invasion Churchill pledged to help Russia in their common struggle, and the Americans followed suit. In his momentous speech of 3 July Stalin mentioned the significance of the British and American declarations of support for which, he said, the Soviet people should be grateful.[19] Initially there does indeed seem to have been a sense of relief and perhaps also of gratitude: 'That Britain should be an Ally – yes, an Ally – was more than we had ever hoped for.'[20]

Soviet propagandists now began to depict in a more flattering light the countries which they had been vilifying a few months earlier. After the Anglo-Soviet agreement on joint action of 14 July, Britain began to be described as 'powerful' and 'freedom-loving'. The press regularly highlighted support for the Soviet Union from certain acceptable sectors of the British and American population such as workers, youth and the intelligentsia. Numerous articles focused on the 'solidarity movement' (*dvizhenie solidarnosti*) with the Soviet Union. This was manifested in a variety of ways including Soviet film shows in New York, letters of support, and public meetings. Political differences were minimized, with prominence being accorded to cultural and scientific links between the countries.

What is striking about the coverage is the way it tended to be unidirectional, with the focus on praise for the USSR from the Allies, rather than vice-versa. This was a pattern which remained fairly constant throughout the war. Soviet propaganda accorded primary importance to extolling the *Soviet* people and their achievements and heroism. In *Pravda*, information about Allied action was usually confined to the back page, where it was recorded in a factual, unemotional way. As Barghoorn points out, there was little attempt to convey the contribution to the war of ordinary people and words like 'heroic' were rarely applied to the Allies.[21] Another form of propaganda, the TASS windows (propaganda posters put out by the TASS news agency), which did sometimes portray the Allied contribution, adopted a quite abstract approach. The Allies were usually symbolized by their flags alone – only occasionally were actual Allied soldiers represented.[22]

Why was there so little attempt to popularize the Allies in official propaganda? It was doubtless partly because of reluctance to glorify countries with an antithetical social system, a dilemma which the Allies themselves faced.[23] It was probably also because the Allies were felt not to be pulling their weight and making the kinds of sacrifices demanded of the Soviet people. For the Soviet people this was above all a 'patriotic war' and the emphasis in the propaganda was upon the 'motherland' and native achievements. Excessive stress on the contributions of the Allies would have undermined this stance and brought into question the strength and capabilities of the USSR itself.

There is little evidence of great enthusiasm for the Allies amongst Soviet citizens in the early period of the war. By the autumn of 1941 Soviet forces had suffered serious reverses. Leningrad was completely cut off at the end of August and Moscow came under attack in October. The mood was depressed and Allied support was regarded as largely insignificant. In this period many assumed that the USSR would be defeated and that Moscow and Leningrad would be forced to surrender. One of the reasons advanced was that the help given by Britain and America was not particularly effective.[24] In Moscow, the journalist N. K. Verbitskii wrote in his diary for 17 October 1941:

> We have the military industry of the whole of Europe which is in the hands of the most expert organizers raining down on us. And where is the help from Britain? But perhaps British imperialism wants to stifle us with the hands of Hitler, weaken him and then crush him? Surely that is logical from the point of view of the British imperialists? The whole world knows how subtly the 'English woman plays tricks.'[25]

This comment reveals some important themes which would recur in popular opinion, including the idea that British 'imperialists' were determined to destroy both Germany and the Soviet Union and the notion that the British were notorious for their trickery.

In his morale-boosting speech of 6 November 1941, Stalin also attributed the reverses in part to the lack of a second front, and stressed that another front in Europe must appear in the near future. However, he portrayed the Allies in a favourable light, contrasting them with the Nazis. Jettisoning any language of 'imperialism' and 'aggression', he noted that 'in Britain and America there are elementary democratic freedoms, there are trade unions of workers and employees, there exist workers' parties, there exist parliaments, while in Germany under the Hitler regime, all these institutions have been destroyed'. He empha-sized the strength of the coalition and the American loan of $1 milliard (one of the results of the Beaverbrook–Harriman mission to Moscow at the end of September). Far from being aggressive, the USSR, Britain and the other allies were conducting a war of liberation and had no designs on others' territories.

The speech created much speculation about whether a second front would be opened and if so, where it would be, with suggestions including North Finland (good for Leningrad), or along a Norway–Murmansk line or a Balkan–Italian front. Some were very confident, especially because Stalin had pledged it would happen: 'if he (Stalin) said that there'll be a second front, that means there's an agreement with the British'.[26]

However, negative comments about the Allies could already be heard. These centred on the unacceptable behaviour of the British: 'the existence of one front and the forthcoming opening of a second front is a fine hint on the part of Stalin to Britain – that her behaviour is unbecoming' and on the unlikelihood of a second front actually being opened, despite Stalin's pledges. Some feared that the USSR would end up bearing 'all the burden of war'. One person remarked scathingly:

> As far as help from Britain and the United States is concerned, then it can be compared with the acid pillow which you give to the sick and dying man to calm the relatives and allow them to talk with the sick man for an extra hour. We can't expect real help from these countries.

This evaluation reveals the depth of the pessimism about Soviet strength which prevailed in this critical period of the war. Another commented in a similar vein: 'Stalin has now openly acknowledged the USSR's total weakness in the war with Germany. From the speech it seems that every-thing depends on the help of America and Britain.'[27] Nevertheless, despite some despondency about the possibility of real Allied help, it is clear that Stalin's speech did raise the hopes of many desperate people, for whom the prospect of a second front represented a lifeline.[28]

The treaties

Spring 1942 was an unimaginably horrific time for Leningrad in partic-ular. With the blockade intact, and literally thousands dying each day from malnutrition, cold and disease,[29] a report of April 1942 recorded much despair amongst the intelligentsia and an assortment of rumours about peace being made with Germany given the unlikelihood of Allied help. A rumour also spread about the possibility of Leningrad being leased to the Allies for 25 years. Apparently talks were being conducted about this matter, with the Soviet government insisting on a period of ten rather than 25 years. The origins of this rumour are unknown, although clearly it was related in some way to the intensive Anglo-Soviet discussions taking place at this time. One comment reveals a fairly common perception of the Allies as prosperous: 'In Leningrad there'll be much food and various goods because the city will be leased to the British and Americans.'[30]

Stalin tried to raise morale in his *prikaz* of 1 May, mentioning the 'freedom-loving countries' first among which were Britain and the United States 'who are rendering our country ever-increasing military assistance ...'. This increased popular expectation of a major breakthrough. On 26 May an agreement with Britain was finally concluded, and a Soviet–American agreement followed on 11 June. The same day saw the publication of the notorious 'Second Front Communiqué', engineered by Molotov during meetings with Roosevelt, which stated that 'full understanding was reached with regard to the urgent tasks of creating a second front in Europe in 1942'. On 18 June a special session of the Supreme Soviet ratified the Anglo-Soviet Alliance. Apart from Ehrenburg's enthusiastic description of London and the British character, 'Heart of England', published in *Pravda* on 19 June, there was a distinct lack of pro-Allied propaganda to mark the occasion. According to Werth, many Soviet flags were on display during the ratification, but no Union Jacks:

> In June there were a few posters – one of three darts of lightning, with the Soviet, the American and the British flags striking down a toad-like Hitler, green with fear. Except for some newsreels of the Molotov visit to the USA and England, nothing much was made of the alliance in either cinemas or theatres; and the only 'pro-allied' show I remember was a variety show at the Moscow Ermitage – which ended, somewhat fatuously, with an exotic-looking young woman playing *Tipperary* on an accordion, and singing in a mixture of broken English and Russian, after which the whole company burst into what was meant to be a sort of Anglo-Soviet-American dance, in the setting of a great display of allied flags. The audience showed very little enthusiasm. This was at the beginning of July; the

show was stopped soon after, and the three dart-of-lightning posters also disappeared, as well as the displays of the 'Victory in 1942' slogan.[31]

News of the alliance generated a fresh wave of anticipation with some clearly interpreting it as the opening of a second front and the imminent end of the war. One worker reported that when she and fellow-workers heard the news about the treaty on the radio, many had tears of joy in their eyes. Molotov's speech to the Supreme Soviet on the ratification of the treaty convinced even more about the approach of a second front and the end of the war. A nurse related: 'When we heard that Molotov's speech would be on the radio we could not sleep. Early in the morning all the sick got up themselves to hear Molotov's speech on the radio. In the afternoon I got hold of a newspaper and read the speech out to the sick. Now we really hope that the war will end quickly.' In some ways this wave of expectation was dangerous, particularly as it was so closely linked in people's minds with the person of Stalin. As one commentator put it, 'America and Britain will open a second front in 1942 – this is the realization of comrade Stalin's plan, the result of his wise strategy for the rout of Hitler in 1942', while another stated: 'The treaty strengthens my firm belief that Hitlerism is inevitably doomed and will fall and that Stalin's historic prognosis will be realized soon.'[32] In staking his own reputation on the opening of a front, Stalin was clearly taking a considerable risk. If the Allies failed to deliver, his own credibility might be tarnished too.

Some enthusiasts of the treaty took the opportunity to snipe at Britain, contrasting her current behaviour with her earlier prevarications: 'the treaty is a reality and not the empty words which Britain allowed before. Now the Soviet Union will get real help.' One worker recalled previous British policy: 'The treaty with Britain and the United States is a great victory for the Soviet Union. It's a serious blow for Germany and her allies. It's clear that Britain has abandoned the policy of the Chamberlains who liked to skim off the fat with other people's hands, now the far-sighted Churchill is in power, who understands with whom one should be in alliance.'[33]

Not surprisingly, there were numerous reservations. An academic expressed concern about the timing and cast doubt on the seriousness of Allied intentions:

Everything seems great and joyful for us on the surface. But in essence we ought to react to the alliance with Britain with caution.

The question is – when will the second front be opened? Maybe in December, when we need it now to weaken German forces and raise morale in the army and in the population. The next two months will reveal all. If a second front hasn't opened by then, it means that the British and Americans are playing with us.[34]

There was also some cynicism because of the failure of previous agreements to bring about anything worthwhile. According to one artist:

The most important aspect of these treaties is the question of the second front in Europe, but the rest adds little to the situation which has been established in the last months of the war. Britain and the US have accepted our demands for more real help. The only thing that's in doubt is whether a second front will be opened. The British are great masters at promising help in words – that was the case with Czechoslovakia, Poland and Greece. We will bear all the burden of the war, in those circumstances Britain might fight for another five years, but will we last out, if the war doesn't end in 1942 that's doubtful.[35]

The last assessment contained the familiar stereotypes that Britain was all words and no deeds, that it broke its promises, and allowed others to fight its wars for it. Someone else expressed doubts about the efficacy of the treaty given the failure of anything to materialize from earlier arrangements and also highlighted the weakness of Britain. 'This treaty is like the one signed last year with Britain, it won't bring anything new. The British won't open a second front, and what kind of fighters are they if they didn't get any results in Libya against a small German force. This is all to drag us into a war with Japan, that's necessary for America and Britain.'[36]

Fears were also expressed that the Soviet Union would become economically dependent on the Allies. Underlying this apprehension were the stereotypes about imperialist, capitalist countries exploiting others for their own profit. Echoes of the 'parasite' and 'slave-owning' imagery which had characterized official propaganda of the 1930s re-emerged. The treaty with Britain was seen as 'a new servitude. Now we won't end the war. All the time Britain and America will live off us and push us towards new wars. In a while we'll expect a war with Japan as a result of the pact with Britain.' As a result of the treaty it was feared that 'the Soviet Union has lost its independence. Our state will exist only for Britain, and we will work without putting our hands down. All the dreams that socialism will be built in one country have collapsed, capitalist encirclement allows itself to be felt.' The signing of the treaty was seen as meaning 'the enserfment of the USSR into dependence on Britain. Britain will betray us and we'll have to fight for long until the United States and Germany are weakened and then Britain and America will dictate their conditions to us and Germany.' Some people pointed more specifically to a fear that concessions were being made to the Allies and, by implication, to capitalism. It was thought that the treaty implied giving American bankers concessions which would lead to the expansion of private enterprise within the Soviet Union. A constructor suggested: 'The treaty includes a number of unpublished conditions relating to the future structure of Russia. Clearly the British asked Molotov for changes to be introduced to the Constitution. I think that Britain will open a second front only after we are completely bled white and they will get the chance of presenting us with any conditions.'[37]

Distrust of Britain's motives was widespread and was reinforced by the resurrection of traditional stereotypes about British diplomacy. One person alleged: 'The British are cunning diplomats and can get out of difficult situations with exceptional skill', and proceeded to demonstrate that when the Nazi–Soviet pact led to the defeat of France and Britain, the latter had conspired to break up the pact and drag the USSR into war with Germany. He ended: 'Here you can see Britain's old principles in all wars "fight one's allies to the last soldier".' Another recalled that Britain was an 'ancient enemy' of Russia and therefore not to be trusted: 'In the tsarist period and now Britain always was the behind-the-scenes leader of all the intrigues against our country.' Britain was hoping that the war would lead to the weakening of both Germany and the USSR and this treaty was designed to prevent a separate peace being concluded with Germany. A professor at Leningrad State University stated bluntly: 'I don't believe the British. They'll betray us just like they betrayed a range of countries at the start of the war. And in general the treaty has been concluded as a fiction on the part of the British, as throughout history it's been impossible to trust the British.'[38]

The question of the second front

The summer of 1942 was dominated by the question of the second front. Werth noted 'a clamour which became strident and abusive in the summer and autumn of 1942. Much of this anger was worked up by the Soviet press; but it would have been there anyway.' As he explained, terrible losses on the Soviet side meant that most people had lost a relative and for them the front was 'almost a matter of life and death'.[39] The continued failure of the front to materialize generated a little irony, as well as anger. Ehrenburg recalls that in this period when soldiers opened American tinned meat they would say 'here goes, let's open the second front!'[40]

After a spate of exasperating correspondence with Stalin in July and August, Churchill came to Moscow on 12 August to tell Stalin in person that there would be no second front in 1942. He informed him about the prospective landings in North Africa, Operation Torch, while also hinting at a cross-Channel operation in 1943. The visit caused some excitement.[41] One section of the public continued to express optimism, regarding it as a sign that a second front would appear soon. There were suggestions that it was the British *workers* who were demanding the second front, a notion amply supported by propaganda which in this period focused on the strong movements for another front amongst ordinary people. This language of class also emerged in the continuing scepticism about the front: 'you can't completely trust the British government, it's a bourgeois government after all', while: 'The capitalists of Britain and America will not allow their governments to open a second front.' The usual stereotypes about the Allies resurfaced: they were poor fighters and having problems in India, Australia, Singapore and Africa, so Churchill had come to say he could not help. They were rapacious, intent on dismembering the USSR and, according to one professor, Churchill's visit was related to the introduction of British forces into the Caucasus, which they intended to occupy permanently. A nurse expressed the common paranoia that 'nothing real will come of these talks. Britain and America intend to stay passive in Germany's war against the USSR. They are waiting for the USSR to be bled white, then they want to divide it up.'[42]

By autumn, Allied–Soviet relations had deteriorated sharply. Popular expectations had been dashed, and the battle for Stalingrad was going badly. An anti-Allied propaganda campaign was launched in the press. On 3 October, in published replies to Associated Press correspondent Henry Cassidy, Stalin stressed the importance of a second front and claimed that in comparison with the aid being offered to the Allies by the Soviets, the Allied aid to the Soviet Union had been not very effective. 'In order to amplify and improve this aid only one thing is required: that the Allies fulfil their obligations completely and on time.' His replies won popular approval: the Allies were all words and no action, Britain was fighting its battles, as usual, 'with other hands', unwilling 'to spill her subjects' blood', wanting 'to go to heaven on another's back'. One worker contrasted Allied behaviour with their own: 'Stalin gave those British and American chatterers a good dressing-down. Today they are discussing, tomorrow they are speaking, but nothing on the second front. No, with us we don't have conversations, with us we have to act and not carry water in the mouth.' Some felt that Stalin should have been even more severe. The widespread view was that the Allies wanted the USSR to be ultimately defeated. As someone pointed out: 'There's no mutual trust.'[43]

In October the Hess affair resurfaced. When Hess had originally flown to Britain in 1941, the Soviets had been terrified that his mission was to make a separate peace with the British. This story now re-emerged in connection with an official campaign on the punishment of war criminals. On 19 October *Pravda* published a vitriolic article pressing for Hess to be tried as a war criminal. Britain was described as a 'haven for gangsters' and it was implied strongly that Hess was a representative of the Nazi government in Britain. These themes were echoed in public opinion. The Hess affair was regarded as a test of the fragile alliance. Why were the British not putting Hess on trial? Was there a deal being done between Britain and Germany? According to one engineer: 'If the British are really our allies they should give up Hess for trial. This step should clear up whether there is a deal between the British and Germans against us.' It was suspected that, since Hess was well aware of secret Soviet policies towards Britain from the period of the Nazi–Soviet pact, the British would want to keep him so he could expose these policies and enable Britain to break the alliance with the USSR. The ambiguous, duplicitous nature of British foreign policy was recalled. The head of a workshop concluded: 'The British will not agree to try Hess now and will get off with chattering. They are dishonest in political matters relating to their allies. In general there's no point relying on the British.'[44]

The day after the Hess article appeared, Werth remembers seeing a Polish officer standing in a queue in Moscow. He had been mistaken for a Briton and was being taunted: 'Instead of queuing up for delicacies, you British had better do a little fighting.' When the crowds discovered his real identity, the taunting stopped.[45] This period was perhaps the nadir in the Allies' relationship with the USSR, and probably also in popular perceptions of the Allies (especially Britain). The NKVD, usually laconic as far as numbers were concerned, reported that in the period from 10 to 25 October a significant proportion of workers in Leningrad were expressing lack of confidence in the opening of a second front.[46]

A fighting alliance

The period following the launch of the North African operation and the first signs of Soviet success at Stalingrad marked the start of a gradual increase in Soviet self-confidence and a diminution in public anxiety about allied assistance and the second front in Europe.

In his October Revolution speech Stalin predicted a second front in the near future and emphasized the strength of the coalition. A TASS window displayed a powerful image of Allied unity: the hands of the three Allies, represented by their respective flags, grasping a sword.[47] The public reaction was mixed. Some thought that Stalin's confidence about a second front implied that one would definitely open, while others suggested that Stalin was being more restrained than usual because the failure of previous prognoses to materialize.[48] On 8 November the North African landings began. In his answers to Henry Cassidy on 13 November Stalin spoke warmly about this operation, which he believed created the prerequisites for a second front. Some regarded the operations in North Africa as actually the start of a second front, or at least as a significant gesture. An engineer commented: 'Churchill is exaggerating in his evaluation of the British actions in Africa as a great victory, because as yet those battles cannot be compared with those that our troops are fighting, but even so the Allies' action in Africa should bring us great help in the war with the Germans.' However others were dismissive of the operation, deeming it only a pale imitation of a new front. A white-collar worker felt that the United States' only aim was to acquire new territories, arguing that if the Americans had really wanted to help the USSR, they would have sent troops to the south of France, but in fact they only wanted to grab the French colonies for themselves.[49]

In 1943, official attitudes towards the Allies grew even warmer. After Stalingrad, victory was already in sight and this year also saw substantial increases in Lend-Lease. However this official warmth did not always correspond with popular feelings:

> though between March and June there was an extraordinary display of official cordiality towards the Western Allies, this contrasted strangely with the much more morose attitude towards them on the

part of the general public. The feeling that the Allies were not pulling their weight, despite North Africa and the bombing of Germany, was very widespread.[50]

At the grassroots the familiar calls for a second front continued, albeit less insistently than in the previous year. Any setbacks had the capacity to reactivate misgivings about the Allies. Thus after the temporary reoccupation of Khar'kov in March an accountant concluded that the lack of a second front had enabled the Germans to send their divisions to the Soviet front from Europe and exclaimed 'surely the Allies realize by now that with a combined effort we can finish off the bloody fascist plague more quickly'.[51]

The Polish question, which flared up in April, was sometimes interpreted as another example of deliberate Allied malevolence towards the USSR. In January the Soviet government had stated firmly that Soviet-occupied areas of Eastern Poland should become part of the USSR. The Polish government-in-exile had protested to the Allies, who were in fact reluctant to antagonize the Soviets. After the Polish decision to ask the International Red Cross to investigate Nazi allegations about the Katyn affair in April, the Soviet Union denounced the Polish government-in-exile and formally broke off relations with Poland on 25 April.

The question of England's role in the matter was raised by many. Although some believed that Britain must be backing the Soviet Union, others were more suspicious. One teacher pointed to the fact that the government-in-exile was based in London, and that the border question and Katyn affair could not have been raised 'without the agreement of English ruling circles'. She blamed Britain and the United States, as well as Hitler, for the turn of events and expressed concern that the Red Cross would back the Germans and Poles. This comment was symptomatic of the paranoia of some in the USSR, the feeling that a 'campaign' was being waged against the USSR by a Britain hostile to the Bolsheviks, who might eventually terminate the alliance. The Polish incident exacerbated fears that the USSR would be isolated and that other Allies might follow suit and break off relations.[52]

The official tone remained upbeat however. In his *prikaz* of 1 May 1943, Stalin commended Allied operations in Tunisia and the bombing of Italian and German cities, describing these as foreshadowing the formation of a second front and noting that this was the first time there had been a joint blow from East and West. On 7 May Stalin congratulated Roosevelt and Churchill on 'brilliant victory' in Tunisia. *Pravda* highlighted the anniversary of the Anglo-Soviet treaty on 20 May, although it is perhaps significant that the anniversary of the Soviet–American treaty merited even more fulsome praise:

> the friendly relations between the freedom-loving peoples of the USSR, Great Britain and the USA, which have been tempered in the fire of the noble war of liberation against the Hitlerite tyranny are based on firm foundations ... Soviet–American relations correspond with the historic traditions of the two great peoples, feeding on mutual sympathy and respect. The Soviet people greatly value American efficiency, which, according to Stalin, is 'that indomitable strength which does not know and does not recognize obstacles ...'. It is just these qualities of American efficiency combined with great patriotism, examples of which the Soviet people and her Red Army daily show the world, are necessary as never before in the current war of freedom-loving peoples.[53]

The dissolution of the Comintern, announced in *Pravda* on 22 May, was welcomed by some who felt it would improve relations with the Allies. However, others thought the move had been forced on the Soviet Union under Allied pressure. One asked: 'Is not the dissolution of the Comintern a sign of the Soviet Union's weakness and of capitulation to our allies in capitalist countries?' Some workers spread a rumour that the Comintern was being dissolved because in capitalist countries the church had become more influential than the communist parties, a comment which is interesting for what it reveals about the popular misconception, fuelled by official propaganda, that communist parties had ever been very powerful in, for example, Britain or America.[54]

Some concern continued about the lack of another front. On 2 June Roosevelt disappointed Stalin with the news that a cross-Channel invasion would not take place until spring 1944. From the end of June through August the press was full of pressure for a second front. On 22 June a major Sovinform report, 'Two Years of the Patriotic War of the Soviet Union', concluded with strong admonitions about the need for a second front: 'without a second front victory over Hitler's Germany is impossible'.[55] Many people responded by asking why there was no second front yet. Others questioned whether it was true as, they thought, Stalin had suggested in his speeches and *prikazy* that Hitler could be beaten by the USSR alone, or whether a second front would be needed as the Sovinform announcement implied.[56]

The road to victory

In July, Allied landings in Italy began, and between August and December most of central Russia and Ukraine were liberated. Three-power conferences took place in Moscow in October and then in Teheran in November–December. From the end of 1943 official portrayals of the Allies were extremely flattering. In his speech of 6 November Stalin described Allied action in 1943 as 'something in the nature of a second front', and promised a real second front shortly. The speech ended with slogans which included 'for the victory of the Anglo-Soviet-American fighting alliance'.

Ilya Ehrenburg was instructed by the *Sovinformburo* at the end of 1943 that in his articles for the foreign press he should stress Soviet loyalty to the Allies, while also reminding them about the need for a second front.[57] The Soviet press gave prominence to a decade of American–Soviet relations on 17 November 1943, the second anniversary of the Anglo-Soviet treaty in May 1944 and on 11 June 1944 'two years of Soviet–American agreement'. Stalin's *prikaz* of 1 May 1944 spoke of Soviet victories having been furthered to a 'significant degree' by 'our great Allies' by their holding of the Italian front, their supplies and their systematic bombing of Germany. On 5 June the taking of Rome was described as 'the great victory of the Allies'. *Pravda* of 7 June, devoted to the Allied invasion of Normandy, contained a large picture of Eisenhower which was somewhat reminiscent of the 'cultic' depictions of Soviet leaders. On 13 June Stalin termed the operation a 'brilliant success'. Several TASS windows in May–July highlighted the Allied actions, and in contrast to the usual symbolic representation of the Allies by means of flags, one window of 16 July actually showed Allied soldiers in connection with the Normandy landings, while a window of 1 November celebrating the liberation of Paris also depicted British, American and French soldiers standing under a female 'Liberty'.[58] Stalin's October Revolution speech dwelled on the joint action by the Soviets and the Allies. Admitting clear differences of opinion on some security issues, he nevertheless remained optimistic about prospects for unity.

This focus on co-operation was interpreted by some as a sign that in future the Allies would play an important role in the Soviet Union. A report of 6 November 1944 noted the spread of rumours about the interference of the Allies, especially America, in the internal affairs of the USSR, and the possible end of the *kolkhozy*, Communist Party and so on. One peasant said: 'The war will end soon, but because the British are helping us in the war, after the war they'll have the high posts. They are also angry at us, no less than the Germans.' A *kolkhoz* leader wondered: 'Will there be *kolkhozy* after the war? The boss is America now.' Some were already looking forward to American influence. A *kolkhoznitsa* said: 'Our men are suffering at the fronts and our children are hungry, and many have even died. We ought to write to America so that the bosses know how we are not treated like humans here and are kept hungry', while a worker resurrected the rumour about Leningrad being leased to the Allies: 'After the end of the war America will lease Leningrad *oblast'* for 20 years, under America we'll live more easily, we'll eat white bread, while under Soviet power we're happy if we can eat grass.' It is significant that by this time the United States was beginning to supplant Britain in popular opinion and to be regarded as the most important of the Allies.[59]

With a real second front now in operation, popular opinion became preoccupied with the idea that the Allies would try to thwart Soviet advances into East Central Europe. Soviet agreements with Finland, Rumania and Bulgaria were interpreted in this light: 'We should not ignore the fact that the better things go for us, the more Churchill and especially Lady Astor lose sleep. They are machinating and making plans against us about which we know nothing.'[60]

Similar apprehensions surfaced during the Yalta conference in February 1945 where it was feared that the Soviet Union would be forced into concessions over Poland. However at the same time there was also great confidence in the strength of the Soviet Union, a feeling that to some extent the Allies were dependent on her now. A doctor remarked that 'the war will undoubtedly end in the middle of this year. Our allies cannot get away with declarations anymore. Churchill and Roosevelt know well that Stalin will overturn all their plans if in the future they cling to their tactics of "yards" and "miles".' One professor boasted: 'We occupied the main place at the conference, that's clear from the fact that it took place on our territory, and the whole style of the communiqué is ours – Soviet. Our relations with the Allies have undoubtedly strengthened on the basis of general interests.' Another professor compared the large numbers of Allied advisers at the conference with Stalin's small entourage:

Stalin modestly limited himself to a few helpers, that's Stalin's style and it underlines our strength in the sense that Stalin doesn't need such a quantity of helpers at the conference. It's clear that while the conference went on, his assistants Zhukov and Konev managed to jump far over the Oder.

This feeling of Soviet superiority over the Allies grew more intense during the victory celebrations on 9 May: 'The war was won, above all, by us, we – our army. Our Marshal is the boss in Berlin. Our Marshal is signing the act of surrender. Our position amongst the world powers is so firm that it would be impossible to find another such example in history.' Now the whole world could see that 'Stalin was right. All countries including Britain and America are convinced there is nothing stronger in the world than our state.'[61]

Suspicion of the Allies continued, especially in regard to their aims in the war against Japan, in which the USSR also became involved. The usual stereotypes re-emerged: that the Allies would try to make the Soviet Union bear the burden and that 'they of course hope to drag out the war with our blood'. It was expected that: 'The Allies will take hamlets and we will trample straight in and there'll be a heap of corpses.'[62]

The prevalence of this type of language even after the evident success of Allied co-operation sheds some light on why the rhetoric of the Cold War was accepted so readily by the Soviet population. This rhetoric clearly accorded quite closely with some of the stereotypes of popular discourse. Wartime co-operation with the Allies was not sufficient to dispel the deep-rooted suspicions which had accumulated over many years.

British and American intervention in Russia during the Civil War and the ensuing tensions of the 1920s and 1930s had left a bitter legacy. After 1941 the negative image of the Allies which had been cultivated in the official propaganda of the inter-war period was moderated in the interests of the co-operative effort. From 1943 onwards the tone became increasingly favourable. Yet the sources examined here reveal that at least some sections of popular opinion remained more hostile towards the Allies than the official opinion expressed in propaganda.

While official propaganda was obliged to be diplomatic and bland in its presentation of the Allies' intentions and actions, the language of popular opinion showed no such restraint. People were forthright in their condemnation of the 'duplicitous' and 'treacherous' Allies who could not be forgiven their failure to open more quickly a second front which might have saved the lives of millions of Soviet citizens. The eventual Allied contribution was felt to be too little, too late. For many

Soviet people the war had indeed been a 'patriotic war' which they had won through their own efforts. As the Cold War deepened it did not require a huge imaginative leap to equate the 'Anglo-American warmongers' with the Soviet Union's former enemies, the fascists.

Notes

1. See V. A. Nevezhin, 'Metamorfozy sovetskoi propagandy v 1939–1941 godakh', *Voprosy istorii*, no. 8 (1994), pp. 164–71.
2. Alexander Werth, *Russia at War, 1941–1945* (London, 1964), p. 84.
3. Two works which focus specifically on images of the Soviet Union in foreign propaganda and public opinion are: P. M. H. Bell, *John Bull and the Bear: British Public Opinion, Foreign Policy and the Soviet Union, 1941–1945* (London, 1990); Ralph B. Levering, *American Opinion and the Russian Alliance, 1939–1945* (Chapel Hill, 1976). A couple of recent articles which address the question of Soviet perceptions of Western countries are A. V. Golubev, 'Zapad glazami sovetskogo obshchestva', *Otechestvennaia istoriia*, no. 1 (1996), pp. 104–20 and V. S. Lel'chuk and E. I. Pivovar, 'Mentalitet sovetskogo obshchestva i "kholodnaia voina" ', *Otechestvennaia istoriia*, no. 6 (1993), pp. 63–78.
4. There is not enough space here to elaborate on the nature of these reports and their strengths and weaknesses as sources. For more, see N. Lomagin, 'Nastroeniia zashchitnikov i naseleniia Leningrada v period oborony goroda, 1941–1942 gg.', in V. M. Koval'chuk *et al.* (eds), *Leningradskaia epopeia* (St Petersburg, 1995), pp. 200–59 (which covers the reports specifically during the siege of Leningrad); Markus Wehner, ' "Die Lage vor Ort ist unbefriedigend". Die Informationsberichte des sowjetischen Geheimdienstes zur Lage der russischen Bauern in den Jahren der Neuen Okonomischen Politik (1921–1927)', *Jahrbuch für Historische Kommunismusforschung* (Berlin, 1994), pp. 64–87; N. Werth and G. Moullec, *Rapports Secrets Sovietiques, 1921–1991: La Société Russe dans les Documents Confidentiels* (Paris, 1994); S. Davies, 'NKVD and Party Information Reports on the Mood of the Population, 1934–1941', unpublished paper presented to the AAASS National Convention, Boston (1996).

    The majority of reports I have used come from Leningrad, which it might be argued was a special case because of its particular history and because it was under siege for 900 days. It would obviously be valuable to examine equivalent reports from other parts of the USSR.
5. Russian sources always refer to *Angliia* and *Angliiskii*. These have been translated as Britain and British throughout.
6. *Propaganda i agitatsiia* (henceforth *PA*) 1939, 2, pp. 35–45.
7. *Propagandist* (henceforth *P*) 1940, 20, pp. 21–6. For more on this question see F. Barghoorn, *The Soviet Image of the United States* (New York, 1950), pp. 21–37.
8. Graham Ross, *The Foreign Office and the Kremlin* (Cambridge, 1984), p. 78.

9. *Sputnik agitatora* (henceforth *SA*) 1935, 8, pp. 24–31; *SA* 1937, 10, pp. 12–15.
10. *PA* 1937, 15, p. 47.
11. *PA* 1938, 7, p. 58; *PA* 1938, 19–20, p. 80.
12. *SA* 1938, 8, p. 30.
13. *SA* 1938, 19, pp. 40–1.
14. *Mezhdunarodnoe polozhenie glazami leningradtsev 1941–1945 (iz arkhiva upravleniia Federal'noi Sluzhby Bezopasnosti po g. Sankt-Peterburgu i Leningradskoi oblasti)*, ed. V. S. Gusev *et al.* (St Petersburg, 1996) (henceforth *MP*), pp. 4–5, 8. However it also appears that the Battle of Britain may have evoked some sympathy for Britain amongst Russians, especially intellectuals. Werth, *Russia*, pp. 84, 98–100.
15. On the changes in Soviet propaganda following the pact, see V. A. Nevezhin, 'Metamorfozy'.
16. *P* 1940, 3, pp. 4–10.
17. *P* 1940, 4, p. 1.
18. *P* 1940, 13–14, pp. 18–25; *PA* 1940, 3, pp. 37–43; *PA* 1940, 4, p. 38; *PA* 1940, 10, p. 42.
19. Stalin's wartime speeches, many of which are referred to in the course of this article, may be found in the book: I. Stalin, *War Speeches, Orders of the Day and Answers to Foreign Correspondents during the Great Patriotic War, July 3, 1941–June 22, 1945* (London, 1945).
20. Werth, *Russia*, p. 162.
21. The allied theme was relatively insignificant in most forms of wartime culture and propaganda. See R. Stites (ed.), *Culture and Entertainment in Wartime Russia* (Bloomington, 1995) for analyses which reveal that the Russian theme was overwhelmingly predominant. On the coverage of the allied theme in *Pravda*, see Jeffrey Brooks, 'Pravda Goes to War', in *ibid.*, p. 20; Barghoorn, *The Soviet Image*, pp. 47–9.
22. See the examples in *Soviet War Posters c. 1940–1945: The Tass Poster Series from the Hallward Library, University of Nottingham* (Marlborough, 1992). The 129 'windows' in this collection are admittedly only a small proportion of all the 'windows' produced during the war. About 14 of these include allied themes.
23. See Bell, *John Bull* and Levering, *American Opinion*.
24. *Leningradskaia epopeia. Organizatsiia oborony i naselenie goroda*, ed. V. M. Koval'chuk *et al.* (St Petersburg, 1995) (henceforth *LE*), p. 219.
25. *Moskva Voennaia, 1941–45: Memuary i arkhivnye dokumenty,* ed. M. M. Gorinov *et al.* (Moscow, 1995), p. 477.
26. *MP*, pp. 14, 20–1.
27. *MP*, pp. 15–16, 23.
28. *LE*, p. 223.
29. For some recently published figures, see *Leningrad v osade*, ed. N. I. Baryshnikov *et al.* (St Petersburg, 1995) (henceforth *LO*), p. 298.
30. *MP*, p. 44.
31. Werth, *Russia*, p. 480.
32. *MP*, pp. 47, 51, 54, 59–69.
33. *MP*, pp. 46–7, 51.
34. *MP*, p. 48.
35. *MP*, p. 52.

36. *MP*, p. 48.
37. *MP*, pp. 48–9, 53, 56.
38. *MP*, pp. 52, 56–7, 60.
39. Werth, *Russia*, pp. xviii, 479.
40. Ilya Ehrenburg, *The War, 1941–45* (London, 1964), pp. 77–8.
41. *Ibid.*, p. 78.
42. *MP*, pp. 61–3.
43. *MP*, pp. 65–7.
44. *MP*, pp. 72–4.
45. Werth, *Russia*, p. 487.
46. *MP*, pp. 74–5.
47. TASS window 857, from *Soviet War Posters*.
48. *MP*, pp. 76–9.
49. *MP*, pp. 80–2.
50. Werth, *Russia*, p. 668.
51. *LO*, p. 476.
52. *MP*, pp. 88–90.
53. *Pravda*, 20 May 1943.
54. *MP*, pp. 94–5; *LO*, pp. 480–1.
55. *Pravda*, 22 June 1943.
56. *LO*, p. 485.
57. Ehrenburg, *The War*, pp. 120–1.
58. TASS window 1046, from *Soviet War Posters*.
59. *MP*, pp. 125–6.
60. The reference to Lady Astor is related to persistent rumours about British foreign policy being decided by the 'Clivedon Set' (*MP*, p. 109).
61. *MP*, pp. 134–5, p. 145.
62. *MP*, pp. 138–9, pp. 159–60.

10
Russia and Decolonization in Eurasia

Jean Houbert

Europe lived in fear of Asian invasions until colonial expansions turned the tables. Except for Russia's overland expansion, Europe expanded in Asia by way of the sea. The overland and overseas colonial expansions were of two distinct kinds: settler colonization and 'administrative colonization'.[1] The Russians, unlike other Europeans, appropriated a major part of Asia through irreversible settler colonization while other Europeans implanted the modern state and capitalism in Asia through administrative colonization and decolonization.

Russia created itself through irreversible settler colonization in Europe and Asia. The same process of self-creation through military conquest, followed by settler colonization and assimilation of indigenous inhabitants, was at work from the early stages of Russia's history on the Dnieper until it spanned Eurasia from sea to sea. As a colonizing people the Russians had two outstanding qualities: a dynamic demography and a capacity to absorb extraneous elements into their society. The peoples the Russians encountered in their expansion, on both the European and the Asiatic sides of the Urals, were not as 'foreign' to them as the peoples which Europeans encountered during their overseas expansion. Indeed, one of the peoples the Russians conquered, the Tatars, had ruled over the land of Russia for centuries. Russia also had a relatively free hand in its colonial expansion. Short of defeating and crossing over European Russia, other European states could not have intervened in its colonial expansion in Asia until it reached the sea. The great Asiatic civilizations had isolationist policies and for a long time did not interfere with Russia's expansion. It was much later that Japan, modernized and expansionist, came into conflict with Russia in the Far East. Through the enormous army of the Raj, Britain, the dominant sea power, became a formidable land power in Asia, posing a threat on the 'soft underbelly' of Russia. The tsars responded to this exposure by annexing Central Asia.

Europe, through Russia, expanded its frontier to the Pacific, but Russia's geographical straddling of Europe and Asia did not bridge the gap between the two civilizations. Russia became the bulwark of Europe in Asia and the implacable foe of Ottoman Turkey. The Ottoman Empire was the last Asiatic power to have posed a military threat to Europe. Russia, in all likelihood, would have demolished the Ottoman Empire but for France and Britain preferring to keep alive a weakened Turk on the edge of Europe rather than have an over-powerful Russian Empire in the area. The tsarist empire conquered and annexed all the Turkic-speaking Moslem peoples between Turkey and China. Once the highway of commerce between Europe and Asia – the fabulous Silk Road – the region had fallen into oblivion when trade was diverted to the sea. Russian and other settlers did go into these Asian lands, becoming the majority in Kazakhstan, but Transcaucasia and Central Asia had far too many indigenous inhabitants to be turned into integral parts of Russia. These Asian territories were eventually decolonized through integration into the Soviet Union.[2]

Western decolonization in Asia and the Soviet Union

The collapse of the tsarist empire in revolution and civil war was part of the terminal breakdown of the European-centred interstate system. Russia, however, unlike the other European colonial powers, had been permanently enlarged through settler colonization. Once the Bolsheviks had entrenched their power and the immense country had been industrialized, the tsarist empire, metamorphosed as the Soviet Union, became one of the two super-powers of the new interstate system of the Cold War.

The new interstate system was global in the sense that it was proportional in size to that of its main actors. Once the United States and the Soviet Union became the principal players, with territories and economic potential exceeding those of some continents, the interstate system covered the whole globe. The system was bipolar in the sense that the United States and the Soviet Union outclassed all other states. There could be a balance of power in the system only if the two super-powers were on opposite sides. Thus the very geometry of forces made for a rivalry of the United States and the Soviet Union. But the configuration of power in the interstate system was not a sufficient cause of the Cold War. The system was also heterogeneous in the sense that the internal political regimes and ideologies of the two super-powers were radically different. The Cold War therefore concerned not only interstate relations but internal politics as well. The East–West heterogeneity was not taken to be a permanent feature of the interstate system. The winner of the Cold War would homogenize the system along American or Soviet lines.

The Soviet Union had an overwhelming superiority of military power in Eurasia. Even if all the other states of Eurasia had united they could not have matched the power of the Soviet Union. The Soviet Union, however, unlike the United States in the western hemisphere, did not have an hegemony in Eurasia. There was no Soviet equivalent of the Monroe Doctrine for Eurasia as a whole. The states which were afraid of coexisting with the Soviet Union in a common Eurasian home could 'call on the New World to redress the balance of the Old World'.[3] The United States was able and willing to provide a counterweight to the Soviet Union in Eurasia, a policy underpinned by the so-called doctrine of 'containment'. The objective was to keep the Soviet Union inland in Eurasia, away from the rim of the land mass and the open sea, through a series of military alliances and nuclear weapons used as deterrent.[4] Politically the United States was to extend economic and political help to all who resisted communism. A constant objective of the Soviet Union throughout the Cold War was to break out of 'containment' and to delink the states of the rim of Eurasia from the United States.

Western Europe, where the American settlers had originated, which shared the political values of the United States, and was the original homeland of the capitalist mode of production, had the highest priority in the 'containment' policy of the United States. A number of the West European allies of the United States had non-settler, administrative, colonies in Asia. The decolonization of these colonies became a stake in the East–West Cold War.[5]

Colonial empires were appendages of the European-centred interstate system which ended in the Second Thirty Years War of 1914–45. There was no place for colonial empires in the new global interstate system. The two super-powers were imperial in a sense but they were against colonialism. If only through membership of the United Nations, states the world over had equal sovereignty in the new interstate system. The United States, which saw itself as the first colony to be liberated, exercised its influence on its European allies for the early transfer of sovereignty to moderate nationalists in the colonies. Timely decolonization would pre-empt the likelihood of communists' exploitation of anti-colonial nationalism.

If the new states coming out of decolonization then joined a Western military alliance to 'contain' the Soviet Union in Asia, so much the better. But even when the new states adopted a posture of non-alignment in the Cold War this was still not detrimental to the West, provided the Western model of political regime inherited from decolonization was retained and the new states remained in the capitalist world market. A new state could adopt an external policy on non-alignment, as India did, for instance, but there could be no non-alignment in terms of internal regimes. At the limit states which had both substantial communist parties and pro-West parties were torn apart by civil wars in which the parties were polarized along Cold War lines. The adoption of a regime based on the Soviet model, even if the state was a small Ruritania, was regarded as a loss by the West.[6]

The West was well placed in the rivalry for the allegiance of the new states emerging from decolonization. The colonial authorities had established elements of Western political institutions in the colonies and had implanted the capitalist mode of production. Indigenous elites had emerged more or less in the image of the West. It was from these elites that the leaders of the nationalist movements were drawn. With decolonization, the nationalist elites in power would not need much prompting from the West to crack down on any radical groups in the new states which might be tempted to turn to communism. It was only when the colonial power refused to decolonize, or hesitated over the form it should take, as France did in Indochina, that the communists were able to take the leadership of the nationalist movements and turn to the Soviet Union and/or China.

The Soviet Union was opposed to colonial imperialism in Eurasia for geopolitical as well as for doctrinal reasons. Marx and Engels had regarded colonization as a progressive force in Asia.[7] Lenin originally did not disagree with the founding fathers of Marxism on this. Lenin, however, saw colonialism as an integral part of 'imperialism'.[8] Imperialism, according to Lenin, was the monopoly stage, the 'highest stage', of capitalism. At that stage, which Western Europe was supposed to be in at the end of the nineteenth century, monopoly capital did not find it profitable to invest in Europe. Capital was therefore exported massively to the pre-capitalist parts of the world, to the colonies, where it was profitable to invest. The export of capital went together with the carving of colonial empires in Africa and Asia.[9] For

Lenin, wars flowed inevitably from imperialism and, therefore, the states of the monopoly capitalists would not be able to divide and redivide the world peacefully.[10] This theory of the inevitability of war between imperialist states became part of the doctrine of the Soviet Union but was modified in the context of the Cold War.[11] The imperialist states confronting the Soviet Union would avoid war between themselves. The terror of the consequences of the large-scale use of nuclear weapons ruled out virtually all categories of war between the two sides of the Cold War. Wars of national liberation were the only wars which the Soviet Union approved of during the Cold War. Hence, the doctrine of 'peaceful coexistence' between a 'zone of peace' and imperialism was elaborated: under peaceful coexistence a powerful Soviet Union and its allies – the 'zone of peace' – would prevent war while the class struggle dug the grave of capitalism.

The colonies had a double role in Lenin's theory: that of providing profitable room for investments, and a source of bribes for the European working class. Nationalism and national self-determination in the colonies therefore should be encouraged as this affected the class struggle in Europe. The liberation of the colonies would remove the room for profitable investments of monopoly capital. The means would not be available any longer to bribe the workers in Europe. The question then was: which class should Moscow support in the national liberation of the colonies?[12]

At the Second Comintern Congress, in July 1920, Lenin argued that the proletariat and the communist parties in Asia were too weak to conduct a socialist revolution and that therefore the Comintern should support a two-stage revolution. In the first stage the communists should ally themselves with the national democratic forces led by the bourgeoisie against colonial imperialism. Then, in a second stage, the communists would conduct a revolution against the bourgeoisie. Roy, the leader of the Communist Party of India, disagreed, arguing that the home-grown bourgeoisie was the worst enemy of the communists in Asia and that it would be folly to ally with them. There should not be a two-stage revolution, argued Roy, but a one-stage revolution led by the communists against colonial imperialism and the local bourgeoisie at the same time.[13] The question of a 'one-stage' or 'two-stage' revolution in Asia was to have grave consequences for relations between the Soviet Union and China.[14]

The two-stage revolution supported by the Comintern had been nearly fatal for the Chinese Communist Party in the interwar period. Yet, even though Stalin did not believe in the revolutionary character of bourgeois nationalism in colonies and semi-colonies, Moscow continued to press this policy on the Chinese communists at the beginning of the Cold War, during 1945-7. The victory of Mao in China demonstrated that it was possible for the communists to conduct a successful revolution in a semi-colonial Asiatic country. The Soviet Union now had to coexist in Eurasia with the world's second-largest communist state, where the Communist Party had come to power by its own means and in spite of, rather than because of, Moscow's advice. An independent communist state was most unpalatable for the men in the Kremlin, the more so as China developed a doctrine which on the two key issues of war and national liberation was radically opposed to that of Moscow.[15]

As the Soviet Union and China were ideocratic states, their conflict on the ground had to be interpreted in doctrinal terms. This was more harmful to Moscow than to Peking. China could afford to be more radical than the Soviet Union for it did not have the role of maintaining the overall global balance of power with the United States. The two super-powers had a common interest in avoiding any armed confrontation which might escalate to the nuclear level. Khrushchev had argued that Soviet achievements in modern weaponry, and notably its lead in intercontinental ballistic missiles, meant that the Soviet Union was no longer encircled by imperialism: the mainland of the United States was now within reach of Soviet nuclear strikes. Imperialism would therefore be compelled to keep the peace while it was being surpassed economically by socialism. Moscow was not against reaching an agreement with the West on arms control so that more resources could go to the economy.

Peking on the other hand had interpreted the Soviet lead in space and ICBMs to mean that Moscow would use this advantage in the arms race for the benefit of the communist world as a whole and in particular to help China achieve its goal over Taiwan. The Chinese argued that war remained inevitable so long as imperialism existed. Communists should not seek war but should not be afraid of imperialism for the triumph of the socialist camp was a certainty. It would appear that Moscow had given the Chinese, in a secret treaty in 1957, a guarantee of nuclear coverage in their conflict with the United States over the offshore islands of Quemoy and Matsu. Moscow then had second thoughts and unilaterally withdrew the nuclear umbrella.[16] This incident brought about a definitive break in Sino-Soviet relations, and from then on the two communist states considered each other as enemies. Moscow withdrew its experts from China, aid was halted, and trade between the two countries fell away rapidly. Frequent border incidents ensued.

The break with China was a catastrophe in geopolitical terms for the Soviet Union in Eurasia. Moscow was now faced with a possibility of wars on two fronts, the spectre which had haunted the tsars as well as the Bolsheviks. During the 1960s and 1970s 'approximately one third of the entire Soviet military power was swung round to confront Chairman Mao's yellow peril'.[17] One of Russia's outstanding geopolitical assets, its immense territorial space, became something of a liability. The transport system between the European and Far Eastern fronts of the Soviet Union relied heavily on the Trans-Siberian railway and this runs near the Chinese frontier for long stretches and was vulnerable to attacks from China. At the nuclear level, China was not in the same league as the two super-powers. But Moscow was not able to intimidate the Chinese, for important Soviet areas such as Kuznets, Khabarovsk, Vladivostok, Novosibirsk, and the Fergana Valley were within range of the then primitive Chinese missiles carrying nuclear warheads. Short of an all-out war, Moscow was most reluctant to have these important areas damaged.[18] According to Kissinger, Khrushchev in 1964 reportedly – and in 1969 very definitely – considered 'preventive' nuclear strikes against China's major missile test centre at Lop Nor.[19]

The Chinese model of one-stage revolution was seen as more relevant by the communists in Asia than the two-stage revolution which Lenin had advocated. Lenin had stressed that, in a first stage, the communists should support a bourgeois-led national struggle against colonial imperialism, but had not envisaged that decolonization would take place in Asia without a class revolution taking place in Europe at the same time. After Stalin's death the Soviet leaders returned to Lenin's idea of supporting national revolution in Asia. By then, however, most of the colonies in Asia had been decolonized by the Europeans, who had transferred political power to nationalist elites, and in Lenin's terms that meant the 'bourgeois nationalists' were no longer 'progressive' because the struggle against foreign (European) rulers was now over. Yet, far from attempting to destabilize the national bourgeoisies and help the communists to take power, Moscow provided military and economic aid to the nationalist regimes even when they ruthlessly suppressed the communists. The rivalry between Moscow and the West for the allegiance of the new states, the growing strength of Third World non-aligned countries in the interstate system, and above all the conflict with China, deflected Moscow from the revolution in Asia.

Under the Zhdanov 'two camps' line of 1947 there had been no room in the Cold War for a Third World of non-aligned countries. All states which had not adopted the Soviet model were labelled imperialist. Stalin, for example, considered India's decolonization a sham and Nehru a stooge of imperialism.[20] Khrushchev, however, recognized that this line only consolidated the links between the new states and the West, and the Soviet leader consequently went out to woo the Nehrus, the Nassers, and the Sukarnos. The Soviet Union was prepared to provide military and economic aid 'without strings', that is without making it a condition that the new states joined the Soviet Union in a military alliance or adopt communist regimes. Thus India received modern arms and steel mills, and in Egypt the Soviet Union built the Aswan High Dam when the West refused to finance the project after Nasser had accepted arms from the Soviet bloc. Later, Soviet pilots and other technicians helped Egypt to keep the Suez Canal open during the Suez crisis. Moscow joined Washington in condemning the armed aggression of Britain, France and Israel, three close allies of the United States, on Egypt, a non-aligned state. Soviet help was very attractive to the new states; and although the aid was never more than a fraction of that of the West it nonetheless provided an alternative and a means of blackmailing the West for more aid 'without strings'. Very rapidly Dulles stopped insisting on the new states joining Western military pacts. Once both sides in the Cold War were prepared to give aid unconditionally, virtually all the new states adopted a non-aligned position. States which had already joined a Western military 'containment' pact, such as Pakistan, had to be further rewarded lest they 'delinked'.

India, the leading non-aligned state, occupied a central place in the new Asia policy of Moscow. The Soviet Union was not readily accepted as belonging to Asia. Moscow had not been invited to the Bandung conference, where the Chinese had had the star role.[21] The Soviet leaders thought that being close to India might help their Asiatic credentials. More importantly, India had a border conflict with China and, by taking the side of New Delhi, Moscow might gain an ally to contain Peking. India was also the rival of Pakistan and helping New Delhi was a way of pressurizing Islamabad out of the United States 'containment' pact. Finally, India had a long coastline on the Indian Ocean. In 1968 Moscow sent its 'Blue Water' fleet to the Indian Ocean and from then onwards kept a regular naval presence there. This was not with the intention of interfering with the tankers carrying oil from the Gulf to the West, as was alleged,[22] but was a response to the mortal danger presented by the American deployment of Polaris nuclear submarines in the Arabian Sea.

The Soviet Union was also anxious to have an alternative supply route to its Far Eastern front, in the eventuality of the Trans-Siberian railway being unusable in a war with China.[23] The Indian Ocean route would not be a secure alternative because the Soviet Union could gain access to it only through the 'choke points' of the Bosphorus, Suez and Bab el Mandeb. The Soviet Union was keen to see the removal of the Western presence at these choke points and, for a time, Moscow did succeed in entrenching its own position in Egypt, on the Red Sea and in Aden. However, a naval base on the northern shores of the Indian Ocean, securely linked by road and rail to the Russian mainland, would have obviated the need to go through the 'choke points' and would have greatly reduced the distance to the Far East. There were speculations in the West that the ultimate objective of the intervention in Afghanistan was to obtain an outlet on the Indian Ocean. If this was the case it could have materialized only in the long term, because the transport facilities in Afghanistan could not even cope with the requirements of the intervention force.[24] That the West took the Soviet threat in the Indian Ocean seriously is attested to by the strengthening of the base at Diego Garcia, the deployment of a naval task force and the setting up of a rapid-deployment force and a new Central Command. But India did not provide a base for Admiral Gorchkov's navy, if such a facility was ever requested, while the intervention in Afghanistan reinvigorated the link between Pakistan and the United States.[25]

The price Moscow paid for looking the other way when Nehru and Nasser repressed the communists was the alienation of the communist parties in Asia. These parties turned to China as a much more relevant model to follow than the 'bourgeoisified' Soviet Union which had betrayed the revolution. In Vietnam it was China which provided the model for a successful revolutionary war against enormous odds, while the Soviet Union urged restraint. Stalin had put the interest of getting the French Communist Party into the government in Paris, and trying to keep France out of the American alliance, before that of supporting a communist-led revolution in Vietnam. Later, at the Geneva conference, after the defeat of the French army at Dien Bien Phu, Moscow exercised its influence on the Vietminh to accept the division of Vietnam. In return for Paris torpedoing the European Defence Community the Soviet Union wanted a settlement in Vietnam that spared France too great a humiliation.[26] In Korea, Stalin had given

North Korea the means to invade the South and attempt to unite the country under the communist regime. This was to be done without the involvement of Soviet forces. When the United States intervened it was the Chinese army which pushed the Americans back to the sixteenth parallel, saving the communist regime in the north of the peninsula.

The Soviet Union could not in principle disapprove of wars of national liberation. Moscow however was very anxious lest these wars escalate and pose risks of serious armed confrontations between the super-powers. Thus the Soviet Union supported insurgents only with arms, not Soviet troops. Troops were sent in only when invited to support governments of existing states. Soviet military experts helped Egypt in wars against Israel. In Afghanistan, the Soviet troops went in on the invitation of the communist government. The Soviet Union gave far more help to bourgeois states in Asia than to communist states, let alone communist insurgents.

One of the unwritten rules of prudence in the Cold War was that when one super-power was fully involved in a local war the other super-power provided arms but kept its troops out. Thus, from 1965, Moscow provided Vietnam with ground-to-air missiles to shoot down the American bombers, but no Soviet troops were involved. In Afghanistan, the United States, through Pakistan, provided massive military aid to the anti-government forces but the GIs were not sent in.

Russia and decolonization in the Soviet Union

The tsarist empire had been unique among the European colonial empires in having the geographical and demographic conditions for pursuing decolonization through integration of the colonies with the metropolitan state. This kind of decolonization failed when it was attempted by the overseas colonial empires. In attempting to integrate their colonies, France and Portugal experienced major crises of decolonization, involving the collapse of the metropolitan political regimes. Integration demands a modicum of homogeneity in cultural, demographic and economic terms between the metropolis and the colony, a precondition that none of the overseas colonial empires had achieved. And none of the colonial powers was really capable of the effort that would have been necessary to create the homogeneity. Britain, which had by far the largest colonial empire, did not even attempt to integrate its settler colonies, let alone its administrative colonies. In the end, all the overseas colonial empires adopted the 'Anglo-Saxon' method of decolonization, namely the transfer of sovereignty to the colonies which then became members of the interstate system. This 'normal' method of decolonization was far from satisfactory: many of the new states born of this kind of decolonization were poor 'quasi-states', sovereign only by courtesy of the interstate system.[27]

Of the many peoples which made up the tsarist empire, some were tiny, landlocked, and surrounded by Russian territory. The only form of decolonization there could be for these small peoples was integration with Russia, while having maximum autonomy. The Europeans constituted the overwhelming majority in the tsarist empire, unlike the overseas empires in Asia where Europeans were tiny minorities. The European peoples had not been in a colonial situation in the tsarist empire; they had taken part in Russia's expansion in Asia; some of their elites were in the ruling circles of the empire. Russia's relations with the European peoples in the Soviet Union cannot therefore be considered as decolonization. The Russian land and people transcend the division between Europe and Asia; short of the dissolution of Russia in Europe and Asia there can be no decolonization of the Russian people. This leaves the Asian peoples: the peoples of Central Asia and Azerbaijan in Transcaucasia. These peoples were in a colonial situation in the tsarist empire. Decolonization certainly applies to them. The tsarist empire had acquired these territories in the spate of European expansion which Lenin called 'imperialism'. These Asian territories did not amount to a particularly large colonial empire in comparative terms. Altogether the new colonies of the tsar in Asia amounted to the size of the Congo, which little Belgium carved up for itself in Africa; the French colonial acquisitions at the time were four times as large as the tsar's.[28]

In principle there could be no colonial situation in the Soviet Union. This was the state of the proletariat, therefore it could not be imperialist. The colonies of the tsarist empire were decolonized through integration into the Soviet Union. The proletariat, however, was not undifferentiated in the new revolutionary state but was divided into nations. The nation was not an indifferent value for the Bolsheviks. Lenin was committed to national self-determination not just because this appealed to the minorities during the civil war, but because the nation had a special place in Lenin's doctrine: wars of national liberation were just wars for they were directed against imperialism. National identification was indispensable in the transition to socialism.[29] The 'prison of nations' had to be opened up so that the nations could freely choose to 'fuse' into a larger socialist entity. Encouragement to the nations in the Soviet Union might also be an added incentive for others to join. It was the East European version of nation which was adopted; that is, nation as defined by culture, language and territory, rather than the French republican idea of the nation as the collective will of people to live together as citizens of a democratic state. The latter concept was reserved for the Soviet Union as a whole.[30]

The Soviet Union was organized with the twin objectives of preserving the nations temporarily and developing an overall allegiance to the socialist state. The nations had their own Republics, the principal ones had Union Republics. In some cases nations were reinvented or created almost artificially. In Central Asia the strategy of 'divide and rule' may not have been totally absent in the artificial creation of nations with their own Union Republics. There had never been nation-states in Central Asia. The tsarist empire had not interfered much in the traditional way of life of the indigenous inhabitants, who identified themselves primarily as Moslems.[31] The Soviet leaders preferred to have a number of 'nations', each with its own Union Republic, rather than having one large Islamic entity in a region bordering the world of Islam. The state went to great lengths to cultivate nationalities in Central Asia. National cultures and languages were fostered. Education at all levels was provided in the national languages. Books, newspapers, and films appeared in each of the languages. The policy of fostering nations was a success in that elites emerged with vested interests in identifying themselves with their nations and less with transnational Islam.[32]

The organization of the state as a Union of Republics, and the initial policy of reinvigorating the nations, turned out to be too much of a success for the project of creating a new 'Soviet Man'. The nations, far from withering away, as the Bolsheviks had envisaged, pressed for more power to be devolved to their Republics and for less authority at the centre in Moscow. This centrifugal nationalism was more marked in the Republics where traditions of independence as nation-states existed – such as Georgia and the Baltic Republics – than in Central Asia. The nations were not so much against integration in a Union of Soviet Republics as against assimilation in an over-centralized state.[33] The Soviet Union was a state which absorbed not only the economy but the whole of civil society. The resilience of the nations maintained an element of pluralism which was not part of the programme and which the regime wanted to eradicate. It was this propensity of the party-state for total control rather than russification that motivated the regime. Russia also came under the totalitarian inclination of the regime, although as the majority nation it was viewed somewhat differently by the rulers; and the other nations certainly identified Russia with the regime.[34]

The nations objected the more vigorously to fusion in the Soviet Union because for the non-Russians this was perceived as assimilation into a larger Russia. The powerful central institutions of the Soviet Union – the Communist Party, the army, the KGB – were all dominated by Russians. Lenin had advocated a federal state but had insisted that the Communist Party remain a highly centralized organization for the USSR as a whole and not a federation of parties of the Republics. The communist parties of the Republics were no more than branches of the central party. At the levels where power was really concentrated – the Central Committee, the Secretariat, the Politburo – membership was exclusively or overwhelmingly Russian. Even at the level of the Republics, the powerful post of Second Secretary – which could overrule the First Secretary, a national – was always occupied by a Russian. Likewise, the army was regarded as an instrument for the assimilation of the nationalities. Stalin had ruled out Sultan Galiev's proposal to have a Moslem army. The Red Army was to be the army of the Soviet Union as a whole, with a unified command. At the highest level, the officers who were members of the Supreme Soviet and those elected to the Central Committee of the Communist Party, were Slavs, the Russians predominant. Russian was the language of the army and also the language used for communications between the nations.[35]

Russian domination was partly policy and partly a function of structure. The Russian territory was considerably larger than the territories of all the other nations put together. Most of the USSR's resources and productive capacities were in Russia. Russia, with nearly half the total population of the USSR, was by far its most numerous nation. If Belarus – a nation almost as artificially created as the nations of Central Asia – was added to Russia along with the Ukraine, these three Slav peoples formed an overwhelming majority of the USSR. Lenin had stressed that Great Russian chauvinism had to be avoided but there could have been no Soviet Union, let alone a future world of communism, without the support of Russia. Stalin, especially during the Second World War, explicitly appealed to Russian nationalism. This was toned down later but, for the regime, the Russians remained the 'elder brothers' in the Soviet Union, notably with regard to the peoples of Central Asia. The colonization of Central Asia by the tsarist empire, which the Bolsheviks initially condemned as an absolute evil, was later reinterpreted as an absolute good, for it gave the peoples of Central Asia the opportunity of becoming part of the Soviet Union.[36]

If the Soviet Union was to remain a super-power it was imperative that its economy continued to grow; and one of the key resources for growth was people. The state, which had absorbed the economy and virtually the whole of civil society, was used to deploy labour as if it was not a scarce resource. The spectacular success of industrialization had been largely based on the collectivization of agriculture and the forced proletarianization of the Russian peasantry. Likewise at the military level the glorious victories of the Second World War were won at the cost of incredible human losses. The enormous Red Army, in the age of high technology, remained dependent on massive recruitment. Indeed, the primary cause of the economic difficulties of the Soviet Union was too much military consumption of material and human resources, and consequently not enough investment elsewhere.[37]

A fundamental demographic shift was under way in the Soviet Union during the last decades of its existence, a shift which was particularly relevant for the Republics of Central Asia and Azerbaijan. The Russian population, which had always enjoyed high levels of growth, had stopped growing with industrialization and urbanization. The Moslem Republics were the only parts of the Soviet Union where modernization had not resulted in a slowing down of population growth.[38] The leaders of these Republics were conscious of the leverage that their expanding populations gave them in a Soviet Union running out of human resources. They wanted more jobs transferred to their Republics. Unlike the Russians, who were great migrants, the Moslem peoples, accustomed to the mild climates of Transcaucasia and Central Asia and attached to the way of life in their Republics, were reluctant to move to the big cities, or to Siberia and the Far East, where their labour was most needed. Creating more jobs in Central Asia meant greater investment and this had to come from Russia. Yet the urbanized Russians were increasingly eager to emulate the way of life in the West, and not so willing to foot the bill of decolonization through integration of the rising numbers of Asians.[39]

There was concern in some circles that in the long run the growing number of Asians would displace the Russians as the majority nation of the USSR. This was unfounded, for if the demographic pattern remains the same well into the next century the Moslem peoples will constitute no more than one-third of the total population of the former USSR. It would have taken a very long time indeed, if ever, for the Russians to have become a minority in the USSR.[40] The growing number of Asians was an asset rather than a liability for the Soviet Union, if not for Russia, for they represented a source of labour and soldiers. Central

Asia also provided a suitable role model for the external decolonization policy of the Soviet Union.

Soviet leaders were proud to take visitors to the Moslem Republics, pointing out what could be achieved under socialism without capitalist exploitation. Guests from the new states of the Moslem world were particularly welcome. The Soviet regime did not encourage religions but there was no discrimination in this respect against Moslems. The Orthodox Church in Russia had not fared as well as Islam in Central Asia. Religious leaders had succeeded in adapting the interpretation of Islam to avoid conflict with the doctrine of the state. If decolonization is measured by the yardstick of equality between the ex-colonizers and the ex-colonized then Central Asia had been thoroughly decolonized under Soviet rule. Massive investments, primarily in agriculture but also in industry based on agricultural resources, on oil in Azerbaijan, and mining in Kazakhstan, had raised production to the level of the European parts of the USSR. In a country as vast as the Soviet Union regional differences in standards of living were inevitable. But United Nations observers had found that they were not larger than in other developed countries.[41] When the greater possibilities of producing their own food and of making extra income through unofficial channels are taken into account, the Asians were as well off as the Russians. Universal education had virtually eliminated illiteracy. Under Soviet law, women had been – relatively – liberated. Clean water, drains, sanitation and free medical care had reduced infant mortality and had greatly increased life expectancy. Central Asia and Azerbaijan had achieved higher standards of living than neighbouring Turkey and Iran, and were beyond all comparison with a Moslem country such as Afghanistan. The communist elites who had emerged owed a great deal to the Soviet Union and did not relish its demise. More confident of the resilience of their Islamic cultures than Belarus and Ukraine were in the face of Russian assimilation, and unlike the Baltic Republics in the assurance that their growing numbers ruled out being swamped by Russian settlers, the Asians advocated more autonomy for their Republics *within* the USSR, which they wished to retain.[42] Independence for these Asian Republics was a consequence, not a cause, of the disintegration of the Soviet Union.

Concluding remarks

Colonization and decolonization formed a continuous process whereby two outstanding institutions of modernity – the nation-state and the capitalist mode of production – were transferred from Europe to Asia.

Russia was unique as a European nation which created itself through irreversible settler colonization in Europe and Asia. The Russian people was itself the principal part of a tsarist empire consisting of European and Asian peoples. Within the empire, only the Asian minorities could be said to have been in a colonial situation.

The Russian revolutionaries were dedicated to end imperialism and the emergence of a new stage of modernity, one that superseded the nation-state and capitalism. To advance this grandiose objective the Soviet state, from its very inception, was forced to compromise with nationalism in its external policy. Moscow supported the nationalists rather than the communists in Asia on the grounds that this was the more effective way to end imperialism. Decolonization under 'bourgeois nationalists' was a further stage in the development of the modern state and capitalism in Asia. By supporting this kind of decolonization the Soviet Union was, perhaps unconsciously, helping history to advance. This certainly would be in line with Marx's thoughts, although not with those of Lenin. The more immediate aim of Moscow in supporting the 'bourgeois nationalists' was to win – or at least not lose – its geopolitical conflict with the West, as well as winning allies in its conflict with China. Both objectives lead away from the revolution in Asia. Non-aligned but bourgeois states were more acceptable for Moscow than independent communism.

Inside the Soviet Union also, communist parties at the national level, not totally controlled by Moscow, were unacceptable. Moscow countenanced nations in the transition stage but not as permanent features of the USSR. A weak federation or confederation of communist nations would perhaps have stood a better chance of keeping the Soviet Union together. This could have been an attractive model to the world outside; but probably the Soviet Union would not then have achieved the rank of super-power.

The nations did not wither away and were unwilling to fuse into one Soviet people in part because they perceived this as assimilation by Russia. This was much more marked in Europe than in Asia. The Russians themselves, with their loss of demographic vitality, had also lost their propensity to assimilate extraneous elements. Russia was no longer prepared to foot the bill of decolonization through integration of the Asian nations when the Soviet Union most needed their manpower. Russia played the decisive role in the process of unravelling the Soviet Union. Decolonization of the Asian nations then reverted to the cheaper, more selfish, 'normal' Anglo-Saxon way of transferring sovereignty in the interstate system.

The Russians might come to regret the loss of the Asians of the Soviet Union. Without sufficient population, the immense territory of Russia is not necessarily an asset in the post-Cold War world. Empty land and vast distances can hold Russia behind in a globalized market economy. The Russian Far East, for instance, geostrategic stronghold of the erstwhile super-power, thinly populated and thousands of kilometres from Moscow, remains an economic backwater in sharp contrast with other parts of the Pacific Rim. The table might turn again, with the demographic vacuum of Russia's vast Asian land being filled by China.[43]

Notes

1. The original meaning of 'colony', in Ancient Greece, was a group of settlers which left the parent city-state to settle abroad in an empty land and form a new city-state. Cultural and sentimental links were maintained with the parent state but no political domination was involved. 'Administrative' colonization entailed the maintenance by a few European administrators, soldiers and entrepreneurs of colonial rule with the collaboration of indigenous elites. An intermediate situation was when settlers were present but not in sufficient numbers to make colonization irreversible. Algeria and Rhodesia are overseas examples, and Kazakhstan an overland example, of territories which came near the margin of irreversible settler colonization.

2. The following works are particularly useful on the themes set out in this introduction: W. Gurian *et al.*, *Soviet Imperialism, its Origins and Tactics* (Indiana, 1953); E. H. Carr *et al.*, *Nationalism* (London, 1939); H. Seton-Watson, *The New Imperialism* (London, 1961); A. Watson, *The Evolution of International Society* (London, 1992); A. Wood (ed.), *The History of Siberia: From Russian Conquest to Revolution* (London, 1991).

3. Recalling Canning's statement to the House of Commons (12 December 1826) concerning the Monroe Doctrine, see H. Bull and A. Watson, *The Expansion of International Society* (Oxford, 1988), p. 136.

4. 'Containment' as the concept behind the United States' foreign policy in the Cold War was coined by George Kennan in an article signed 'Mr. X' in *Foreign Affairs* (July 1947). Much later Kennan had second thoughts about containment – see *Encounter* (March 1978). A good collection of documents on the containment policy: T. H. Etzold and J. L. Gaddis, *Containment: Documents on American Policy and Strategy* (New York, 1978).

5. On international systems the works of Raymond Aron are most useful. See in particular: R. Aron, *Paix et Guerre entre les Nations* (Paris, 1962) and *Les Dernières années du siècle* (Paris, 1984). See also A. W. Deporte, *Europe between the Super Powers* (London, 1979). On decolonization in the Cold War interstate system see P. Hassner, 'Le systême international et les nouveaux états', in *La Communauté Internationale face aux Jeunes Etats*, ed. J. B. Duroselle and J. Meyriat (Paris, 1964), pp. 11–59.

6. Non-alignment of new states is discussed by P. Hassner, 'La montée des jeunes états et les relations entre les deux blocs', in *La Communauté Internationale face aux Jeunes Etats*, ed. J. B. Duroselle and J. Meyriat (Paris, 1964), pp. 294–400.

7. 'The bourgeoisie ... draws all, even the most barbarian, nations into civilisation ... it forces the barbarians' intensely obstinate hatred of foreigners to capitulate. It compels all nations, on pain of extinction, to adopt the bourgeois mode of production... . In one word, it creates a world after its own image' (K. Marx and F. Engels, 'The Manifesto of the Communist Party', in *The Essential Left*, London, 1971). See also the articles of Marx and Engels in the *New York Tribune*, in particular 'The Future Results of the British Rule in India' (London), Friday 22 July 1853: 'England has to fulfil a double mission in India: one destructive, the other regenerating ... the laying of Western society in Asia ... we may safely expect to see ... the regeneration of that great and interesting country... .' (reprinted in K. Marx and F. Engels, *On Colonialism* (Moscow, 1976), pp. 81–7).

8. V. I. Lenin, *Imperialism, the Highest Stage of Capitalism* (Moscow, n.d.). The two recent Marxist critiques of Lenin which are most helpful are G. Arrighi, *The Geometry of Imperialism: The Limits of Hobson's Paradigm* (London, 1978), and B. Warren, *Imperialism, Pioneer of Capitalism* (London, 1980).

9. Lenin, *Imperialism*, p. 128.

10. V. I. Lenin, *Lenine sur la Guerre et la Paix Recueil de Trois Textes* (Peking, 1975). Aron has argued that Lenin's theory of war was based on a synthesis of Marx and Clausewitz. See R. Aron, *Penser la Guerre: l'Age Planètaire* (Paris, 1976).

11. D. Armstrong, *The Revolution and World Order: The Revolutionary State in International Society* (Oxford, 1993), *passim*, but see especially pp. 139–51.

12. Lenin had reconciled his condemnation of the Second International for supporting the First World War with support for nationalism in the colonies with the argument that the war was between imperialist states, not nations. See Aron, *Penser la Guerre*, pp. 69–75.

13. See Warren, *Imperialism*, pp. 94–109.

14. G. Jukes, *The Soviet Union in Asia* (London, 1973), p. 7.

15. On war, in doctrinal terms: if war flowed from imperialism, then war was inevitable. Furthermore, war was unthinkable between socialist states. If war was thinkable between China and the USSR then at least one of them must have been imperialist.

16. Jukes, *The Soviet Union in Asia*, p. 224.

17. M. Hauner, *What is Asia to Us: Russia's Asian Heartland Yesterday and Today* (London, 1990), p. 233.

18. Jukes, *The Soviet Union in Asia*, p. 78.

19. Hauner, *What is Asia to Us*, p. 233. See also P. Kennedy, *The Rise and Fall of the Great Powers* (London, 1988). According to Kennedy, Kissinger had said that the United States could not allow the Soviet Union to obliterate China (*The Rise and Fall of the Great Powers*, p. 514).

20. Jukes, *The Soviet Union in Asia*, p. 9.

21. 'Les relations entre Grande Puissances communistes face au pays du Tiers Monde', in *La Communauté Internationale face aux Jeunes Etats*, ed. J. B. Duroselle and J. Meyriat (Paris, 1964), pp. 161–96.

22. See, for instance, P. Wall (ed.), *The Indian Ocean and the Threat to the West* (London, 1975), *passim*, but see especially pp. 67–137.

23. Hauner, *What is Asia to Us*, p. 120. See also Kennedy, *The Rise and Fall of the Great Powers*, p. 662.

24. Hauner, *What is Asia to Us*, pp. 118–20.

25. For more on the Cold War in the Indian Ocean see D. Braun, *The Indian Ocean: Region of Conflict or Zone of Peace* (New York, 1983); G. Jukes, 'The Indian Ocean in Soviet Naval Policy', *Adelphi Papers*, no. 87 (London, 1972); M. Bezborath, *Strategy in the Indian Ocean: The International Response* (London, 1977).

26. Jukes, *The Soviet Union in Asia*, pp. 205–7. See also the chapter on Ho Chi Minh in J. Lacouture, *Cinq Hommes et la France* (Paris, 1961). Much later, in 1978, Vietnam had a war with China over Cambodia. Moscow supported Vietnam, which provided naval facilities for the Soviet navy.

27. See R. H. Jackson, *Quasi-States: Sovereignty, International Relations and the Third World* (London, 1990).

28. N. S. Timasheff, 'Russian Imperialism or Communist Aggression', in Gurian (ed.), *Soviet Imperialism*, p. 25.

29. Aron, *Penser la Guerre*, p. 75

30. H. Carrère D'Encausse, *L'Empire Eclaté* (Paris, 1978), pp. 271–2. For a post-Soviet criticism of the nationalities policy of the USSR see A. S. Barsenkov *et al.*, *Towards a Nationalities Policy in the Russian Federation* (Aberdeen Centre for Soviet and East European Studies, 1993).

31. R. E. Pipes, 'Russian Moslems before and after the Revolution', in Gurian (ed.), *Soviet Imperialism*, pp. 75–90.

32. W. Fierman (ed.), *Soviet Central Asia: The Failed Transformation* (Oxford, 1991).

33. Carrère D'Encausse, *L'Empire Eclaté, passim*.

34. A. Rahr, 'Russia', in *The Demise of the USSR: From Communism to Independence*, ed. V. Tolz and I. Elliot.

35. Carrère D'Encausse, *L'Empire Eclaté, passim*. See also J. Keep, *Last of the Empires* (London, 1995).

36. S. M. Schwarz, 'Revising the History of Russian Colonialism', *Foreign Affairs*, vol. 30, no. 3, pp. 488–93.

37. Aron, *Les Dernières Années du Siècle*, p. 142.

38. Carrère D'Encausse, *L'Empire Eclaté*, pp. 45–91.

39. Rahr says that by the mid-1980s the RSFSR was producing two-thirds of the USSR's GNP, but that 61 per cent of its earnings went to the other Republics. See Tolz and Elliot, *The Demise*, pp. 109–10. See also D. Lieven, 'The Russian Empire and the Soviet Union as Imperial Polities', *Journal of Contemporary History*, vol. 30 (1995), pp. 607–36.

40. Jukes, *The Soviet*, p. 56

41. Seton-Watson, *The New Imperialism*, p. 69.

42. H. Malik (ed.), *Central Asia: Its Strategic Importance and Future Prospects* (New York, 1994); G. W. Lapidus *et al.*, *From Union to Commonwealth: Nationalism and Separatism in the Soviet Republics* (Cambridge, 1992).

43. The 300 million people being added to the Chinese population in the last two decades of this century are roughly double Russia's total population. See 'Russia & China' in *The Economist*, 26 April 1997, pp. 21–3.

11
Concluding Remarks

James D. White

The theme of Russia and the world in historical perspective is a particularly challenging one, approaching it, as we do, in the aftermath of the Soviet Union's demise, when it is no longer clear what this 'Russia' is, what place it occupies in the world, or what historical traditions it embodies. As long as Russia formed the heart of the Soviet Union it had – or seemed to have – a particular identity as a country, the Cold War alignments defined its place in the world, and Russian history was mainly concerned with the processes which had produced the Soviet regime and determined its subsequent fate. Historians, as A. J. P. Taylor stated, ask themselves the question: 'How did this state of affairs come about?'[1] Until a decade ago historians of Russia had the Soviet Union as a relatively solid starting point. But the present-day Russia is still in flux, so that what Taylor calls 'this state of affairs' is as yet an unknown quantity.

For what one thinks the proper place of post-Soviet Russia in the world is, it is possible to construct a corresponding historical heritage. A striking example of this phenomenon is the modern version of the 'Eurasian' theory of Russian history. The interpretation was first elaborated by émigré historians between the two world wars. Its revival is prompted by suspicion that the West, following its victory in the Cold War, intends to foment antipathy between Slavs and Moslems in post-Soviet space. The Eurasian interpretation of Russian history is concerned to show that Russia is a country situated between Asia and Europe, with its own particular national characteristics. It holds that the shared experience of Slavonic and Moslem peoples transcends obvious differences in religion. The implication also is that Russia's expansion towards the east was not the kind of colonialism characteristic of European powers, but altogether a much more peaceful and

209

organic type of absorption of non-Russian peoples. (This position is to some extent supported by Jean Houbert's paper in the present volume.) It also regards the Mongol invasions in the thirteenth century as an integral part of Russian history rather than as a break in its continuity.[2]

Though it over-states the case, the Eurasian interpretation of Russian history is a useful corrective to the view that assumes that progress in Russian history was necessarily associated with Westernization, the adoption of practices and institutions from Western Europe or, in its most recent version, from the USA. It is also a useful reminder that there was a time when the Russians looked to the East for their economic ideas and improvements in lifestyle. The Russian words for 'money', 'warehouse', 'horse', 'overcoat' and 'shoe', are taken from Turkic languages. The words for 'tea' and 'silk' come from Chinese.[3] It was only because in more recent times the great Eastern civilizations fell into stagnation while the European countries forged ahead intellectually, technically and economically, that Russia turned towards the West for models to emulate.[4] To put Russia's Westernization process fully in its context would thus involve examining developments in Asia.

Until the time of Peter the Great, Russia's contacts with the West were seriously impeded by its neighbours the Swedes, the Turks and the Poles. It was only at the start of the eighteenth century that Russia was able to make its entry onto the European stage suddenly and dramatically, in Pushkin's words 'Like a ship being launched, to the thud of axes and the roar of cannon'.[5] The attempts to assimilate Western accomplishments and civilization also came just as suddenly and dramatically rather than gradually and piecemeal as they no doubt would have if Russia's interaction with the countries of Western Europe had been of longer standing.

It is interesting to note in this connection what Lindsey Hughes says about the grounds on which Peter the Great's opponents resisted the introduction of Western fashions and practices. The objections were not ones that were peculiar to Russia or which were only characteristic of Asiatic societies. They were rational ones that had been repeatedly voiced in comparable situations in the countries of Western Europe in pre-modern times. Opponents of Peter's reforms proceeded from the assumption that all aspects of the life of society were interrelated, each one interacting upon the other. Consequently, any innovation could not be seen in isolation, but had to be viewed as a factor likely to disrupt the equilibrium of social life in general. These were considerations which might be alien to a Western European of the eighteenth century, but only because the Reformation and the Enlightenment, and with them the rise of moral and economic individualism, had superseded thinking of that kind; not because Western Europeans had never reasoned in that way.

The possibility of accounting for differences between Russia and the West in terms of different rates of development helps evaluate the interpretation of Russian history which maintains that Russia's place in the world is by nature non-European. This is a theory commonly propounded by countries of the former Soviet bloc and some newly independent countries of the former Soviet Union. They argue that whereas these countries and peoples undoubtedly belong to Western European civilization, Russia just as indubitably does not. The theory draws a line of demarcation between Russia and its East and Central European neighbours, and is used to justify the expansion of NATO to Russia's borders.

An example of this current of thought is the article 'Russia's Route' by the Polish historian Jan Kieniewicz, which appeared in a collection of papers from an international conference on political geography.[6] Kieniewicz argues that the direction Russia will take in the future depends upon the nature of Russian civilization, and considers that 'Russia spawned a civilisation which is distinct from that of Europe'. One of the basic impulses of this civilization is territorial expansion, and in this respect there is striking continuity between the Muscovite, Russian and the Soviet states. Russia aspired to come into direct contact with Europe by pushing her frontiers westwards. By this process, however, Russia did not become any more European; rather the contrary, with its expansion Russia became Messianic and tried to spread its peculiar kind of civilization. As for the Petrine reforms, Kieniewicz contends, these did not bring about the Westernization, only the modernization of Russia. Noting that Russia's western borders have now been pushed back to where they were in the first half of the seventeenth century, Kieniewicz fears that the country's colonizing tendencies might re-emerge, but consoles himself with the thought that Poland, as part of Europe, will return to its traditional role as an opening to Europe for Russia. The implication is that Russia's situation outside Europe will be confirmed and perpetuated.[7]

Kieniewicz's interpretation of the relationship between Russia and the West lacks an essential element: it lacks a definition of what 'European' means in this context. If one knew what characteristics were peculiarly 'European', one could then go on to examine how the characteristics of Russian civilization differed from the European ones.

But since 'European' is not a precise term, and any definition would be a purely arbitrary one, the Kieniewicz interpretation has no real foundation. One suspects too that Kieniewicz would be extremely hard put to show that 'Westernization' and 'modernization' were not in effect synonyms.

The corrective to interpretations of Russian historical development which stress its position outside the mainstream of Western civilization is the work of Paul Dukes. When in 1955 Godechot and Palmer elaborated their concept of an eighteenth-century Atlantic revolution, they dealt with the impact of the American and French revolutions throughout the Western world, but paid little attention to developments beyond Western Europe. First in *The Emergence of the Super-Powers* and then in *October and the World* Dukes showed that the great upheavals of the USA and Western Europe had their counterparts in Russia and Eastern Europe.[8] When these books were written the impulse to exclude Russia from the general course of world history had a Cold-War inspiration. Kieniewicz's essay shows that even in the post-Soviet era this kind of interpretation persists.

Another kind of study which Paul Dukes has specialized in, and which reflects Russia's integration into European history, is the investigation of Russia's links with Scotland.[9] As Dmitry Fedosov shows in his paper, Scotland's connections with Russia are long-standing and on many levels, testifying to a certain affinity between Scots and Russians. In this respect Graeme Herd's paper on Patrick Gordon is very instructive. For it shows that Gordon's being in the service of Peter the Great was not a chance phenomenon, but the outcome of long-term historical circumstances which obtained at that time in Britain and Russia. Like other Royalists and Catholics, Gordon left Scotland following the execution of Charles I in 1649 and the creation of the Commonwealth. After studying in the Jesuit College at Braunsberg he – again like many Scots of his generation who lacked career openings at home – entered Polish and Swedish mercenary service. As the Restoration promised no better prospects for military employment in Britain, Gordon entered the service of Russia. Because Russia had been cut off by its neighbours from the latest developments in military technology the country had a need for modern military expertise, and with that expertise it could attempt to end its enforced isolation from Western Europe. In Russian service Gordon, as a Jacobite, attempted to promote the cause of the Stuarts in Russia. In its way Gordon's career is simultaneously the extension of British history on Russian soil and a characteristic expression of Russian development of those times.

Peter the Great's victory over Sweden gave Russia control over part of the Baltic littoral, a 'window on the West'. This was recognized in the Treaty of Nystadt of 1721. But in it Peter confirmed the existing privileges of the Baltic nobility, so that the social structure of Estland and Kurland remained as it had been under the Swedes. On these territories events took a course relatively unaffected by Russian rule and were more exposed to German than to Russian influences. Riga was home both to Herder and Hamann, and was the place where Kant's *Critique of Pure Reason* was published in 1781. As Roger Bartlett shows, Germanized Britons could carry on religious and Masonic activities much as they might if they lived in Germany or Britain.

Some of the great intellectual movements of nineteenth-century Russia had their origins in the Scottish Enlightenment and made their way into Russia via Germany. David Hume made the discovery that though the human mind understood things in terms of cause and effect there was no guarantee that the real, external, world functioned in the same way. Hume's discovery was appreciated less in his own country than it was in Königsberg by Immanuel Kant (who believed that his own ancestry was Scottish).[10]

Kant made use of Hume's idea to show that, whereas the human mind could not know for sure what the external world was actually like, it was able to define the scientific laws which governed that world. Kant's *Critique of Pure Reason* inspired a succession of German thinkers including Schelling and Hegel, who in turn served as an inspiration for the Russian Slavophiles and Westerners.

The element which made German philosophy so relevant to the Russian situation was its reaction to the work of another figure of the Scottish Enlightenment – Adam Smith. Smith's *Wealth of Nations* provided a lucid and persuasive picture of how a market economy works, presenting its various aspects as an integrated self-regulating system. Smith's account of a market economy was profoundly shocking to many of his contemporaries. It depicted a society in which the bonds of loyalty and affection between people had been replaced by commercial transactions, a soulless world in which calculations of profit and loss were the governing principles. Schelling and his disciple Adam Müller elaborated critiques of this 'mechanical society', and pointed up virtues of the feudal order which were threatened by the spread of market relations.[11] Their ideas inspired the investigations of August von Haxthausen into the structure of peasant societies first in Germany and then in Russia. The book which he published between 1847 and 1852 brought to general notice the fact that Russian peasants lived a communal existence in their villages, holding the land in common, and deciding matters of common concern in a democratic way in meetings of their village assembly, the *mir*. Although Haxthausen's description of the *mir* was quite brief,[12] it had enormous significance, because it identified in a readily observable way how precisely Russian society differed from that of the West (and for that matter from the Baltic provinces). The Slavophiles were able to elaborate on this distinction, contrasting the Russian spirit of fellowship with the selfishness and egotism of the West.

A contrast that was made by some Russian historians in the nineteenth century between Russia and the West was that whereas in the West initiative for change came from below, from society, in Russia it was the state that set changes of all kinds in motion. Boris Chicherin argued in this way and so did Kliuchevskii and Miliukov. They were liberals who wanted to believe that transformations in Russia could take place without the kind of social upheavals that had shaken the countries of Western Europe.[13]

The implication of this doctrine, however, was that since Russia had a relationship between state and society that was altogether different from that in the West, parliamentary institutions of the English kind were impossible in Russia. The desire to demonstrate that this kind of reasoning was erroneous, by showing that England too in earlier times had institutions resembling the Russian *mir,* inspired a school of Russian historians represented by Maksim Kovalevskii and Paul Vinogradov to make comparative studies of village communities in different parts of the world.

Underlying these studies was the assumption that all countries passed through the same historical stages, and that in this respect Britain had reached a later stage than Russia. In the introduction to a volume of essays by liberal scholars published in 1905 M. A. Reisner outlined what he thought these historical stages were. The 'tribal' stage was the first form of social organization. This was followed by 'feudalism', and this gave rise to the third stage, the 'military–national state'. This in its turn gave way to the 'industrial-law-governed state', the phase of development reached by the most advanced countries in the West.[14]

Reisner contended that although no doubt Russia would pass through these historical stages after its own particular fashion, it would nevertheless undergo them, just as every other state would. The military–national state which Russia now was, was not Russia's original form of social organization, had not existed throughout Russia's history, and would not be the phase at which the country's political evolution would end. Reisner considered that the difference between Russia and the West in this respect was that in Russia the military–national state was more unstable than its Western equivalents had been, and more likely to change in a liberal direction.[15]

In his contribution to that volume Vinogradov illustrated how the democratic Anglo-Saxon township (which he translated as *sel'skaia obshchina*), on which the manor was later superimposed, had co-existed with the growth of a centralized state organization. This, Vinogradov implied, was much in the same manner as the *mir* now co-existed with the autocracy. And if parliamentary democracy had arisen in Britain, what prevented the same kind of development taking place in Russia?[16]

It was possibly because the Russian liberals had such high expectations of constitutional government in their country that when Russia's own 'constitutional experiment' was set up in 1906 they tended to emphasize its limitations rather than compare the new regime with the constitutional arrangements of other European states. Had they done so they might have discovered, as Robert McKean has done in his essay for the present volume, that the Russian constitutional monarchy emerged rather well from the comparison.

Russia's process of Westernization (or modernization) was to acquire an international significance. For Asian peoples it became a model for their own attempts to overcome backwardness and isolation. The Russian revolutionary movement also attracted considerable interest in Asian countries, as this was viewed as the attempt by Russians to overthrow an autocratic regime and institute a democratic constitutional government. To many Asians this seemed a noble cause worthy of emulation by themselves. Many young Japanese and Chinese, for example, had a fascination with the Russian revolutionary movement, and at the beginning of the twentieth century the radical Japanese and Chinese press contained numerous articles on Russian 'Nihilism' and Anarchism, the exploits of Russian terrorists, and the biographies of socialist thinkers. This interest in Russia prepared the ground for the reception of the 1905 revolution not only in Asian countries, but in countries throughout the world.[17]

Even more than the Russian revolution of 1905 that of 1917 had world-wide ramifications. Although Soviet historiography paid lip-service to this facet of the Russian revolution, they never gave it the attention it merited. The main reason for this is that from its very inception in 1920 Soviet historical writing presented the revolution as an episode in which the Bolshevik party had led the way, and in doing so had established certain principles that other revolutionary parties were expected to follow. This approach limited severely the scope for historical investigation, and tended to equate the international aspect of the Russian revolution with the history of the Comintern. Paul Dukes is one of the very few historians to take up the challenge of placing the Russian revolution in its international context, and in *October and the World* has shown how the Russian revolution resonated not only through Europe and the USA, but through corners of the globe as remote as the Cook Islands as well.

Soviet historical writing obscured the international aspects of the Russian revolution by creating the impression that it was an essentially Russian phenomenon which radiated outwards to other peoples. It played down the contribution made to the revolution by non-Russian communities and overlooked the fact that the participation of each of these national communities had its own peculiar dynamic, and the revolution impacted on each of these communities in a particular way.

Moreover, Russians, Poles, Latvians, Lithuanians, Jews and other peoples from the Russian Empire had émigré communities in European countries, the USA and even farther afield. These émigré communities maintained a constant dialogue with their fellow countrymen who remained in the Russian Empire. Publications printed abroad could be smuggled into the country; fund-raising could be carried on abroad to help those in need at home; grievances suffered at the hands of the tsarist authorities could be given publicity on the world stage. This kind of interchange forms part of the context in which the Russian revolution and Civil War took place, adding to its international character.

When the Russian revolution broke out in 1917 many émigrés from the Russian Empire returned home to take part in the momentous events. The group which came from the USA seems to have been numerous, judging by the impressions of *The Times* (London) correspondent who reported that many of the anarchists he had encountered in June 1917 were refugees who had returned to Russia from America. He added that when asked why they did not carry out their theories in free America, one of them replied: 'You do not know the American police.'[18] It is significant that when Bertrand Russell visited Russia in 1920 he formed the opinion that the ruling group of Bolsheviks was composed of 'Americanised Jews' who had the aim of making Russia as 'industrial and as Yankee as possible'. Russell's conclusion was that the process of Westernization in Russia was going too far, and this was the lesson of the Russian revolution which he conveyed to the Chinese when he went to lecture in Beijing later in the year.[19]

The young Chinese whom Russell addressed did not, however, take his message to heart and their reception of the Russian revolution represented an extension of their acceptance of Western models. It is interesting to note in this connection that when Qu Qiubai, an aspiring Chinese journalist who had recently taken part in the May the Fourth Movement, set out from Beijing to visit Soviet Russia in 1920, his first stop was Chita in the Far Eastern Republic. The person who explained the workings of the Republic's economic system to Qu and his friends was its transport commissar Bill Shatov, a Russian who had recently returned from the USA. Qu also interviewed the President of the Far Eastern Republic, Alexander Krasnoshchekov,[20] who had been an associate of Trotskii's in Nikolaev before settling in Chicago, where he graduated in law. Krasnoshchekov too had returned to Russia in 1917.[21]

Some returnees to Russia were Lithuanians from Scotland, many of whom had settled there after the 1905 revolution. Between 1,500 and 1,800 Lithuanian men were deported from Scotland to Russia in October 1917 to fight in the Russian army. By the time they reached Russia, however, the Provisional Government had fallen and some attempted to leave Russia through Vladivostok to Japan, China or the USA. Many became involved in the Civil War in Siberia. At the beginning of 1920 Chicherin, the Soviet Commissar for Foreign Affairs, received a telegram from Juozas Steponaitis, one of the Scottish Lithuanians, giving a laconic account of how his contingent had joined a Lithuanian battalion formed in Novonikolaevsk and brought it over to the Red side. The battalion had then fought with the local partisans against Kolchak's regime. They had, in the words of Steponaitis, 'carried out the duty of workers who for many years have slaved in the Scottish coal mines'.[22] These Scottish Lithuanian former miners from Lanarkshire were among the many nationalities which fought with the Reds in the Civil War. Just how international the Red forces were is shown by John Erickson in his paper.

The Cold War is an aspect of Russian history which is world-historical by definition. It is also the one which presents the greatest challenge to historians by its scope and variety. But the rewards would be commensurate; a great deal could be learnt about history as a discipline by tackling the subject of the Cold War in the way it merits. It is an illustration of Marc Bloch's idea that the only true history is universal history. The principle of universal history would serve as the starting-point of historical investigation, so that episodes with national locations would not be considered as disparate entities, but component elements of the totality of world history.

It is instructive to follow the route by which Paul Dukes refined his ideas on Cold-War history over the three works *The Emergence of the Super-Powers*, *October and the World* and *The Last Great Game*. The first of these draws suggestive parallels between Russian and American history, while the second puts modern Russian history in a world context. *The Last Great Game* builds on the previous two books by suggesting a framework for how the Cold War could be studied as a genuine totality. By doing so, it provides an explanation for why the historical parallels between Russia and the USA should exist and why there is no obvious explanation for the existence of the Cold War.

Following Braudel, Dukes argues that history functions at many levels, some of them on the surface as events, some on a longer time-scale as cyclic movements in economics or politics, and some as basic underlying factors which operate over centuries. These levels all interact with each other to provide the phenomena of history, and of the Cold War in particular.[23]

This hierarchy of levels in history is applicable not only to the Cold War, but to the post-Cold War world as well. With the end of communism the ideological surface layer of the Soviet regime has been removed, and with it its integrative function in the Soviet state. But the deeper cycles and structures remain in place, so that the geopolitical confrontation between the USA and Russia remains, and with it the somewhat modified system of international alignments. The end of the Cold War has only led to a 'Cold Peace'.

In 1979 Paul Dukes concluded *October and the World* by calling for 'a revision of our historical consciousness which will help to avoid conflict and promote progress'.[24] That plea has lost none of its force in the intervening period, since the end of the Cold War. The point of view of the historian, in our dangerous age, must be the universalism of world history. It is an ambitious objective, and one that is demanding and responsible. But it is not unattainable, and we are indebted to Paul for showing us how to get there.

Notes

1. P. Dukes, *The Last Great Game: USA versus USSR* (London, 1989), p. 91.
2. 'Evraziistvo: za i protiv, vchera i segodnia (Materialy kruglogo stola)', *Voprosy filosofii*, no. 6 (1995), pp. 3–74.
3. See T. Wade, *Russian Etymological Dictionary* (London, 1996).

4. Paul Dukes, *October and the World: Perspectives on the Russian Revolution* (London and Basingstoke, 1979), p. 11.

5. Quoted in L. A. Nikiforov, 'Rossiia v sisteme evropeiskikh derzhav v pervoi chetverti XVIII v.', *Rossiia v period reform Petra I* (Moscow, 1973), p. 9.

6. J. Kieniewicz, 'Russia's Route', in *European Space – Baltic Space – Polish Space*, part two, ed. A. Kuklinski (Warsaw, 1997).

7. *Ibid.*, pp. 248–56.

8. P. Dukes, *The Emergence of the Super-Powers* (London, 1970); Dukes, *October and the World*. See also P. Dukes (ed.), *Russia and Europe* (London, 1991) and P. Dukes, *World Order in History: Russia and the West* (New York and London, 1996).

9. See, for example, *The Caledonian Phalanx: Scots in Russia*, by Paul Dukes and others (Edinburgh, 1987); P. Dukes, 'Scotland and the Slavic World: An Introduction', *Coexistence*, vol. 29 (1992), pp. 107–12.

10. K. Fischer, *Immanuel Kant* (Mannheim, 1860), pp. 47–8. Fischer explains that the original spelling 'Cant' had been altered to 'Kant' to conform with German orthography. Some doubts are raised on this matter in E. Cassirer, *Kant's Life and Thought* (New Haven and London, 1981), pp. 12–13.

11. P. Kluckhohn, *Persönlichkeit und Gemeinschaft: Studien zur Staatsauffassung der deutschen Romantik* (Halle, 1925).

12. A. von Haxthausen, *Studien über die inneren Zustände, das Volksleben und insbesondere die ländlichen Einrichtungen Russlands*, 3 vols (Hannover, Berlin, 1847–52), vol. 1, p. 124.

13. P. Struve, 'B. N. Chicherin i ego mesto v istorii russkoi obrazovannosti i obshchestvennosti', in *Sotsial'naia i ekonomicheskaia istoriia Rossii* (Paris, 1952), p. 327.

14. M. A. Reisner, 'Vvedenie', *Politicheskii stroi sovremennykh gosudarstv: Sbornik statei*, vol. 1 (St Petersburg, 1905), p. vi.

15. *Ibid.*, p. vii.

16. P. G. Vinogradov, 'Gosudarstvennyi stroi Anglii', *Politicheskii stroi sovremennykh gosudarstv*, pp. 191–8.

17. See Ivar Spector, *The First Russian Revolution* (Englewood Cliffs, NJ, 1962); D. C. Price, *Russia and the Roots of the Chinese Revolution, 1896–1911* (Cambridge, Mass., 1974).

18. *The Times*, 26 June 1917.

19. B. Russell, *Autobiography* (London, 1978), pp. 354–5.

20. Qu Qiubai, 'Exian jicheng' [Journey to a Hungry Country]', *Qu Qiubai wenji* [Selected Works of Qu Qiubai], vol. 1 (Beijing, 1953), pp. 64–7.

21. H. K. Norton, *The Far Eastern Republic of Siberia* (London, 1923), p. 171.

22. V. Kapsukas, *Raštai*, vol. 7 (Vilnius, 1964), pp. 364–5.

23. Dukes, *The Last Great Game*, pp. 158–9.

24. Dukes, *October and the World*, p. 189.

Paul Dukes: a Select Bibliography

The following bibliography of Paul Dukes's main publications excludes many smaller articles, notes and comments which he has written for an eclectic array of publications.

Books

Catherine the Great and the Russian Nobility: A Study Based on the Materials of the Legislative Commission of 1767 (Cambridge, 1967).

(Joint editor with R. C. Bridges, J. D. Hargreaves and W. Scott), *Nations and Empires: Documents on the History of Europe and on its Relations with the World since 1648* (London, 1969).

The Emergence of the Super-Powers: A Short Comparative History of the USA and USSR (London and New York, 1970); translated as *Amerika-Rusland* (Amsterdam, 1972).

A History of Russia: Medieval, Modern, Contemporary (London and New York, 1974; 2nd edn, 1990; 3rd edn, 1997).

(Editor and introducer), *Russia under Catherine the Great*, vol. II: *Catherine the Great's Instruction (Nakaz) to the Legislative Commission, 1767* (Newtonville, Mass., 1977).

(Editor, introducer, and translator), *Russia under Catherine the Great*, vol. I: *Select Documents on Government and Society* (Newtonville, Mass., 1978).

October and the World: Perspectives on the Russian Revolution (London, 1979).

The Making of Russian Absolutism, 1613–1801 (London, 1982; 2nd edn, 1990).

A History of Europe, 1648–1948: The Arrival, the Rise, the Fall (London and New York, 1985).

The Last Great Game: USA versus USSR. Events, Conjunctures, Structures (London and New York, 1989).

(Joint editor with J. Dunkley), *Culture and Revolution* (London, 1989).

(Editor), *Russia and Europe* (London, 1991).

(Joint editor with T. Brotherstone), *The Trotsky Reappraisal* (Edinburgh, 1992). (Trans. into Japanese, 1994.)

(Editor), *Aberdeen Universities and Europe: The First Three Centuries* (Aberdeen, 1995).

(Editor), B. F. Porshnev, *Muscovy and Sweden in the Thirty Years War, 1630–1635* (Cambridge, 1995).

World Order in History: Russia and the West (London, 1996).

(Editor), *Frontiers of European Culture* (Lampeter, 1996).

Articles

'Russia and the Eighteenth Century Revolution', *History*, vol. 56 (1971), pp. 371–86.

'History Congress in Moscow', *Russian Review*, vol. 30 (1971), pp. 240–9.

(With J. W. Barnhill), 'North-East Scots in Muscovy in the Seventeenth Century', *Northern Scotland*, vol. 1, no. 1 (1972), pp. 49–63.

'Ossian and Russia', *Scottish Literary News*, vol. 3 (1973), pp. 17–21.

'Russia and the General Crisis of the Seventeenth Century', *New Zealand Slavonic Journal*, No. 2 (1974), pp. 1–17.

(With B. Meehan-Waters), 'A Neglected Account of the Succession Crisis of 1730: James Keith's Memoirs', *Canadian–American Slavic Studies*, vol. 12 (1978), pp. 170–83.

'Some Aberdonian Influences on the Early Russian Enlightenment', *Canadian–American Slavic Studies*, vol. 13 (1979), pp. 436–51.

(With J. W. Hiden), 'Towards a Comparison of the Soviet Union and Nazi Germany in the 1930s', *New Zealand Slavonic Journal*, No. 1 (1979), pp. 45–77.

'The Leslie Family in the Swedish Period (1630–5) of the Thirty Years War', *European Studies Review*, vol. 12 (1982), pp. 403–24.

'Paul Menzies, 1637–1694, and his Mission from Muscovy to Rome', *Innes Review*, vol. 35 (1984), pp. 88–95.

'Patrick Gordon and his Family Circle: Some Unpublished Letters', *Scottish Slavonic Review*, no. 10 (1988), pp. 19–49.

'Scotland and the Slavic World: An Introduction', *Coexistence*, vol. 29 (1992), pp. 107–12.

'Contacts and Integration: Some Scottish Examples' [Noblesse, état, et société en Russie, XVI – début du XIX siècle], *Cahiers du monde russe et soviétique*, vol. 34 (1993), pp. 227–32.

(Guest editor), 'Eastern Approaches to European Culture', *Coexistence*, vol. 32 (1995).

(Guest editor), 'The Russian Revolution in Comparative Perspective', *International Politics*, vol. 33 (1996).

Contributions to books

'Catherine II's Enlightened Absolutism and the Problem of Serfdom', in *Russian Law: Historical and Political Perspectives*, ed. W. E. Butler (Leyden, 1977), pp. 93–115.

'Towards a Comparison of the Jacobite and Pugachev Revolts', in *Britain and Russia: Contacts and Comparisons, 1700–1800*, ed. A. G. Cross (Newtonville, Mass., 1979), pp. 279–94.

'The Russian Enlightenment', in *The Enlightenment in National Context*, ed. R. Porter and M. Teich (Cambridge, 1981), pp. 176–91.

'How the Eighteenth Century Began for Russia and the West', in *Russia and the West in the Eighteenth Century*, ed. A. G. Cross (Newtonville, Mass., 1983), pp. 2–19.

'A Defence of Armageddon: Two Discourses containing some American Ideas of Absolutism in Mid-Nineteenth-Century Russia', in *Russian Thought and Society, 1800–1917: Essays in Honour of Eugene Lampert*, ed. R. Bartlett (Keele, 1984), pp. 23–41.

'Problems Concerning the Departure of Scottish Soldiers from Seventeenth-Century Muscovy', in *Scotland and Europe, 1200–1850*, ed. T. C. Smout (Edinburgh, 1986), pp. 143–66.

'Aberdeen and North-East Scotland: Some Archival and Other Sources', in *The Study of Russian History from British Archival Sources*, ed. J. M. Hartley (London, 1986), pp. 51–66.

'Scottish Soldiers in Muscovy', in *The Caledonian Phalanx: Scots in Russia*, by Paul Dukes and others (Edinburgh, 1987), pp. 9–23.

'The Social Consequences of World War II for the USSR', in *Total War and Social Change*, ed. A. Marwick (London, 1988), pp. 45–57.

'Some Cultural Aspects of the Context of Von Grimm's Prediction', in *Russia and the World of the Eighteenth Century*, ed. A. G. Cross, R. P. Bartlett and K. Rasmussen (Columbus, Ohio, 1988), pp. 45–57.

'The Emergence of a Modern Vernacular Culture in North-East Scotland', in *Interpretation and Cultural History*, ed. J. H. Pittock and A. Wear (London, 1991), pp. 269–96.

'The First Scottish Soldiers in Russia', in *The Scottish Soldier Abroad, 1247–1967*, ed. G. G. Simpson (Edinburgh and Maryland, 1992), pp. 47–54.

'Nationalism and the Fall of Multinational Empires', in *Vampires Unstaked: National Images, Stereotypes and Myths in East Central Europe*, ed. A. Gerrits and N. Adler (Amsterdam, 1995).

'Globalization and Europe: the Russian Question', in *Globalization and Europe: Theoretical and Empirical Investigations*, ed. R. Axtmann (London, 1998), pp. 93–108.

Book reviews

Paul Dukes is a prolific reviewer of books. It would be a nearly impossible task to list the many reviews he has written. Here we can merely refer to some of the main journals for which he has reviewed.

American Historical Review, American Political Science Review, British Journal of Eighteenth-Century Studies, English Historical Review, Europe–Asia Studies, European Studies Review, History Today, International Affairs, Irish Slavonic Review, Journal of European Studies, Revolutionary Russia, Scottish Slavonic Review, Slavic Review, Slavonic and East European Review, Study Group on Eighteenth-Century Russia Newsletter, Times Higher Education Supplement, Times Literary Supplement.

Index